AF556356

COOPERATIVE ENTREPRENEURSHIP

COOPERATIVE ENTREPRENEURSHIP

By

Dr. M.Karthikeyan

Associate Professor
Department of Cooperatives
Institute of Cooperatives & Development Studies
Ambo University
P.B.No:19, Ambo, Ethiopia
Email: mkeya2003@gmail.com

DISCOVERY PUBLISHING HOUSE PVT. LTD.
NEW DELHI-110 002

Published by:
Tilak Wasan
DISCOVERY PUBLISHING HOUSE PVT. LTD.
4383/4B, Ansari Road, Darya Ganj
New Delhi-110 002 (India)
Phone : +91-11-23279245, 43596064-65
Fax : +91-11-23253475
E-mail : discoverypublishinghouse@gmail.com
sales@discoverypublishinggroup.com
parul.wasan@gmail.com
web : www.discoverypublishinggroup.com

First Edition: **2014**

ISBN: 978-93-5056-445-5

Cooperative Entrepreneurship

Printed at:
Aditi Fine Art Press
Delhi

Preface

Dear readers and entrepreneurs! It is my pleasure to introduce the book on "**Cooperative Entrepreneurship**" to you. It has been designed in a detailed manner so as to help you understand the basic concepts of Entrepreneurship and practice of Entrepreneurship in Cooperatives. This book has additional information on cooperative entrepreneurship, is a development of my book "Entrepreneurship in Cooperatives".

This work is based on my experience as teacher, trainer, entrepreneur and researcher in the field of cooperatives for more than 16 years. The present work is the outcome of my experience and many articles published in reputed journals. This book is very unique in the field of cooperative entrepreneurship. Few attempts have been made in cooperative entrepreneurship and in a book form this is the pioneering effort. This book will be very much useful to the entrepreneurs and cooperative stakeholders, the trainers who are working in various training establishments and the students of management and cooperatives both at under graduate and post graduate levels, and for cooperative researchers. I have drawn the inputs from various materials; papers, journals, books and I have consulted several of our friends, colleagues and field experts. I am ever grateful and thankful to them for their immense support and healthy criticism. I hope that the readers of this book will get knowledge on entrepreneurship in cooperatives. Any useful comments, suggestions to improve the present version are welcome and solicited from the readers. I am thankful to Discovery Publishing House Pvt. Ltd., India for publishing this book neatly under their renowned label for the cooperative entrepreneurs.

—M.Karthikeyan

Contents

Part III – Cases in Cooperative Entrepreneurship

Part – I
Entrepreneurship

Entrepreneur

Evolution of the term "Entrepreneur"

Before having the present definition the term of entrepreneur was related to a lot of assertions. The following are among the significant developments that gave the present form to entrepreneur.

- The word entrepreneur first appeared in the French language as "entreprendre", which means, "to undertake".
- From the 14th up to the end of the 17th century, the term entrepreneur was applied to persons like leaders of military expedition, tax collectors, adventurers and architects who were responsible for construction of roads, bridges, and buildings.
- Writers of 17th and 18th century stressed on the two essential characteristics of entrepreneur was taking of risks and creating innovation.
- Richard Calliton became the first person to relate entrepreneur to economic activities, because he defined entrepreneur as a person who buys service factors at certain prices and sell products at uncertain price in the future. By this definition, we can observe that entrepreneur surely face risk as there is possibility of bankruptcy and inconsistent demand.
- J.B. Say defined entrepreneur as "Economic agent who unites all means of production, the labour, the capital or the land of the other and who finds in the value of products which results from their employment, reconstitution of the entire capital that he utilizes and the value of the wages the interest and the rent which he pays as well as profit belonging to himself."

- FH Knight (1921), in his book referred entrepreneurs as specialized group of people who bear risks and deal with uncertainty.
- Leon Walras (1945) considered entrepreneur as a coordinator of the factors of production. He treated entrepreneur as the fourth factor of production, as one who hires factors of land, labour and capital.
- Schumpeter (1960s) defined entrepreneur for developed and developing nation.
- For developed countries.
- Entrepreneur is the one who innovates; raises money assembles inputs chose manager and sets the organisation with his ability to identify them.
- For developing countries.
- Entrepreneur is the one who start an industry (old or new) undertake risk, bears uncertainty and also perform managerial function of decision-making and coordination.

In general Schumpeter regarded entrepreneur basically as an innovator who carries out new combination to initiate and accelerate economic development. This is the intersection point of his two definitions.

As we can see from the selected evolutions, the aspects given to the entrepreneur has expanded as the evolution continues to get modernized. Anciently, entrepreneur was referred to people that are not considered as entrepreneurs today. Also, the importance given to entrepreneur in terms of economic enhancement and development has significantly upgraded by the trend of the evolution. To sum up in the light of the developments, there are four key elements of entrepreneurs. These are:

1. Vision (identifying emerging opportunities).
2. Innovation (creating new business or new ways of doing something).
3. Risk bearing (taking risk and facing uncertainty).
4. Organising (collection and coordination of the necessary resources).

The Entrepreneur

Entrepreneurs have many of the same character traits as leaders. Similarly to the early great man theories of leadership, however, trait-based theories of entrepreneurship are increasingly being called into question. Entrepreneurs are often contrasted with managers and administrators who are said to be more methodical and less prone to risk-taking. Although such person-centric models of entrepreneurship have shown to be of questionable validity, a vast but clearly dated literature studying the entrepreneurial personality found that certain traits seem to be associated with entrepreneurs:

- For example, in 1961, David McClelland described the entrepreneur as primarily motivated by an overwhelming need for achievement and strong urge to build.

- Collins and Moore (1970) studied 150 entrepreneurs and concluded that they are tough, pragmatic people driven by needs of independence and achievement. they seldom are willing to submit to authority.
- Bird (1992) sees entrepreneurs as mercurial, that is, prone to insights, brainstorms, deceptions, ingeniousness and resourcefulness. they are cunning, opportunistic, creative, and unsentimental.
- Busenitz and Barney (1997) claim entrepreneurs are prone to overconfidence and over generalisations.
- According to Cole (1959), there are four types of entrepreneur: the innovator, the calculating inventor, the over-optimistic promoter, and the organisation builder. These types are not related to the personality but to the type of opportunity the entrepreneur faces.
- Burton W. Folsom, Jr. distinguishes between what he calls a political entrepreneur and a market entrepreneur. The political entrepreneur uses political influences to gain income through subsidies, protectionism, government-granted monopoly, government contracts, or other such favorable arrangements with government(s) (see crony capitalism and corporate welfare). The market entrepreneur operates without special favours from government.

Definition of Entrepreneur

(a) an entrepreneur is a person who organises and manages any enterprise, esp. a business, usually with considerable initiative and risk;

(b) an employer of productive labour; contractor;

(c) he is the one to deal with or initiate as an entrepreneur.

Entrepreneur, just like management, has no single definition. It can be defined from different perspectives. The most important perspectives from which entrepreneur can be defined include the following

➢ **For an Economist**
  - Entrepreneur is one who brings resources and assets into combination that makes their value greater than before and is also one who introduces change and new order while contributing to economic development of a nation.

➢ **For a Psychologist**
  - Entrepreneur is a person that is typically driven by certain internal forces- need to obtain something, experiment and escape authority of others

➢ **For a Businessman**
  - Entrepreneur is either a threat (aggressive competitor) or an ally (source of supply, customer, etc.)

➢ **To a Capitalist Philosopher**
  - Entrepreneur is one who creates wealth for others, who produces jobs others are glad to get.

Definitions by some Authors

Schumpeter – *"Entrepreneurship essentially consists in doing things that are not generally done in the ordinary course of business routine"*.

Ronstadt – *"Entrepreneurship is the dynamic process of creating incremental wealth. This wealth is created by individuals who assume the major risks in terms of equity, time, and career commitment of providing value for some product or service."*

Peter Drucker – *"An entrepreneur is one who always searches for change, response to it and exploit it as an opportunity."*

Robert Hisrich – *"An entrepreneur is the person who will establish a successful new business venture. Besides, he must also be a visionary, leader – a person who has great dreams."*

From the above definitions, we can explain the meaning of entrepreneurship as follows:

1. An entrepreneurship function is undertaken in extraordinary course of business.
2. It is a process of creating wealth.
3. An entrepreneur is one who searches for change and convert it as an opportunity.
4. Innovation is the tool of entrepreneurs.
5. An entrepreneur will search for success.
6. He/she is also a visionary and leader who has great dreams.

Characteristics of an Entrepreneur

The characteristics, nature, feature or qualities of entrepreneur as an individual are essential to contribute to the success of an enterprise. Mc Celelland stated the characteristic of successful entrepreneur as an individual with technical competence, risk taking, high initiative, good judgment, intelligence to analyze and solve problem areas, leadership qualities, confidence, positive attitude high level of energy, creativeness, honesty integrity, emotional stability and fairness.

An entrepreneur should have the first hand knowledge of the product, process and end uses to bring inventive ability and sound judgment of the planned project. Flexibility, good social behaviour, open mind and the desire to take personal responsibilities will fit in the qualities of a true entrepreneur. There is no one universally accepted approach that best describes the traits and characteristics of entrepreneurs. But every approach has their own significance.

Some Authors' point of view the following are characteristics of an Entrepreneur:

- The entrepreneur has an enthusiastic vision, the driving force of an enterprise.
- The entrepreneur's vision is usually supported by an interlocked collection of specific ideas not available to the marketplace.

- The overall blueprint to realize the vision is clear, however details may be incomplete, flexible, and evolving.
- The entrepreneur promotes the vision with enthusiastic passion.
- With persistence and determination, the entrepreneur develops strategies to change the vision into reality.
- The entrepreneur takes the initial responsibility to cause a vision to become a success.
- Entrepreneurs take prudent risks. They assess costs, market/customer needs and persuade others to join and help.
- An entrepreneur is usually a positive thinker and a decision maker.

Characteristics denote qualities, features, attributes, and traits. The characteristics of an entrepreneur are developed on the basis of:

1. the history of thought on the term entrepreneur;
2. studying the characteristics of the successful entrepreneurs;
3. differentiating the term entrepreneur from related terms such as manager;
4. myths on entrepreneur;

Some of the characteristics of the entrepreneur are as follows:

1. *Self confident and optimist:* An entrepreneur is having more confidence on himself and thinks positively.
2. *Taking risk:* An entrepreneur is willing to take risk so that he can achieve things.
3. *Respond positively to changes:* An entrepreneur is also ready to face challenges in his business.
4. *Flexible and adapt:* An entrepreneur is flexible to changing needs and times.
5. *Knowledgeable of markets:* He knows better about the market and the changes that are taking place in the market.
6. *Able to get along well with others:* He moves closely with others and creates friendship and business relationship with others.
7. *Independent minded:* In taking decisions, he is quite independent.
8. *Knowledge:* He is very particular to know the latest knowledge on all aspects of his business.
9. *Energetic and diligent* – He works hard using all his intelligence.
10. *Creative:* He introduces creativity in planning, execution, and management of his business and venture.
11. *Dynamic leader:* He is a leader, who gives leadership to people around him.
12. *Responsive to suggestions:* Any useful suggestion is welcomed by him.
13. *Take initiatives:* For new programmes he himself takes initiatives.
14. *Resourceful and persevering:* He is ready to work hard.

15. *Perceptive with foresight:* Future is always his concern.
16. *Responsive to criticism:* He is ready to face criticisms positively to improve his business.

Traits of a True Entrepreneur

Several research studies have been carried out to identify the traits of a true entrepreneur. A distillation form fifty research studies reveals the following entrepreneurial traits.

- Capacity to take risk
- Capacity to work hard
- Above average intelligence and wide knowledge
- Self (inner) motivation
- Vision and foresight
- Willingness to defer consumption
- Imagination, initiative and emulation
- Inventive ability and sound judgment
- Flexibility and sociability
- Desire to take personal responsibility
- Desire to seek and use feedback
- Persistence in the face of adversity
- Innovativeness and future-orientation
- Mobility and drive
- Creative thinking
- Storing need for achievement
- Ability to marshal resources
- High degree of ambition
- Will to conquer and impulse to fight
- Will to prove superior to others.

Why do People Want to Become Entrepreneurs?

Today, people are becoming entrepreneurs at an alarming rate. The fact that the number of today's entrepreneurs when compared to the figure before ten years is almost quadruple tells too much about the increasing number of entrepreneurs. These days, many people share a dream of becoming entrepreneurs. This shows, there are a lot of factors that push ordinary people to become entrepreneurs. This ranges from the tangible and psychological benefit of putting themselves in the world of entrepreneurship. In brief these factors are:

➢ **Opportunity**

Chance to be part of a new environment or to be exposed to a new environment.

Chance to share the dream of many people

- **Profit**

  Fast road to richness
- **Independence**

  Not working for others. Some people have a phobia of being a servant of others.
- **Challenge**

  To take risk. People like to take risks to test themselves and to get the happiness after surpassing those risks.

Who are entrepreneurs?

Let us have a look at some of the approaches that tried to give answer to our big question: who are entrepreneurs?

Approach 1: Entrepreneurs are:

- **Self-directed (self-disciplined)**
  - Entrepreneurs have independent mind, i.e. mind that is not drive and manipulated by others. Their mind is not pushed by anyone's.
- **Self-nurturing**
  - Entrepreneurs believe in their ideas even if no one else does.
- **Action oriented**
  - Entrepreneurs have a burning desire of building their dreams in to reality.
  - They understand that business ideas are not enough by themselves unless they are implemented.
- **Highly energetic**
  - Entrepreneurs are emotionally, mentally and physically able to work long and hard.
- **Tolerant of Uncertainty**
  - Entrepreneurs have the ability of taking risk and facing uncertainty.

Approach 2: Entrepreneurs have the following qualities:

- Strong mental ability, intelligent, creative and analytical.
- Clear Objectives (Entrepreneurs chase clear purposes).
- Business Secrecy (Ability to guard trade secrets).
- Human relation ability (Entrepreneurs display polished behaviour while dealing with customers, employees, suppliers, government etc.)
- Communication Skill (Entrepreneurs are excellent communicators).
- Technical knowledge (Entrepreneurs have sound knowledge about production process and techniques).

Approach 3: Entrepreneurs have the following psychological qualities:

- High need for achievement

  - Every human being posse's three basic needs. These are need for power, need for affiliation and need for achievement and only one is dominant. For entrepreneurs need for achievement is dominant.
  - Entrepreneurs need to be successful in all assignments.
- High Self determination (Internal locus of control)
  - Entrepreneurs are quite confident in their ability to perform and succeed which gives rise to external locus of control, i.e. blaming others for failure and take credit for success.
- Desire for Self independence
  - Entrepreneurs act according to their personal vision, analysis and decision making. They don't want to work under other's influence.
- Innovative and Action oriented
  - Entrepreneurs are always ready (impulsive) to implement their ideas
- High tolerance for ambiguity
  - Entrepreneurs can work under dynamic and uncertain environment
- Moderate risk takers
  - Entrepreneurs are not gamblers (not high risk takers)

Myths of an Entrepreneur

Myth denotes the beliefs of an entrepreneur. Certain myths may be right or wrong; certain myths may become true or become a dream.

1. *Entrepreneurs are driven by money:* Money is the main motivation for an entrepreneur. Some people are driven for money but some may not go after money.
2. *Entrepreneurs are high risk takers:* By nature, an entrepreneur has to take risk to achieve things and earn money. Sometimes, even without taking risks entrepreneurs may succeed.
3. *All entrepreneurs are wealthy and successful:* It may be true in a country like America, but in developing countries this may not be true. Many new entrepreneurs are self-made people.
4. *Entrepreneurs are born not made:* Here also comes the difference between developed countries and developing countries, between the rich families and poor ones.
5. *Anyone can start a business:* Anyone can start a business, but to survive in the business and make it a success is a great thing.
6. *Entrepreneurs are gamblers:* Successful entrepreneurs take calculated risks. Gamble may lead to success or total failure.
7. *Entrepreneurs want the whole show to themselves:* Some entrepreneurs may think that they have done everything by themselves for their success. But many think their success was made by others also.

8. *Entrepreneurs are their own bosses and completely independent:* An entrepreneur has to serve many masters like partners, investors, customers, suppliers, employees, etc.
9. *Entrepreneurs work longer and harder than managers:* Many entrepreneurs work more than their managers but some may not.
10. *They face great deal of stress and pay a high price:* An entrepreneurship is stressful, painful, and demanding. But many entrepreneurs work hard and they take no rest.
11. *Starting a business is risky and ends up in failure:* Those who failed in their ventures say like this.
12. *Money is most important to start a business:* More than money, courage, faith, risk-taking, etc. are important for entrepreneurship.
13. *Entrepreneurs should be young and energetic:* This may not be true in all cases.
14. *Entrepreneurs seek power and control over others:* Some may like power and some entrepreneurs may want to share it.
15. *Any entrepreneur can raise money:* Through confidence and leadership, an entrepreneur can raise money.

Background of Entrepreneurs

Background means origin. Under this title, we will try to look at the common origins that holds true on the majority of entrepreneurs, as justified by various researches.

- Childhood background
    - Most entrepreneurs are the either the first child or the only child for their family.
- Parental background
    - The parents of most entrepreneurs are self-employed running their own business.
- Age Background
    - Most male entrepreneurs became entrepreneurs in their early 30s.
    - Most female entrepreneurs become entrepreneurs in their late 30s.
- Educational Background
    - Most entrepreneurs at least hold 1st degree (more usually BA degree). In other words, people with first degree become entrepreneurs than any other qualification.
- Marriage Background
    - Most entrepreneurs are married.
- Parental Relationship Background
    - The relation of most entrepreneurs with their parents is proved to be strong.

- Work History
  - Most entrepreneurs have some previous work experience especially the type of work that resembles to their present business
- Work Environment Background
  - The work environment under which most entrepreneurs had been working under was more presumably unsatisfying. That is one of the push factors for becoming an entrepreneur.

Role of Entrepreneur in an Organisation

An entrepreneur is someone who organises a system.he is the person who creates a product or service in order to gain profit. However, there is a general sense that entrepreneurship involves the establishment of a new venture while adopting some of the risk and being ready for failure. There is no general definition for the word, as it has been used in a large variety of ways. Some scholars of entrepreneurship, such as Prof. W. Long have tried to develop a specific definition by studying the evolution of the word's usage "ENCYCLOPEDIA"

Entrepreneur as a Risk Bearer

An entrepreneur is an agent who buys factors of production at certain prices in order to combine them into a product with a view to selling it at uncertain prices in future. Uncertainty is defined as a risk, which cannot be insured against and is incalculable. There is a distinction between ordinary risk and uncertainty. A risk can be reduced through the insurance principle, where the distribution of the outcome in a group of instances is known. On the contrary, uncertainty is a risk, which cannot be calculated. The entrepreneur, according to Knight, is the economic functionary who undertakes such responsibility of uncertainty, which by its very nature cannot be insured, or capitalized or salaried to. Mark Casson has extended this notion to characterize entrepreneurs as decision makers who improvise solutions to problems which cannot be solved by routine alone.

Entrepreneur as an Organiser

An entrepreneur is one who combines the land of one; labour of another and the capital of yet another, and, thus, produces a product.

By selling the product in the market, he pays interest on capital, rent on land and wages to labourers and what remains is his or her profit.

Entrepreneur as a Leader

Scholar R.B. Reich considers leadership, management ability, and team-building as essential qualities of an entrepreneur.

Entrepreneur is sometimes mistakenly equated with "opportunist". An entrepreneur may be considered one who creates an opportunity rather than merely exploits it, though that distinction is difficult to make precise.

Types of Entrepreneurs

There are so many ways of classifying entrepreneurs. The most important bases are discussed below.

Classification by Danhof: Danhof classified entrepreneurs as follows:

(a) *Innovative entrepreneurs:* an innovating entrepreneur is the one who introduces new goods, inaugurate new method of production discovers new market and recognizes the enterprise. It is important to note that such entrepreneur can work only certain level of development is already achieved, and people look forward to change and improvement.

(b) *Imitative entrepreneurs:* imitative entrepreneurs do not innovate the change themselves, they only imitate techniques and technology innovated by others. Such type of entrepreneurs are particularly important for under developed region for bringing mushroom drive of imitation of new combination of factors of production already available in developed regions.

(c) *Fabian entrepreneurs:* Fabian entrepreneurs are characterized by very great caution and skepticism in experimenting any change in their enterprises. They imitate only when it becomes perfectly clear that failure to do so would result in a loss of the relative position in the enterprise.

(d) *Drone entrepreneurs:* these are characterized by a refusal to adopt opportunity to make change in production formulae even at the cost of severely reduced returns relative to other producers.

Classification according to Type of Business

When we divide entrepreneurs by type of business they engage in, we have the following:

- *Business entrepreneur:* These entrepreneurs are individuals who conceive an idea for a new product or service and then create a business to materialize their ideas in to reality. They have both production and marketing resources in their search to develop a new business opportunity.
- *Trading entrepreneur:* is the one who under takes trading activities and is not concerned with the manufacturing work he or she identifies
- *Industrial entrepreneur:* essentially a manufacturer who identifies the potential needs of customer and sales a product or service to meet the market need. The entrepreneur is a product-oriented person who starts an industry unit because of the possibility of making some new product.
- *Corporate entrepreneur*: is an individual who plan and develop and manages a corporate.
- *Agricultural entrepreneurs:* are those entrepreneurs who undertake agricultural activity such as raising and marketing of crop and agricultural input.

Classification according to Motivation

Entrepreneurial classification based on motivation: Motivation is the force that influences the effect of the entrepreneur to achieve his or her objective.

- *Pure entrepreneur:* is an individual who is motivated psychological and economic reward. The entrepreneur undertakes the enterprise for his personal satisfaction.
- *Induced entrepreneur:* is the one who is induced to take up entrepreneurial task due to the policy measures of the government that provides assistance, incentive and necessary overhead facilities to start a venture.
- *Motivated entrepreneur:* motivation is the desire for self-fulfillment. They come into being because of the possibility of making and marketing some new product.
- *Spontaneous entrepreneur:* is one who is motivated by his/her natural talent to begin a business. This kind of entrepreneurs is very confident in their natural blessings from God and wants to undertake business because they believe their natural gifts will enable them to do so.

Classification according to use of Technology

- *Technical Entrepreneurs:*
  - Have technical knowledge regarding innovation of new products
  - Concentrate on manufacturing (technical aspect) rather than marketing
- *Non technical Entrepreneurs*
  - Are not concerned with technical aspect of a product.
  - Concentrate on developing alternative marketing, distribution and promotion aspects of their product rather than manufacturing aspect.
- *Professional Entrepreneurs*
  - Are interested in neither the technical aspect nor in the non technical aspects of a product.
  - Are interested in establishing a business but doesn't have the interest to manage or operate once a business is established. Professional entrepreneurs sell their business ideas and look on to creating another business.

Classification according to Stage of Development

- *First Generation Entrepreneur*
  - Starts an industrial unit by innovative skill i.e. combines different technology to produce marketable product.
- *Modern Entrepreneur*
  - Undertake those ventures which go well along with changing demand in the market i.e. he or she chooses those ventures that suit to current marketing needs.

➢ *Classical Entrepreneur*
   - Is stereotyped business who is only motivated by economic gain i.e. they run businesses that give them the maximum economic benefit?
   - Tries to increase their profit by developing self supporting ventures

Classification according to Growth

- Growth Entrepreneurs
- Super growth Entrepreneurs

Classification according to Area

- Urban Entrepreneurs
- Rural Entrepreneurs

Classification according to Gender and Age

- Men Entrepreneurs = Young, middle-aged and old entrepreneurs
- Women Entrepreneurs

Classification according to Scale of Operation

- Small scale Entrepreneurs
- Large scale Entrepreneurs

Some more categories

1. *Individual and institutional entrepreneurs:* In the small scale sector individual entrepreneurs are dominant. Small enterprises outnumber the large ones in every country. Such entrepreneurs have the advantages of flexibility, quick decision- making and state patronage. But a single individual can establish, operate and control and organisation up to a limit. Thereafter, it becomes necessary to institutionalize entrepreneurship. A group of entrepreneurs has to be developed to handle the increasingly complex network of decision-making. The central function of the entrepreneur remains the same but the basic decisions like the line of business, the amount of capital employed, etc. Are taken collective by the group of promoters at the helm of affairs. Thus, individual entrepreneur and institutional entrepreneur coexist and support each other. Corporate sector is the symbol of institutionalize entrepreneurship.
2. *Entrepreneurs by inheritance:* At times, people become entrepreneurs when they inherit the family business. In France and India, there are a large number of family-controlled business houses. Firms in these houses are passed form one generation to another.
3. *Technologist entrepreneurs:* With the decline of joint family business and the rise of scientific and technical institutions, technically qualified persons have entered the field of business. These entrepreneurs may enter business to commercially exploit their inventions and discoveries. Their main asset is technical expertise. They raise the necessary capital

and employ experts in financial, legal, marketing and other areas of business. Their success depends upon how fast they start production and on the acceptance of their products in the market.

4. *Forced entrepreneurs:* Many persons become entrepreneurs on account of the circumstances. The money lenders of yesteryears enter into business due to decline of money lending business wit the growth of Banking and Government regulations. Neo rich Ethiopians returning form abroad (NREs) and educated unemployed seeking self-employment may also be descried as forced entrepreneurs. This class of entrepreneurs accounts for the maximum number of failures because there is no proper screening of misfits.

Behavioural Pattern of Entrepreneurs

This title focuses on the socio economic factors that affect the type activities of entrepreneurs. People with diverse backgrounds enter into different types of industry depending on their experiences. The following are among the behavioural patterns of entrepreneurs.

- People from agricultural background usually gravitate towards industries, where technology is elementary and capital requirement is the modest.
- Off springs (sons and daughters) of professional and skilled craftsmen are usually attracted towards undertakings that have complex production methods because they have specialised knowledge.
- People from commerce are likely to set up large sized firms with the help of their accumulated wealth.
- Professionals and craftsmen have little opportunity for accumulation of wealth and are likely to begin small scale firms.

Entrepreneur Vs. Enterprise

According to the classical economists, entrepreneur is one who provides the fourth factor of production, namely 'enterprise'. As the fourth factor, it assembles, coordinates and manages the other factors namely land, labour and capital.

But in a true sense, an enterprise consists of a group of dedicated people who work together in the organisational structure primarily for the purpose of making and/ or selling a product or service by pooling their recourses (skills). Entrepreneurs create an enterprise as one part of organising function.

Entrepreneurs Vs. Managers

An entrepreneur is different form a manger. But it doesn't mean that they are entirely different from each other. That means they also have their own intersection points.

Similarities

- Both make decisions

- Both are visionary
- Both are accountable for their actions
- Both work under constraints
- Both are organisers
- Both perform management functions

Differences

The main points of difference between the two may be described as follows:

1. *Primary Motive:* The entrepreneur is primarily driven by innovation, profit and need for independence. On the other hand, the manager is driven by power and compensation
2. *Focus:* Entrepreneurs focus more on exploiting new opportunities. But managers focus is more on optimising the existing resources
3. *Risk taking:* An entrepreneur takes calculated risks of a business venture. He may jeopardize his own financial security for losses that may occur. By contrast, the manger does not face the uncertainty of a new venture with its potential for failure and financial loss. He does not share any business risks.
4. *Reward:* An entrepreneur is motivated by profits while the manger is motivated by externally imposed goals and rewards. The gains of an entrepreneur are uncertain and irregular and can at times be negative. The salary of a manger is on the contrary, fixed and regular and can never be negative.
5. *Skills:* An entrepreneur needs intuition, creative thinking and innovative ability among other skills. On the other hand, a manger depends more on human relations and conceptual abilities.
6. *Status:* An entrepreneur is self employed and he is his own boss. On the contrary, a manger is a salaried person and he is not independent of his employer, the entrepreneur.

Functions of Entrepreneurs

General Functions

Broadly speaking, there are three most important general functions performed by entrepreneurs. These are:

1. *Innovation:* Innovation implies doing new things or doing of things that are being done in a new way. It includes introduction of new products, creation of new markets, application of new process of production, discovery of new and better sources of raw materials and developing a new and better form of industrial organisation.
2. *Risk taking:* Risk taking or uncertainty bearing implies assuming the responsibility for loss that may occur due to unforeseen contingencies of the future. An entrepreneur provides or invests capital in order to establish and run the enterprise. He guarantees interest to lenders, wages

to employees, rent to the landlord. After making payment to these persons little or nothing may be left for him. Thus business is a game of skill wherein risks and rewards both are great.

3. *Organising:* organisation and management of the enterprise is the main function of an entrepreneur. It implies bringing together the various factors of production. The purpose is to allocate the productive resources in order to minimize losses and reduce costs in production. While organising, human resource and physical resources are among the two types of resources that are coordinated. Entrepreneurs coordinate human resources to create enterprise or a group of committed people.

Specific Functions

Kilby identified thirteen functions of an entrepreneur, which included some of the managerial functions also. These functions are as follows:

1. Perceiving market opportunities
2. Gaining command over scarce resources
3. Purchasing inputs
4. Marketing of the products and responding to competition
5. Dealing with the public bureaucracy (concessions, licenses and taxes)
6. Managing human relations within the firm
7. Managing customer and supplier relation
8. Managing finance
9. Managing production (control by written records, supervision, coordinating input flows with orders, maintenance).
10. Acquiring and overseeing assembly of the factory
11. Industrial engineering
12. Upgrading process and product quality, and
13. Introducing new production techniques and products

Kilby has classified the above functions into four groups viz., Exchanges relationship (1-4), political administration (5-7), management control (8-9), and technology (10-13). He has suggested that in the strict sense entrepreneur will perform only first two functions listed above and for the other eleven functions, he will employ experts in the related lines.

Arthur H. Cole has described the following functions of an entrepreneur:

1. The determination of those objectives of the enterprise and the change of those objectives as conditions required or made advantageous.
2. The development of an organisation including efficient relation with subordinates and all employees.
3. Securing adequate financial resource, the relations with existing and potential investors.
4. The requisition of efficient technological equipment and the revision of it as new machinery appeared.

5. The development of a market for the products and the devising of new products to meet or anticipate consumers demand.
6. The maintenance of good relations with public authorities and with society at large.

Based on the above discussion, each specific functions of an entrepreneur can be grouped in one of the general functions. In other words the above list is of no exception to the general functions list.

Responsibility of Entrepreneurs

To the Nation	To the Enterprise
Tax timely	Survival and growth
Follow rules and regulation	Profit
Adding to the nation l wealth	Company image
	Fair compensation

To the Society	To their Business Associates
Using resources properly	Profit or dividend fairly
Employment	Future certainty
Minimising toxic levels	Fair knowledge of company performance

2

Entrepreneurship

Evolution and Development of Entrepreneurship

Just like a human being gets born, gets young and flourish, entrepreneurship as a discipline and as a practice have grown. The earliest practice of entrepreneurship was observed 4000 years ago witnessed by a piece of writing on small business describing how banker's loaned money on interest. In fact the Arabs, Babylonian, Egyptians, Jews, Greeks, Romanians, Indians and Jews were among pioneers as entrepreneurs some 2500 BC. But the true development of entrepreneurship is best signified and initiated by small businesses. Small businesses flourished in all civilization. Industrial revolution kicked up entrepreneurship in a big way and due to liberalization policy by most countries, small businesses has got special emphasis and now contributes majority in employment and economic activities. During 1980's and1990's small business began to enjoy more esteem and prestige's than ever, due to its ability to invent new products, create new jobs, customize products and respond quickly to changes. Even today, fortune 500 companies depend heavily on small business for parts and equipment for creating their own products. Previously, entrepreneurship was the last option and people used it if there is no job opportunity. But today, undertaking entrepreneurship is the dream of many people.

Definition of Entrepreneurship

Entrepreneurship, like an entrepreneur, has no single definition. The main difference between entrepreneur and entrepreneurship is their attachment. Entrepreneur is a person while entrepreneurship is a process. When it is put in other way, entrepreneurship is a process undertaken by entrepreneur to augment his/her business interest. Broadly defined:

- Entrepreneurship is a dynamic process undertaken by an entrepreneur to create incremental value and wealth by discovering investment opportunities, organizing an enterprise, undertaking risk and economic uncertainty and there by contributing to economic growth. or
- Entrepreneurship is the process of creating something different with value by devoting the necessary time and effort, assuming the accompanying financial, psychic and social risks, and receiving the resulting rewards of monetary and personal satisfaction and independence.

When the first definition is explained in other words, entrepreneurship is a function of seeing investment and production opportunity, organizing an enterprise to undertake a new production process, raising capital, hiring labour, arranging for the supply of raw materials and selecting managers for the day to day operation of an enterprise (Higgins). i.e. through the process of entrepreneurship, entrepreneur organises an enterprise that is committed to undertake the basic activities essential in making and selling entrepreneur's product.

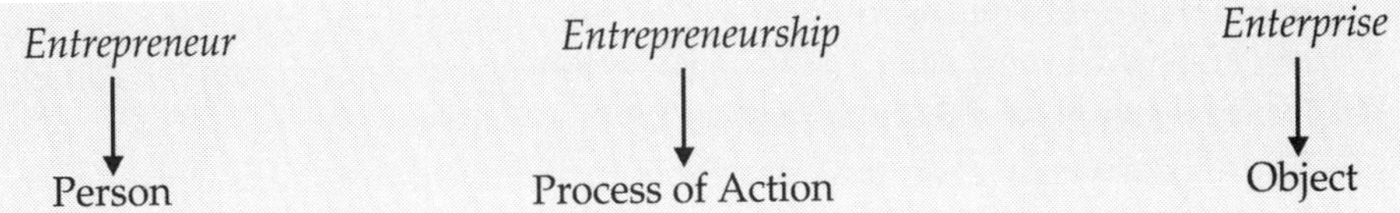

So, entrepreneurship:

- Is both a science and an art.
- Involves vision and passion of innovation and creation.
- Requires willingness to undertake calculated risk.
- Involves building a committed and dedicated team.
- more over involves accepting challenges, managing skills and organisation of resources.

In general the four key elements in entrepreneurship are:

1. Vision (Identifying emerging opportunities)
2. Innovation (Doing some thing new)
3. Risk taking (Assuming different types of risks: financial, psychological, social)
4. Organising (Coordinating resources and creating enterprise)

What is entrepreneurship?

In a narrow sense, the term "entrepreneur" refers to the individual "who undertakes an enterprise, especially a commercial one, often at personal risk"

1. This definition is clearly inappropriate for cooperatives. A more comprehensive definition has been offered by Robert E. Nelson:

"An entrepreneur may be defined as a person who is able to look at the environment, identify opportunities to improve the environment, marshall resources, and implement action to maximise those opportunities. The term is used in its broadest sense and includes persons who work in large, medium and small enterprises, as well as those who work in cooperatives and government."

2. Increasingly therefore, "entrepreneurship" is being used to describe a set of skills employed by persons working in large, medium and small enterprises, cooperatives, public institutions, non-commercial undertakings such as community associations, charitable foundations and others. These skills usually include the ability to search for new opportunities and to respond effectively to these opportunities in an innovative and purposeful manner.

   What therefore are the core competencies needed by entrepreneurs? Nelson and Nguiru list these characteristics:

   "Initiative, sees and acts on opportunities, persistence, information seeking, concern for high quality of work, commitment to work contract, efficiency orientation, systematic planning, problem solving, self-confidence, expertise, recognizing own limitations, persuasion, use of influence strategies, assertiveness, monitoring, credibility, integrity, sincerity, concern for employee welfare, recognizing the importance of business relationships, building capital, concern for the image of products and services".

3. Therefore we can see that psychological factors are considered to be the central entrepreneurial characteristics without which the would-be entrepreneur is unlikely to be successful. These factors are many but perhaps the most important are: personal motivation, a positive self-concept, initiative, innovation, problem-solving tendencies and risk-taking. David McClelland has emphasized the importance of "achievement motivation", or a subconscious "need to achieve".

4. The abilities needed to perform these functions effectively may in some cases be "inborn", but a more reasonable and modern approach recognizes that training can play an important role in developing the necessary competencies for successful entrepreneurship.

Elements of Entrepreneurship

Entrepreneurship has certain elements, which are noted below:

1. *Innovation:* Innovation refers to the new ideas or solutions found by an individual entrepreneur for his industry or for the whole industries in a locality. Innovation refers to new product developments, finding new markets, finding new processing technologies, finding new markets abroad, etc.
2. *Risk taking:* This element of entrepreneurship is related to the particular individual. That individual should have courage to face problems, confidence in himself to meet challenges like labour problems, government regulations, threat from competitors, etc.

3. *Vision:* Vision denotes the forecasting of future. An entrepreneur should forecast a positive vision to expand his business and find out ways and means to achieve them. Sometimes, a vision may become a dream.
4. *Ethics:* Ethics denotes the good qualities of an entrepreneur, which includes character and values in life. They are inherent qualities and inner strength of an individual. They are influenced by family atmosphere, culture, and beliefs of an entrepreneur.
5. *Organising skills:* These are certain abilities, which may be found within an individual or can be learned through experience. Organizing skills are managerial skills required for the success in terms of coordination, control, direction, and communication.

Benefits and Drawbacks of Entrepreneurship

Truly speaking, when most entrepreneurs start operating entrepreneurship, they more presumably start from a scratch. That means at the first glance of living in the world of entrepreneurship, they will only be the owners of small business. Of course, this may be an exception when businesses are inherited from rich parents. But the true adventure of entrepreneurship is observed when businesses start from a scratch or small businesses. That is why we will discuss the general benefits and drawbacks of entrepreneurship from the stand point of small entrepreneurs.

Benefit and Opportunity of Small Business Entrepreneurship

Pull Factor

- Opportunity to gain control over your own destiny: owning a business gives the entrepreneur the independence and the opportunity to achieve what is personally important.
- Opportunity to reach your full potential: small business is an instrument for self-expression and self-actualization. Many entrepreneurs don't enjoy working for some one else. No body limits you because you are independent and there is likely that you have challenging job.
- Opportunity to reap unlimited profit: although money is not the primary force driving most entrepreneurs, their ability to keep the money their business earns certainly is a critical factor in their decision to create companies.
- Opportunity to contribute to the society: small business owner enjoy the recognition they received from customers whom they have served faithfully over the years.
- Opportunity to turn previous work experience into business for self and family.

Push Factor

- Redundancy (unable to recycle a job)

- Job insecurity or unemployment
- Disagreement with previous employer

Potential Draw Backs of Small Business Entrepreneurship

- *Uncertainty of income:* The entrepreneur of small business cannot be 100 per cent sure about the level of revenue that he will earn because there could be more powerful competitors.
- *Risk of losing entire capital:* Small businesses fail more than any other business type. If they completely fail, their owner looses hi entire capital.
- *Psychological and Social Tensions:* When you run a small business, you question yourself whether it will be successful or not i.e. torturing your psychology. On the other hand, there could be some social out castings. Others may neglect you and even laugh at you when you start your own business because they may feel that you want to be special from them and this results in some social tensions
- *Long hours and hard work:* Opening small business needs a devotion of your entire time. You may work for more than 60 hours per a week.
- *Lower quality of life until the business get established:* Your frequent food and drink can be "shiro" and "water" till your financial power gets more enhanced.
- Complete responsibility on those issues which you don't have a complete knowledge.
- *Tremendous competition:* Stiff competition from established businesses can be faced by small business entrepreneurs.

What is Small Business?

Small business is a business which is independently owned and operated, not dominated in its field of operation and meets certain standard of number of employee and capital. In Ethiopian case, small businesses have the following criteria. There are two approaches to the criteria.

Size Criteria

Less than 50 employees.

Less than 50000 birr of sales volume

Economic/Control criteria

Market share: Low, not dominant

Personalized management: Not professionals

Independence: Independent

Reasons for Failure of Small Business

Many small businesses fail due to various reasons. Presumably, most of the reasons are artificial i.e. the majority of the reasons are created by faults and mistakes of human beings. Some of the reasons include the following:

- Management incompetence
- Poor financial control
- Lack of adequate capital
- Over investment in fixed asset
- Failure to plan current as well as future operation
- Failure to adopt proper of inventory control system
- Improper Attitude (The entrepreneur may not respect time, employees and may have lazy lifestyle and dictatorial style of work)
- Inadequate marketing plan
- Incorrect market identification
- Poor distribution channel
- Weak marketing communication or promotion

How to Avoid the Pitfalls

Know your business in depth: Knowing your industry well can be one of the ways of minimizing the failures of small businesses. Also knowing your business well by preparing documented business mission, objective, strategies and policies is another method.

Have a Good Relation with Stake Holders: Personal contact with suppliers' customers, trade association and even competitors is one of the ways to get knowledge.

Prepare business plan: A well-written plan is a crucial ingredient for the success of small business. Answering, "what business I am in?" leads to the establishment of goals and objectives. In turn these serve as aids in creating strategies policies and procedures.

Managing financial resources: The first step in managing financial resource is to have adequate start up capital. The most valuable financial resource to small business is cash. You cannot maintain control over a business unless you are not able to judge its financial health.

Understanding financial statement: To understand what is truly going on in the business you must have at least basic understanding of accounting and finance that would help to recognize the financial position of your business from time to time.

Learn to manage people effectively: Every business depends on a foundation of well-trained, motivated employees. You would only do this if you learn how to manage people more effectively.

Keep in tune with yourself: The success of your business will depend on your constant presence and attention and so it is critical. As an entrepreneur you must always physically and mentally fit through adjusting yourself with time.

Take up short professional courses in management (entrepreneurship): To improve your managerial skills.

Be sensitive to your customers: Your best opportunity lies within your customers. If you loose them, you will be hurt. So as an entrepreneur, don't ever give yourself a chance to disappoint them. The other is being wise in identifying the present and future needs of your customers through the analysis of the changes in their interests.

Importance of Entrepreneurship

One of the important inputs in any economic development of a country is entrepreneurship. More the entrepreneur activity betters the development. Entrepreneurship is the life blood of any economy and it applies more to a developing economy like Ethiopia. The areas of development are:

- Taking to higher rate of economic growth by creation of value.
- Speed up the process of industrial use of the factors production.
- Creation of employment opportunity
- Dispersal of economic activities to different sectors of the economy and identifying a new venue s of growth.
- Development of back word and tribal areas.
- Better social changes
- Improvement of the standard of living of different weaker section in the society
- Bringing social and political change in the society
- Develop technological know how
- Improve culture of business and expand commercial activities
- Entrepreneurship acts as a change agent to meet the requirement of the change markets and customer preferences.

The Process of Entrepreneurship

The decision about weather to start a new business is best considered in light of an understanding of the entrepreneurial process. The entrepreneurial process has four steps.

1. Identifying and evaluating business opportunity;
2. Developing business plan;
3. Determining the resources required for business; and
4. Managing the enterprise.

1. Identifying and evaluating business opportunity

Although most entrepreneurs do not have formal mechanism for identifying business opportunities some sources are: consumers and business associates member of distribution system and technical people. New business opportunity may be the result of technological change, market shift, government regulation, or computation. It is important to understand the cause of the opportunity. Since this factors and the resulting opportunity have a different market size and time dimension.

Whether the opportunity is identified with the input from customers, business associates, channel member or technical people; each opportunity must be carefully screened and evaluated. This evaluation of the opportunity is perhaps the most critical element of the entrepreneurial process as it allows the entrepreneur to assess whether the specific product or service has the return needed for the resource required. This evaluation process involve looking at the creation and length of the opportunity, its real and perceived value, its risk and returns, its fit with the personal skills and goals of the entrepreneur, and its differential advantage in competitive environment.

2. Develop a business plan

A business plan is a document the entrepreneur prepares before going to the implementation stage. It details every aspect of the business the entrepreneur aspires to establish: description of the business and the marketing, financial, organisational and operational plans necessary for the foundation of the venture. A good business plan is important in developing opportunity and also important in determining the resource required, obtaining those resources and successfully managing the resulting venture.

3. Determining the resources required

The resource needed for the opportunity must also be assessed. The process started with an appraisal of the entrepreneur's present resources. Care must be taken not to underestimate the amount and variety of resources needed. An entrepreneur should strive to maintain as large an ownership position as possible, particularly in the start up financing stage. As the business develops, more funds will probably be needed to finance the growth of the venture, requiring more ownership to relinquish.

4. Managing the enterprise

After resources are acquired the entrepreneur must employ them trough implementation of business plan. The operational problem of the growing enterprise must also be dealt with. These involve implementing a management style and structure, as well as determining the key variable for success. A control system must be identified so that any problem areas can be carefully monitored.

Entrepreneurship as a "Principal Equation"

Entrepreneurship suffers greatly from the lack of common understanding as to what, exactly, it is. Before describing a model for entrepreneurship, therefore, it may therefore be useful to say briefly what it is not:

- It is not innovativeness or creativity. Innovation and creativity are one of the hallmarks of entrepreneurship, but they are a response to the entrepreneurial equation, rather than an input. For entrepreneurship to exist and to function, it needs a context that includes a specific project with measurable outcomes, inadequate resources and clear ownership. There are countless examples of creative people doing innovative things that are worthy or essential, but have nothing to do with entrepreneurship, because they lack one or more of these contextual imperatives.

- Entrepreneurship is not about an organisation, nor is it about an individual. It is about the development of an organisation under the leadership of an entrepreneur. The entrepreneur is inseparable from the organisation - the organisation is defined by the entrepreneur's individual vision, which cannot be realized without the organisation.
- Entrepreneurship does not have to exist in the context of an entire organisation - it can function in a discrete part of a larger organisation, as long as that part meets the criteria of a specific project, inadequate resources and clear ownership. This means that numerous independent entrepreneurs can exist in the context of a firm led by someone who may or may not be an entrepreneur - so that each entrepreneurial part is lead by an entrepreneur, without there having to be an entrepreneur at the top (although it helps if there is one at top).
- Entrepreneurship is not a personality stereotype. Despite thousands of hours of research, no-one has found a personality template that fits all entrepreneurs - they come in every size, shape, gender, race, IQ, EQ, background, training, personality and character. They may be born entrepreneurs (many show signs of it at a very early age), but there are also countless examples of people who have become entrepreneurs through their life experiences. Entrepreneurship is a behavioural phenomenon, not a personality type.

In proceeding to describe what entrepreneurship is, it is helpful to think of it as a "principal equation" that can be activated only with certain necessary inputs. The principal equation is the specific project, which starts with an idea, is made possible by attracting the necessary resources and is brought to fruition through concerted, competent effort at combining the resources and the idea to produce a measurable outcome. The project can be of short duration or it can last a lifetime. Or it can be a series of short-term projects that goes on for a lifetime.

Before this chain reaction can occur, however, there have to be two necessary catalysts - an entrepreneur with an appropriate set of core characteristics and motivations and an environment that allows entrepreneurship to breathe and survive.

For the organisation to succeed, the entrepreneur must have a strong need to achieve (which alone provides the resilience and stamina to overcome all the hurdles), must be a leader in order to attract resources and must be an owner in whatever sense ownership may apply to the project (more about that shortly). Equally, entrepreneurship can be sparked only in a market characterized by instability. There are two aspects to an unstable market - first it is a free market, where people have the right to choose or not choose whatever suits them best, and second, it must be unstable, because stable markets are always dominated by large organisations that do not have to be entrepreneurial to survive.

This combination of the principal equation and its two catalysts are illustrated in the model below.

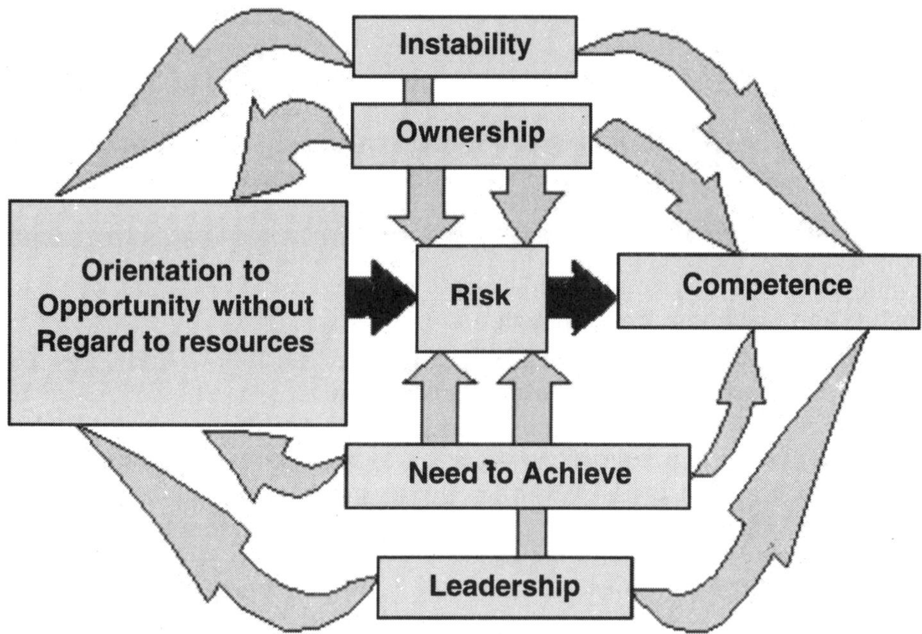

There is a high degree of interaction between all the elements of entrepreneurship. However, the core is the principal equation of entrepreneurship, which is a sequence of three elements running through the centre of the model - opportunity orientation without regard to resources, risk and competence. Before embarking on a more detailed discussion of the principal equation, we will review the role of the market, since the assumptions inherent in a market environment inform much of the model's functioning.

Entrepreneurship, Economic Development and Business Environment

Factors for Economic Development

In manufacturing a commodity or service, the following factors are needed. They are called as factors of production:

1. *Land:* Land is the basic factor for organizing a concern or undertaking activities like agriculture
2. *Labour:* Ideologists like Karl Marx insisted that, among all the factors of production labour is the supreme one. All other factors of production must be subordinated to labour
3. *Capital:* In free enterprises or capitalistic order of the society, capital is given more importance. Capital may be in the form of cash, finances and natural resources
4. *Organisation:* Organisation denotes the managerial ability of an enterprise.

In a country all factors of production may not be available. So entrepreneurs apply the resources that are available abundantly to the maximum extent. The scarce resources are used to the minimum. The following are the factors for economic development.

1. *Natural resources:* Natural resources make a country rich. By means of using the natural resources industries and business concerns can be organised. The important natural resources are agricultural resources, metal and mineral resources, oil resources and sea/water resources.
2. *Human resources:* In developed countries human resources form the major part of economic development. Human resources are expressed in educated manpower, skilled manpower and the development of Science and technology. The factors that decide the human resources in a country are:

(a) *Population* - within the population the size of age group is important. If a country has young people with good education, it is a great assets to the country. The second aspect of human resource is level of education. Education can be classified as formal education, higher education and technical education.

3. *Industrialisation:* For the fast growth of an economy and to have higher income for the population, a country should have industries. The following factors decide the industrialisation of the country:
   (a) Availability of raw materials
   (b) Infrastructure facilities (road, transport, communication, sea port, airport etc.)
   (c) Skilled manpower
   (d) Labour intensity
   (e) Technology (traditional, intermediate, latest)
   (f) market (local and foreign)
4. *Poverty and unemployment:* For the economic development of the country poverty must be abolished and the rate of unemployment must be kept low. Poverty is contributed by factors like illiteracy, low development of agriculture, lack of industrialization, political instability etc. Unemployment is caused by heavy dependents on agriculture, low level of industrialisation, lack of technical education etc.
5. *Cultural factors:* Cultural factors are decided by the hereditary of the country, religion, family etc. In advanced countries, culture allows equal opportunity for all types of population. Gender equality, giving equal freedom to human, is one of the factors for economic development. Women must be given equal rights and opportunities in the fields of education, employment, administration and politics.
6. *Foreign private investment:* These are the days of economic liberalization. Developing countries have the freedom to invite foreign private investment and start industries and business in their own countries. Developed countries extend their investments in poor and developing countries. This opportunity must be used by the developing countries for their industrialisation, employment, export trade and general economic development.
7. *Globalisation:* Globalisation implies the movement of goods and services, industries and businesses to move from one country to another country, By means of globalization consumers can get all types of goods from various countries at a lower price. But globalization led to the disappearing of local industries. Because local industries with their low technology, low investment and limited market could not compete with foreign goods.

Role of Entrepreneurs in Economic Development

Entrepreneurs are the pioneering people who take the initiative to organise the new industries and business.

(a) *Increasing per capita income:* Entrepreneurs through their hard work increase their income and the income of the workers they employ. Through this process per capita income in a country increases.

(b) *Wealth creation and distributions:* When new entrepreneurs enter the new fields, income and wealth of the country increases. Entrepreneurs are small-scale industrialists who distribute the wealth equitably. Through them industries are started through out a country which avoids regional imbalances

(c) *New products and services:* Entrepreneurs go for innovations and they produce new goods and services, which helps the economic development.

(d) *Employment generation:* Small-scale industries organised by new entrepreneurs create a lot of employment opportunities. They also use the locally available raw materials.

(e) *Better production methods:* New entrepreneurs are innovators and they introduce better production methods through which the cost of production is reduced.

(f) *Conversion of natural resources:* Natural resources available from agricultural and related areas are converted into finished forms, which provide employment, income generation, marketing etc.

(g) *Abolition of monopoly:* Entrepreneurship is encouraged in small scale and medium industries. Large industries create monopoly and concentration of industries in few places. But small-scale industries can be located in all parts of the country and can abolish monopoly.

(h) *Export:* When new products are manufactured such products will have export market also.

(i) *Development of complimentary goods:* When one industry is coming up, based on it so many other industries will also be developed. When a sugar factory is organised, based on it liquor factories, paper factories etc can be organised.

(j) *Business opportunities:* when new industries are coming up business opportunities increase. A network of suppliers, wholesalers and retailers are appointed and they provide employment opportunity and regulate the flow of goods.

(k) *Revenue to government:* Entrepreneurs provides income to government by paying various types of taxes like income tax, excise duties, VAT etc.

Employment

Employment has three parts namely unemployment, underemployment and full employment. Unemployment denotes jobless nature.

Underemployment denotes a qualified individual getting a low salary for a low level of job. Full employment denotes work for all people. The causes for unemployment are as follows:

1. *Low level of education:* If a country has low level of education, it will lead to unemployment.
2. *Natural resources:* Non availability of natural resources may lead to poor industrialization and unemployment.
3. *Lack of industries:* Only industries can provide more employment opportunities compared to agriculture.
4. *Low income and low purchasing power:* Lower income of the population leads to lower purchasing power and further employment opportunities cannot develop.
5. *Population:* Huge population and high density of population may also lead to unemployment.
6. *Lack of competition:* If competition is not there, industries and business cannot grow fast which may lead to stagnation in employment.
7. *Hard working:* hard working nature of people can provide good employment. Otherwise it may lead to unemployment.
8. *Lack of EDP:* lack of entrepreneurial development and new entrepreneurs may lead to unemployment.

Entrepreneurship and Society

Entrepreneurship helps the society as well as the entrepreneur, itself. The benefits of an entrepreneurship may be divided into three distinct categories that include the benefits to the nation, benefit to the society and the benefit to the individual.

As already discussed, an effective entrepreneurship venture fosters the production of wealth for a nation. When many of the entrepreneurship produce an output greater than the input, the economy of the nation is directly bolstered. Another advantage to the nation is the creation of jobs for its people. Such a job creation utilizes the human resources of that particular country and helps the natural talent materialize. With the new inventions and development in the new technology a nation can use its resources more effectively. Since, a majority of the entrepreneurship projects are private; it provides an environment of competitiveness which further increases the quality of the products in the national markets. By privatizing the local economy, entrepreneurship ventures help attract eager foreign firms who are otherwise reluctant to do business with the government subsidized economy.

The income level of the average person and the standard of living of a society increase with every successful entrepreneurship project that is undertaken. There is an increase in the employment level on the regional scale. It is also noticeable that an entrepreneurship helps develop other entrepreneur businesses because of the extra incentives that it can provide to a new entrepreneur in the shape of capital, knowledge and technology. Entrepreneurship helps the societies to fulfill its basic needs in the world that calls for the 'survival of the fittest'. Entrepreneurs lead by example in assisting the society and therefore boost the moral of the public.

An entrepreneur helps himself while creating opportunities for others. It is a fact that by doing so an entrepreneur fulfills his creative urge. Each successful project carried out by the entrepreneur leads to self satisfaction. The greatest satisfaction is derived from the fact that the individual is his own boss and therefore can use its creativity without any fear of repercussion. The quality of every good entrepreneur project is the profit and the fame that such a career provides. Infect, entrepreneurs always enjoy respect and high status in their communities.

Entrepreneurship and Business Environment

The state of the society and the government are interdependent on the many entrepreneur projects being undertaken around the world. The role of each entrepreneurship projects differs widely on a global scale due to the disparities in the local business environment. In developing countries, the process of privatization has helped to eliminate restrictions on the kind of opportunities that exist in the market. Whereas, socialist countries have historically helped entrepreneurs who have shown keen interest in optimizing the plans of the government. On the other side, less developed counties have rarely provided the entrepreneur a thriving atmosphere.

The major hurdles that the new entrepreneurs face are the availability of resources to carry out such a business. The most important is the allocation of funds that comes in the form of money to research and development. Another largely ignored factor is the availability of knowledgeable partners who can run a successful entrepreneurship after its initial stage. This is so because there is a great tendency for the entrepreneur to move from one project to another. The lack of knowledge on part of the management can halt the development process, if adequate training is not provided. Historically, women owned businesses have not been successful even in the developing countries due to the lack of government support. It remains the most significant problem in mainly the theoretical and male dominated societies.

Governments can help improvise the entrepreneurial spirit by not only removing the hurdles described above but by creating an industrial atmosphere that is favorable to the structural change. If the resources are allocated from the losers to gainers by purchasing the sales of assets, the entry and exist of the firms and rise and fall of the industries, the governments can effectively allocate resources to the successful entrepreneurs.

Experts agree that the most effective method of managing the entrepreneurship industry is to foster the start-ups. Among other techniques, this can be achieved by minimizing the paper work and formalities for the new starter. A single identification number should be issued to every new entrepreneurial project to track down each case. The authorization process should not take long and the case decisions should be made by a fixed date. Tax treatment of the new subsidiaries and the policies on induction of new employees should be simplified.

Rural Entrepreneurship

These days rural entrepreneurship is seen as the largest force in the development of the rural areas. Infect, many of the developing countries in the world have use the concept of rural entrepreneurship as a very successful method of deterring rural unrest. The greatest asset that the rural areas have in not the natural resource but it is the vast uncultivated land. Due to the ever growing population of the world and the expansion of the metropolitan areas, government's reliance on the rural land has significantly increased. These lands are used in the development of industry and establishing manufacturing base. Many countries have used these lands to establish recreational and educational facilities. This is one of the primary reasons that most new institutions of higher education are opening in suburbs and small towns.

Another great advantage in the rural entrepreneurial projects is the availability of cheap labour that can reduce the cost of production. It is also well known that the less technical projects have a chance of success in rural communities because of the closely knit together communities that can carry out the communication much better than the workforce in the cities. The production plants of many large entrepreneur projects are always located in these rural communities because not only does these projects provide employment opportunities but also prosper on behalf of the hard working labour force.

Governments and companies are promoting rural entrepreneurship by providing extra incentives to women who have been allocated to the traditional feminine jobs. Many companies have established training centers in order to educate the rural workforce on technical matters. Historically, governments have eliminated many of the requirements for the rural entrepreneurs who want to set up an industry in their regional areas. Similarly, many of the entrepreneurs, who want to set up rural industries, are exempt from strict laws that govern the urban development.

Problems of Rural Entrepreneurship

Rural entrepreneurship has its own drawbacks. Policies such as keeping of land in protection when there is already an over production and pricing subsidy policies that helps to retain the minimum income are two of the greatest threats to rural development. Due to the remote access and unavailability of knowledgeable labour, it is difficult to advise the local entrepreneurs who are willing to take risk. Access to capital labour, commercial markets and the managerial staff are hindered due to the remote locations.

In order to alleviate the problems of rural agriculture, a competitive agriculture entrepreneurship under the government supported resources in needed. The government should set aside a quota for the rural entrepreneurship projects and select only the very best ideas that directly benefits not only the community but can compete on a global scale. It is also vital for the success of the rural communities that the development of each rural project remains in the hand of the local agencies which in return cooperate with the government to oversee the entire project. Entrepreneurship education is the leading factor that can help develop the rural areas. Governments should encourage the foundation of a local network that can communicate with the rural population and try to abridge the gap between the extended and remote communities.

Theories of Entrepreneurship

Entrepreneurship Theories

Business academics have two classes of theories of how people become entrepreneurs, called supply and demand theories, after Economics. In the supply theory, entrepreneurs arise as they are born, with personality traits which drive them to become entrepreneurs. In the demand theory, anyone could be recruited by circumstance or opportunity to become an entrepreneur.

Several research studies have shown that entrepreneurs are convinced that they can command their own destinies. behavioural scientists express this by saying that entrepreneurs perceive the "locus of control" to be within themselves. It is this self-belief which stimulates the entrepreneur, according to supply-side theorists.

A more generally held theory is that entrepreneurs emerge from the population on demand, from the combination of opportunities and people well-positioned to take advantage of them. The entrepreneur may perceive that they are among the few to recognise or be able to solve a problem. In this view, one studies on one side the distribution of information available to would-be entrepreneurs (see Austrian School economics) and on the other, how environmental factors (access to capital, competition, etc.) change the rate of a society's production of entrepreneurs.

Apart from the above some authorities have given the following theories:

1. Economic Theory
   - Economists view entrepreneurship as a process where entrepreneurs are driven by profit motive and maximization of wealth by combining different factors of production.

2. Socio-cultural Theory
    - Sociologists view entrepreneurship as a process where an entrepreneur acts as a role model, senses expectations of society and tries to bring about products/services as per culture, norms and tradition of society.
3. Psychological Theory
    - Psychologists view it as a process where4 an entrepreneur acts as a change agent with tremendous psychological drive (need) for innovation, experimentation and seize unusual opportunities of environment.
4. Managerial Theory
    - Professional managers view entrepreneurship as a process where an entrepreneur performs managerial functions (planning, organizing, staffing, leading and controlling) to make new products for business to compete (a rival) and an ally (business associate).

There are many theories of entrepreneurship; in some authors' view the important ones are as below:

1. Schumpeter's Theory of Innovation

According to his theory, economic development of an entrepreneur takes place through innovation. Innovation takes place under the following five categories.

(a) Introduction of new products
(b) Introduction of new technology
(c) Opening a new market
(d) New source of raw material
(e) Creating new forms of organisation – mergers, acquisitions, etc.

2. McClelland's Theory of Achievement

According to his theory, an individual has a desire to achieve, i.e., achievement motive. For an entrepreneur, the achievement motive comes through the following sources.

(a) Taught by parents
(b) Profit is not the main motive
(c) Takes calculated risk
(d) Have high inner spirit

According to him, aimless life is a goalless game.

3. Peter Druckers' Theory of Innovation

Drucker also insists innovation as the basis for entrepreneurship. He puts the following conditions for innovation.

(a) It requires knowledge and ingenuity
(b) It must be built on one's own strength
(c) It should be closer to market

4. Harbinson's Theory of Organisation Building Function
   According to him, an entrepreneur must have the organizing skill. His theory is opposite to Schempeter's theory and Drucker's theory of innovation. An entrepreneur must be an organizer and he must be a leader. Through organizing abilities, an entrepreneur can come up. So, for Harbinson, managerial skill is important.

Moreover, there are contributions in the form schools by different authorities on entrepreneurship. The following are some of the entrepreneurship theories emerged out of different schools:

The Neoclassical School

The literature on innovation and technical change is discussed from our perspective in Devine (forthcoming); see also Metcalfe (1995). The standard theory views the firm in purely technological terms, with the management knowing the firm's cost and revenue functions and performing a mathematical calculation in order to achieve optimal values for all its decision variables. Management is nothing in this setting but 'a passive calculator that reacts mechanically to changes imposed on it by fortuitous external developments over which it does not exert, and may not even attempt to exert, any influence' (Baumol, 1993, p. 13). Thus, there is no need, indeed no room, for entrepreneurial action. It is evident that this fundamental characteristic remains intact even if the model assigns to the objective function a task other than profit maximisation.

The neoclassical approach also recognises that there may be government failure, a consequence of which is that profits might be maximised not from the rules of economic rationality applied to production but from a patron-client network. In this regard, Baumol's (1993) argument that how a firm acts will depend heavily on the reward structure in the economy is telling. He concludes that, although entrepreneurial activity per se cannot be analysed within a neoclassical framework, the allocation of entrepreneurial ability between productive and unproductive activities will be profoundly influenced by the rules of the game. However, although this approach, and more generally the literature on rent–seeking and bribery, offers an understanding of the optimal behaviour of firms under different settings, at an epistemological level it is no different from the standard neoclassical theory of the firm.

All decisions are construed as constrained maximisation problems, with the constraints known beforehand, at least in probabilistic terms. The outcome, therefore, is that 'automaton maximizers the business people are and automaton maximizers they remain' (Baumol, 1993, p. 14). There have also been attempts within a game theoretic framework to analyse innovative activities undertaken in an imperfectly competitive environment. These may be classified under three headings. First, given that the less successful rivals of successful innovators may use their capabilities to launch countermeasures to neutralise or even destroy the innovators' competitive advantage, innovative effort and 'enterprising' sabotage have been analysed as an interactive game (Baumol, 1993, Chapter 5). Second, in other game theoretic models of innovator–imitator interactions (Dasgupta & Maskin, 1987; Dasgupta, 1988), firms either race for a patent on a winner-take-all basis or firms wait for someone else to incur the bulk of the risk. Finally, technology-sharing consortium situations have been analysed in which firms will benefit by sharing complementary information but will be even better off if they retain their information while others share, with the outcome depending on whether the game is finite or infinite (Baumol, 1993). While neoclassical models such as these may offer some insights into various aspects of the innovative process, they contribute nothing to an understanding of the dynamics of entrepreneurship, since in all such models the outcome is predetermined, the rules of the game having been set in advance. Returning to Kirzner's quotation, mistakes in a neoclassical setting occur if and only if there are 'mistakes in arithmetic'. The neoclassical models discussed so far remain essentially production functions and assume away the existence of firms and the relationships between individuals within them. However, building on the work of Coase (1937), neoclassical models have been developed that explain the existence and boundaries of the firm as the outcome of maximising individuals' decisions in conditions of opportunistic behaviour, asymmetric information, bounded rationality or incomplete contracts, and asset specificity. Two strands have emerged in this literature. First, the 'nexus of contracts' or 'property rights' approach (associated with Alchian & Demsetz, 1972, and Jensen & Meckling, 1976), emphasises the residual rights of control over the firm's physical assets or the property rights of the 'indispensable agent'. Second, the 'transactions costs approach' (associated with Williamson, 1985, 1989), focuses on the relative efficiency of different governance structures. The relevance of these developments within neoclassical theory for the purpose of this paper is whether they provide scope for introducing an analysis of entrepreneurship.

Both perspectives rest on the concept of a 'contract' between various input owners to create an optimal governance structure, under the assumption that inputs, outputs and production technology are well-known (Aoki, Gustaffson & Williamson, 1990; Milgrom & Roberts, 1992). The contractual approach, according to Witt (1998, p. 161), 'has been increasingly attracted to one theme: how is opportunism kept under control so that it cannot eat up the gains on transaction costs that can be achieved by setting up a firm as a special way of coordinating individual economic activities [and so that it cannot] discourage asset-specific investments by the firm members where these create potentially sizeable quasi-rents?' These attempts certainly lead to a richer and more realistic portrayal of firms than the production function versions of neoclassical theory, but they again fail to create room for entrepreneurial activity since the outcome of the interactions between the various actors is nothing but the result of a contract assumed to be optimally designed. As Foss (1996, pp. 8-9) emphasises, 'It is outside the prerogative of standard contractual analysis to examine how new resource uses are discovered, how resources are accumulated, how firms learn, which governance structures best promote learning under which circumstances, etc.

To sum up, the neoclassical approach is incapable of usefully addressing the issue of entrepreneurship due to its epistemological standpoint. We now turn to the ways in which the Austrian approach deals with entrepreneurship.

The Austrian School

According to the Austrian school the economic problem consists of the social mobilisation of tacit knowledge, by definition fragmented and dispersed, through the interaction of rival entrepreneurial activities. Thus, the two core concepts in the Austrian approach are the tacitness of knowledge, as elaborated by Hayek, and entrepreneurship, as emphasised by Mises. The social mobilisation of tacit knowledge occurs via entrepreneurial actions, with entrepreneurs directing their efforts toward the achievement of potential profits and thereby discovering what is and what is not possible. The discovery of tacit knowledge in a world that is inherently in a process of continuous change (Hayek, 1937, 1945) is therefore the starting point of the Austrian approach. Since the world is characterised by uncertainty, the discovery process necessarily involves failure as well as success. Entrepreneurs act on their perceptions, or their hunches, and discover whether they were well-founded or in error, in which case they are revised. Thus, the Austrian view of entrepreneurship also has built into it a process for the correction of error. The epistemological standpoint underlying this approach is quite distinct from that underlying the neoclassical school. As Kirzner (1997, p. 64) has recently put it: 'In the neoclassical world, decision makers know what they are ignorant about. One is never surprised. For Austrians, however, to abstract from these qualities of imagination, boldness, and surprise is to denature human choice entirely.' In this regard, it was Knight (1921) who elaborated the concept of unmeasurable uncertainty, separating it from risk which is defined as measurable uncertainty. He stressed that change in line with known laws does not cause uncertainty and that predictable events present no problem of action. Problems of action arise out of departures from routine, from the possibility or occurrence of unpredictable events. Entrepreneurship, therefore, is human action 'seen from the aspect of the uncertainty inherent in every action' (Mises, 1949, p. 254).

In this setting, the Schumpeterian entrepreneur, who plays a disequilibrating role by innovating, and the Misesian–Kirznerian entrepreneur, who plays an equilibrating role by detecting and exploiting? It has been suggested that while the property rights approach remains within an orthodox neoclassical framework, Williamson's transactions costs approach is less neoclassical in that it embraces Simon's concept of bounded rationality (Foss, 1993). It has also been suggested that the transactions costs approach 'by viewing optimal contractual design as a reality that will only be revealed *ex post*, can arguably accommodate a concept of entrepreneurship.' This is an interesting idea which, to be developed, would involve the transactions costs approach moving away from the neoclassical optimising framework within which it is at present firmly located. There is clearly a tension between Williamson's adoption of bounded rationality, which Simon (1979) associates with 'satisficing', and his insistence that opportunistic behaviour is maximising behaviour (Williamson, 1989). We are grateful to Martin Currie for this latter point (see Currie & Messori, 1998). Opportunities that others failed to notice, emerge as the two different types of entrepreneur.

The Early Schumpeterian Entrepreneur

In *The Theory of Economic Development* (1911), Schumpeter outlines a theory of endogenous change in which the entrepreneur, the underlying force in economic development, breaks away from the path of routine. According to Schumpeter, under constant conditions consumers' and producers' goods of the same kind and quantity would be produced and consumed in each successive period, with people abiding by their previous experience and following established methods in familiar ways. Schumpeter then questions what would happen if change occurs, disturbing the smooth flow of economic life. Thus, 'It is the spontaneous and discontinuous change in the channels of the flow, disturbance of equilibrium, which forever alters and displaces the equilibrium state previously existing' (1911, p. 64). Economic development is defined by the implementation of new combinations6 and it is in this context that Schumpeter emphasises the importance of the entrepreneurial function. Entrepreneurial profit is a surplus over costs, as new combinations will persist only if they turn out to be more advantageous. Then, as new businesses arise, entrepreneurial profit disappears as a new equilibrium position is reached. Schumpeter distinguishes the entrepreneur from the capitalist, while acknowledging that entrepreneurs may need to borrow initial capital in order to be able to carry out their new combinations. The Schumpeterian entrepreneur receives profit, but is not the risk bearer in terms of financial responsibility.7 Schumpeter also distinguishes his entrepreneur from the 'inventor' by claiming that 'As long as they are not carried into practice, inventions are economically irrelevant. And to carry any improvement into effect is a task entirely different from the inventing of it, and a task, moreover, requiring entirely different kinds of aptitudes' (1911, p. 88). Thus, for the early Schumpeter, entrepreneurial talents make themselves felt by introducing new ideas, new combinations, with the consequence that established firms are challenged and the pre-existing ways of economic life are disrupted. Schumpeter identifies five types of new combination: the introduction of a new good; the introduction of a new method of production, not yet tested by experience; the opening up of a new market; the conquest of a new source of supply of raw materials or semi-manufactured goods; and the implementation of a new organisation of industry, such as the creation or breaking up of a monopoly position. This point should not be interpreted to mean that the Schumpeterian entrepreneur does not take any responsibility. Schumpeter is careful to point out that the entrepreneur 'may risk his reputation' (1911, p. 137).

The Kirznerian Entrepreneur

Kirzner uses the Misesian notion of 'human action' to analyse the entrepreneurial role: 'the humanaction concept, unlike that of allocation and economizing, does not confine the decision-maker (or the economic analysis of his decisions) to a framework of *given* ends and means' (Kirzner, 1973, p. 33). Thus, the entrepreneurial element in human decision-making is defined by Kirzner (1973, p. 35) as 'the element of alertness to possibly newly available resources and to possibly newly worthwhile goals which is absent from economizing behaviour but present in human action.' The Kirznerian entrepreneur notices 'profit opportunities that exist because of the initial ignorance of the original market participants and that have persisted because of their inability to learn from experience' (Kirzner, 1973, p. 14). In this setting, the knowledge required for entrepreneurship is alertness, defined as 'knowing where to look for knowledge' (Kirzner, 1973, p. 35), and it is assumed that by using this superior knowledge the entrepreneur will capture profits. In answering criticisms that the entrepreneur in many instances creates rather than merely sees a given opportunity, Kirzner replies that the more fundamental function is that of discovery: 'This insight is simply that for any entrepreneurial discovery creativity is never enough: it is necessary to *recognize* one's own creativity' (Kirzner, 1994, p. 109). Although defined in this way the scope for entrepreneurial decision-making may be in danger of disappearing, since the services of individuals with knowledge can be hired, like those of any factor of production, Kirzner argues that the person who hires 'alertness' in fact displays alertness of a still higher order. Kirzner is clear that in an equilibrium state, where there is no lack of coordination and no ignorance, the entrepreneur cannot contribute to the reallocation of resources or products to remove inefficiencies. However, he argues that 'The entrepreneurial market process may indeed reflect a systematically equilibrative *tendency*, but this by no means constitutes a *guaranteed* unidirectional, flawlessly converging trajectory' (Kirzner, 1997, p. 72). Kirzner (1992) emphasises that ownership and entrepreneurship are completely separate functions. The pure entrepreneur starts out with no means and must acquire from the capitalist the capital with which to initiate entrepreneurial activity. However, the capitalist's decision to lend also contains an entrepreneurial element, since in conditions of uncertainty it involves being alert to whether or not an investment offers a real possibility of gain. Kirzner also accepts that entrepreneurship involves an element of risk but argues that this does not mean rejecting the view that the essence of entrepreneurship is perceiving opportunities: 'To recognize that alertness in a world of uncertainty may call for good judgement and lively imagination does not, surely, affect the centrality of the insight that entrepreneurship refers, not to the deliberate exploitation of perceived opportunities, but to the alert perception of opportunities available for exploitation. While the entrepreneur operates under uncertainty, and therefore displays imagination, judgement and creativity, his role is not so much the *shouldering* of uncertainty as it is his ability to *shoulder uncertainty aside* through recognizing opportunities in which imagination, judgement and creativity can successfully manifest themselves' (Kirzner, 1994, pp. 108-109).

A Fusion of the Schumpeterian and Kirznerian Concepts of Entrepreneurship

For Schumpeter entrepreneurial activity involves innovation through the introduction of new goods or methods of production, the opening up of new markets, the conquest of a new supply of materials, the reorganisation of an industry. Kirzner, however, sees entrepreneurial activity as the discovery of opportunities rather than the creation of them: 'the function of the entrepreneur consists not of shifting the curves of cost or of revenues which face him, but of noticing that they have in fact shifted' (1973, p. 81). Thus, arbitrage, in the sense of taking advantage of price differences, would be an entrepreneurial activity for Kirzner, but not for Schumpeter. In Schumpeter's analysis, imitators, who move the economy towards a new equilibrium following a disruption as a result of an innovation, are not engaging in entrepreneurial activity. In Kirzner's analysis, by noticing opportunities and acting to take advantage of them, they certainly are. However, in his more recent work, Kirzner is in the end unwilling to draw a definite line between his concept of entrepreneurship and Schumpeter's concept of creative innovation: 'Discovery would include not only one of hitherto unknown natural resources (as in oil discovery) but also of new kinds of output (as through entrepreneurial product-innovation), or of new additional productivity (of known outputs) available from known inputs (as when an entrepreneur innovates a new productive technique)' (Kirzner, 1997, p. 75).

With regard to the identity of entrepreneurs in the two conceptions, as Witt (1994, p. 541) indicates, 'Being an entrepreneur is, according to Schumpeter, not an occupation or a profession, but rather a unique, and rarely found, capacity to carry out new combinations of resources; that is innovations. The basis of this capacity is held to be a peculiar personality and motivation, an interpretation with obvious elitist connotations. In this respect, Schumpeter clearly contrasts with Mises and Kirzner who interpret the entrepreneurial element as a basic human capacity, an lertness that everyone possesses more or less.' Finally, although for Schumpeter the entrepreneur is the disruptive, disequilibrating force, for Kirzner (1973, p. 127) the entrepreneur remains 'the equilibrating force whose activity responds to the existing tensions and provides those corrections for which the unexploited opportunities have been crying out' (see also Kirzner, 1999). To what extent is a fusion of these two concepts possible? According to Casson (1987, p.151), once the entrepreneur is defined as 'someone who specialises in taking judgmental decisions about the allocation of scarce resources', then the Kirznerian *arbitrageur* and the Schumpeterian innovator can be thought of as 'special cases of the general concept of entrepreneurial speculation based upon self-confident judgement.' We agree with Casson that, while it is necessary to recognize the two distinct functions of entrepreneurship, the umbrella concept of the judgmental decision-maker is a helpful further insight.

The Absence of Firms in the Austrian Approach

Firm behaviour is not theorised in Austrian economics. As Foss & Christensen (1996, p. 11) comment, the Austrians' focus on the study of spontaneous order seems to have 'taken precedence over the study of designed order, such as organisations.' Questions concerning the existence, boundaries and internal organisation of firms have not been addressed; nor, *a fortiori*, have the entrepreneurial activities of firms. The Austrian school's epistemological position concerning the tacit nature of knowledge and the uncertainty inherent in economic life is much more realistic than the over formalised and oversimplified world of the neoclassical paradigm and this *ipso facto* applies to the Austrian approach to entrepreneurial activities. However, by confining themselves to the analysis of individual action in a market process, the Austrian school finds it is difficult, if not impossible, to address entrepreneurial activities within different micro organisational settings. See also McNulty (1987), who suggests that the two concepts are complementary in the sense that disequilibrating and equilibrating activities are part of a single process. For further discussion, see Foss (1994), Loasby (1989) and Minkler (1993). For recent contributions seeking to construct a theory of the firm in the spirit of the Austrian approach, see Foss (1994, 1997), Ioannides (1998) and Sautet (2000). However, such attempts necessarily depart from the Austrian school's basic principle of subjectivism.

Although in his later work Schumpeter focused on the activities of the large corporation, by undermining the individualistic nature of economic dynamism he also distanced himself from the Austrian tradition. In *Capitalism, Socialism and Democracy* (1942) Schumpeter discarded his earlier individualistic conception of the entrepreneur and argued instead that entrepreneurship was increasingly being undertaken by the research and development departments of corporations rather than by individuals. While he recognised that innovating firms might be large or small, he believed that small firms were more and more being pushed to the margin owing to the superior access of large firms to financial resources. Furthermore, although uncertainty provides entrepreneurial opportunities, it may easily become so great as to paralyse action. Hence, increasingly only large-scale enterprises would be ready to undertake entrepreneurial risk. However, once conceived in this way, the Schumpeterian entrepreneur loses his or her defining function, which is to revolutionise the pattern of production and consumption: 'For, on the one hand, it is much easier now than it has been in the past to do things that lie outside the familiar routine—innovation itself is being reduced to routine. Technological progress is increasingly becoming the business of teams of trained specialists who turn out what is required and make it work in predictable ways' (Schumpeter, 1942, p. 132). In fact, Schumpeter and the Austrians from the beginning had little in common apart from a general distancing of themselves from the neoclassical school and, in the early Schumpeter, the issue of entrepreneurship. For discussion of the innovativeness of small versus large firms and of concentrated industries versus atomistic industries, see Loasby (1982), Malerba & Orsenigo (1995), Scherer (1984), Sylos-Labini (1992) and Teece (1996).

The Competence Theory of the Firm

The competence, or capabilities, or knowledge-based theory of the firm emphasises the importance of specific stocks of knowledge that are tacit, socially produced and reproduced, and path-dependent. It seeks to explain on the one hand the sources of competitive advantage and on the other hand the existence and boundaries of firms. The tacit nature of knowledge refers to the non-codifiable, person specific and context-specific dimension of knowledge. The social dimension stems from the interaction between members of economic organisations which creates an accumulation of knowledge that is more than the sum of each individual's personal knowledge and is typically embedded in routines. Pathdependency, finally, arises from the role that each economic organisation plays in providing a unique framework for the generation, mobilisation and articulation of knowledge. The three elements are interwoven, with the possibilities that the firm faces in efficiently using its knowledge base being shaped and reshaped within an interactive process. Thus, the competence perspective provides much greater scope for explaining the dynamics of economic life than the static framework of the neoclassical approach; at the same time, since it focuses on the firm as the site for individual action, it goes well beyond the Austrian approach (Hodgson, 1998a).

The competence theory has roots in both the Austrian and the evolutionary literature. It shares the Austrian epistemological standpoint on the tacit nature of knowledge, but not the Austrian school's subjectivism. One of the key insights of the competence theory is that tacit knowledge does not have to be 'individual' knowledge but may also be 'social' knowledge. It is this insight that enables the competence theory to go beyond the Austrian approach by focusing on the firm as a central part of the social framework within which the actions of individuals are shaped and their individual tacit knowledge is mobilised to produce social knowledge. Competence theorists develop the Austrian approach by arguing that knowledge can be held by both individuals and collectivities in either explicit or tacit form. Tsoukas argues that explicit and implicit knowledge and individual and social knowledge are mutually defined and cannot be separated from one another. He adds that 'a firm's knowledge is distributed in the sense that it is inherently indeterminate: nobody knows in advance what that knowledge is or need be. Firms are faced with *radical uncertainty*: they do not, they cannot, know what they need to know' (1996, p. 22). Since competence is a 'determinant of economic behaviour—meaning that economic competence is embodied in the very ways economic decisions are made' (Pelikan, 1989, p. 283), it must be seen as a scarce resource and hence the process by which it is allocated matters for efficiency. Furthermore, given the nature of their knowledge base, economic organisations 'are [to be] seen as being in constant flux, out of which the potential for the emergence of novel practices is never exhausted' (Tsoukas, 1996, p. 22), i.e. collective or social human action is inherently creative. In this context, the organisational form of the firm is conceptualised as 'a means of acquiring, combining, utilizing and maintaining' knowledge that is by definition not available to any one single agent (Witt, 1998, p. 162). Thus, the firm turns out to be the central entity in the competence approach as the site for generating, mobilising and allocating knowledge—a key input in production. The concept of tacit knowledge was independently developed by Hayek (1937, 1945) and by Michael Polanyi (1962, 1967), who first coined the term. For discussion of the link between them, see Lavoie (1985). 14 In addition, Liebeskind (1996, p. 94) has argued that, in an economy based on private ownership, firms as institutions play a critical role in protecting valuable knowledge from 'expropriation and imitation', since property rights in knowledge, such as patents and copyrights, are very narrowly defined under the law and are costly to write and enforce. From the evolutionary literature, the competence theory takes explicitly the concept of economic development, in particular the development of the firm and its internal organisation. The key authors referred to in this context include Marshall (1920), Nelson & Winter (1982), Penrose (1959), Richardson (1972) and Veblen (1904). Nelson & Winter (1982) note that the firm's explicit and tacit stocks of knowledge are articulated and mobilised in the course of interaction with the external economic environment and what is learnt is then loaded in the firm's 'routines', which makes it available for future use. Since these routines are open to improvement, the firm is conceptualised as a 'learning' body, with organisational knowledge emerging as the outcome of this learning process (Aoki, Gustafsson & Williamson, 1990; Dosi & Marengo, 1994; Lazonick, 1994; Teece & Pisano, 1994). Hodgson (1998a, p. 184) suggests the further clarification that learning should be conceptualised as 'a developmental and reconstitutive process', as opposed to the way in which the neoclassical school (as exemplified by Bray & Kreps, 1987) treats it as 'the cumulative discovery of pre-existing "blueprint" information, or Bayesian updating of subjective probability estimates in the light of incoming data.' The general framework of the competence approach allows a natural role for entrepreneurship, although this has not yet been much elaborated. One reason for this is that the two literatures have developed separately and are based on different discourses, as is evident from the fact that discussions of tacit knowledge in the competence theory rarely make explicit reference to the central role played by tacit knowledge in the Austrian approach, perhaps due to their rejection of the Austrians' subjectivism. It is evident that a concept of entrepreneurship based on the premises of the competence theory would differ significantly from concepts of entrepreneurship based on individualistic premises. One attempt to develop such a concept has been made by Foss. Starting from the position that 'What competence really implies is a view of rationality that is very different from maximisation', he notes that 'Means and ends are not simply given to the decision-maker through some unexamined historical process', with the corollary that 'means-ends-structures have to be set up by the agents themselves' and this, according to Foss, 'is the meaning of the competence known as "*entrepreneurship*"' (Foss, 1993, p. 134). This approach in a sense echoes the much earlier contribution by Penrose (1959, p. 31) on the role of entrepreneurs: 'the introduction and acceptance on behalf of the firm of new ideas.' Penrose's perspective has been confirmed and modified recently by Eliasson (1990) who identifies the competence endowment of firms as the ability to sense direction, i.e. intuition, willingness to undertake risk, efficiency in identifying mistakes, effectiveness in correcting mistakes, effectiveness in managing successful experiments and effectiveness in feeding acquired experience back into intuition.

The competence approach welcomes entrepreneurial inputs from any layer within the firm, as stated by Tsoukas (1996, p. 23): Given the distributed character of organisation knowledge, the key to achieving coordinated action does not so much depend on those 'higher up' collecting more and more knowledge, as on those 'lower down' finding more and more ways of getting connected and interrelating the knowledge each one has. A necessary condition for this to happen is to appreciate the character of a firm as a discursive practice: a form of life, a community, in which individuals come to share an unarticulated background of common understandings. Sustaining a discursive practice is just as important as finding ways of integrating distributed knowledge. For further discussion of the origins of the competence theory of the firm, see Foss (1996, 1998), Hodgson (1998a) and Loasby (1998). However, this does not mean that there is no role for imagination or leadership, even if this dimension has been somewhat neglected in work on the competence theory (Witt, 1998). For early Schumpeter and the Austrians such qualities are theorised within a subjectivist framework, with a role for the firm, if any, only as the vehicle for the implementation of the entrepreneur's pre-existing insight or vision. By contrast, the competence theory implies that imagination draws on and is shaped by the social knowledge embedded in the firm and that leadership takes the form of nurturing the firm's discursive practice and developing consensus around the new means-ends-structures that emerge.

Entrepreneurship in a Participatory Context

An Evaluation of the Literature on Entrepreneurship

What are the implications of this literature for the relationship between entrepreneurial activity and type of economic organisation? Although rarely made explicit, the assumption underlying most, if not all, of the literature is a capitalist system based on the private ownership of capital. Yet, the *raison d'être* of private ownership, the alleged necessity of private ownership for the flourishing of entrepreneurial activity, is never theorised. The Austrian school, of course, constantly claims that social ownership is incompatible with the mobilisation of tacit knowledge through entrepreneurial activity, as in the socialist calculation debate. However, the Austrian contribution to that debate consists of a critique of neoclassical central planning and neoclassical market socialism, both based on state ownership. While we agree with this critique of neoclassical socialism, in our view, as we have argued elsewhere, the Austrian claim that their critique necessarily applies to any form of socialism is mere assertion and has never been theoretically established (Adaman & Devine, 1996). A second implicit assumption in the literature is that entrepreneurial activity is in general socially productive, with the possible relationship between the existence of a capitalist system and unproductive entrepreneurial activity discussed, if at all, only in terms of rent-seeking behaviour. In none of the literature is the possibility even considered that there may be a systemic bias in a capitalist private ownership system towards unproductive entrepreneurial activity. Let us, therefore, summarise the principal themes that have been discussed in the literature on entrepreneurship reviewed in Section 2 and then relate these to different types of economic organisation. Four, possibly complementary, roles for entrepreneurship have been identified:

1. the equilibrating activities of alert individuals in pursuit of their private gain as the essence of the way in which the market process works;

2. the innovative activities of heroic individuals of a special mould forcing through nonincremental change as the way in which the economy develops;
3. decision-making in conditions of uncertainty; and
4. the exercise of individual or collective competence in establishing new means–ends relationships in uncertain, open-ended conditions. In a paper titled 'Why are there no Austrian socialists?', Boettke (1995) cites five propositions offered by Rizzo (1992) as summarising Austrian political economy. The fifth proposition is that socialism is not feasible because of the difficulties of economic calculation without private property and the price system. No supporting argument is provided. In addition to the Austrian school, the other body of theory that makes claims with respect to the question of ownership is the property rights approach. However, property rights analysis is focused on the relationship between residual rights and efficiency within a neoclassical optimizing framework and therefore does not, and cannot, address the issue of entrepreneurship. Furthermore, even within its own framework the property rights approach is unable to 'take account of the separation of ownership and control present in large, publicly held corporations' (Hart, 1989, p.1773).

In the course of the discussion five principal and recurring themes have emerged. First, the tacit nature of much of the knowledge relevant for entrepreneurial activity is recognised by both the Austrian and the competence perspectives. Second, it is central to the competence perspective that tacit knowledge arises in relation to both individuals and organisations and that such knowledge is not only tacit but also social and path-dependent. Third, it is universally agreed that tacit knowledge is generated, mobilised and articulated through a social process—individual rivalry through the market process for the Austrians; the internal processes within the firm, mediated by its routines and discursive practices, for the competence perspective. Fourth, in the literature on entrepreneurship a clear distinction is drawn between the entrepreneur and the capitalist, while in the literature on the competence perspective the issue is rarely explicitly addressed. Of course, it is explicitly or implicitly recognised that entrepreneurial activity requires access to capital, but why this depends on the private ownership of capital is not discussed.

Finally, there is the question of the motivation giving rise to entrepreneurial activity, which is often not made explicit. The Misesian–Kirznerian analysis starts from the premise that since the knowledge required for all effective action, however motivated, is tacit and can only be discovered by acting, through trial and error, all human action has an entrepreneurial element. Yet the Austrian school's analysis privileges a subset of entrepreneurs, who have access to capital and are assumed to be motivated to participate in the market process solely or primarily by the prospect of private financial gain. While this may be a reasonable assumption for some forms of entrepreneurial activity in the institutional context of a capitalist economic system, there is nothing necessary about it. Schumpeterian entrepreneurs, while they may end up with great riches, are motivated more by the need for achievement, while what motivates the actors in the discursive community that constitutes the firm in the competence perspective is typically left unanalysed. It is worth noting that these five themes are also present in the most recent literature on innovation and technical change, even though this literature for the most part does not discuss such change explicitly in terms of entrepreneurial activity (Devine, forthcoming; Metcalfe, 1995).

The Austrian and the competence approaches explicitly or implicitly assume a capitalist institutional framework with privately owned economic units competing against each other. Resources are allocated and reallocated through the operation of market forces in accordance with the discovery of unexploited opportunities or the selection of preferred innovations, as judged in both cases by the criterion of expected and realised profitability. Explicitly or implicitly it is accepted that there is a control group within the firm, i.e. the owner-manager or the management on behalf of the owners, which has the responsibility and the power to make strategic decisions.18 Of course, discussion of different forms of more or less codetermined internal firm organisation has proliferated, as economists have come to recognise the tacit, social, path-dependent nature of knowledge and the discursive practices that generate, mobilise and articulate it. However, in all these forms the owners and their hired managers decide if, when and how the other employees of the firm take part in decision-making and, whatever the subjective motivation of the owners may be, the ultimate criterion of survival and success is profitability. Thus, the internal allocation of resources to potential entrepreneurial and innovative activities, the micro level definition of what are productive and unproductive activities, is determined by judgements of expected profitability. The findings of McCleland's (1961) study as summarised by Baumol (1993, p. 272), 'entrepreneurs are motivated by *n*-achievement (the need for achievement) and not by desire for money. ... In his tests, people with high levels of *n*-achievement do no better when offered larger amounts of money for success, whereas people with low *n*-achievement scores do much better when offered money. ... *n*-achievers choose smaller risks than the average person: they are not gamblers but calculators and planners. ... [T]he *n*-achiever is not an individualist and does not depend for success on private enterprise. ... Such persons get just as much satisfaction from the manipulation of a committee, or for working for a government, since their interest is in results rather than in considerations such as profit or status. This is perhaps one reason why huge committee-run corporations can be successful'. See Ioannides (1998) for discussion of a possible Austrian theory of the firm with a controlling ownership interest; and Ioannides (1994) for an argument that a controlling ownership interest is also required for the We conclude from this evaluation that entrepreneurial and innovative activity requires an organisational context in which:

1. the generation, mobilisation and articulation of tacit, social, path-dependent knowledge is facilitated, which we take to involve participation in the discursive practices and decision making processes within the firm; and
2. there exist (a) criteria embedded in the firm's evolving routines for the internal allocation of resources across potential entrepreneurial activities, (b) selection mechanisms that select across the output of the firms making up the economy according to socially agreed criteria of social productiveness and unproductiveness, (c) processes that allocate capital for future entrepreneurial and innovative activities according to these criteria, and (d) feedback processes which enable the outcome of the selection mechanisms in (b) and the allocation processes in (c) to be used to modify the routines in (a).

While a capitalist economic system clearly constitutes such a context, the necessarily limited participation afforded by private ownership and the one dimensional criterion of profitability that animates processes (a) to (d) above suggest that a participatory economic system based on social ownership may have comparative advantages in contributing to human well-being.

A New Perspective: Participatory Entrepreneurship

We define a participatory economic system, following Devine (1988), as an interlocking network of social relationships, mediated through a set of interlocking institutions, in which the values and interests of people in the different aspects of their lives interact and shape one another in a discursive process of decision-making through negotiation and cooperation. Given this paper's focus on entrepreneurship, participation will be discussed at the intra-firm and extra-firm levels—within the firm, where tacit knowledge is generated, mobilised and articulated; and outside the firm, where the output of the entrepreneurial activities of firms is evaluated and the allocation of, or access to, the capital needed to engage in future entrepreneurial activity is determined. Generalised participation may be thought of as the direct or indirect involvement in social practice, on an equal footing, of all those with either a relevant input to contribute or a legitimate interest in the outcome, i.e. all those who are affected by an activity. With respect to economic activity, the institutional form corresponding to generalised participation is that of social ownership, ownership by those with an interest in the use of the assets involved in the activity in question. Social ownership defined in this way has clear similarities with the concept of stakeholding, with the stakeholders being those inside or outside an organisation who have a specific interest in its activities. Both concepts require criteria for determining the principal interest or stakeholding groups or constituencies, the basis or weight of representation, and the way in which representatives should be chosen. The institutional form through which the social owners at different levels might be determined may be thought of by way of analogy with the bodies that determine the boundaries of electoral constituencies in the UK. Just as such boundaries are changed as population densities and community identities change, so the social owners would change as the activity in question and those with an interest in it changed. Neoclassical firm in both its nexus of contracts/property rights and transactions costs versions. For extended discussion of the concept of social ownership, see Devine (1988, (esp. pp. 149-152), and 9 (esp. pp. 222-234). The concept of stakeholding associated with social ownership needs to be distinguished from *(i)* recent discussion of stakeholding which assumes a capitalist economic system, with the organisational form through which stakeholding is institutionalised at the micro level being some sort of trusteeship or consultative process rather than legal social ownership by the stakeholders (Kay, 1997; Parkinson, 1997; Williamson, 1997), although this would also require a method for determining who the stakeholders were; and, *a fortiori*, from *(ii)* the macro level concept of 'stakeholder capitalism' which seeks to analyse the conditions necessary for social inclusion, with all sections of society having their legitimate interests met to an acceptable level, within a private ownership. Since knowledge is now generally recognised to cover a spectrum from tacit to explicit, with all knowledge consisting of both, albeit in differing combinations, it can be argued that social ownership and the generalised participation that it makes possible are likely to constitute a more efficient form of economic organisation for the social mobilisation of knowledge than either private or state ownership (Adaman & Devine, 1996, 1997). Furthermore, since social ownership involves all those with an interest in the use of the assets that are concerned, the criteria and judgements used in deciding the allocation of those assets across different alternatives can be arrived at through a discursive process of cooperative interaction in which the people constituting the relevant 'community', the social owners, 'come to share an unarticulated background of common understanding' (Tsoukas, 1996, p. 23), which facilitates the more explicit process of negotiation between the different interests. In order to evaluate our claim that a participatory economic system would be more efficient at mobilising knowledge than a capitalist system and would be able to apply wider criteria than profitability for the allocation of resources, we first briefly outline the principal characteristics of such a system. It follows from our definition of social ownership that the social owners will differ according to the nature of the economic activity in question. The participatory model we advocate rests on the distinction between market exchange and market forces. Market exchange involves the use of existing capacity—selling and buying what can be produced using the existing assets of the firm. Market forces are the process through which changes in the structure of capacity are brought about in capitalist societies. Investment or disinvestment is undertaken atomistically by individual capitalist enterprises.

The outcome is dependent on the aggregate effect of these atomistic decisions which are then coordinated *ex post*. In a system based on social ownership, market exchange would continue but firms would be owned by those who are affected by their activities. Market forces, however, would be replaced by a process of negotiated coordination in which those who would be affected, the social owners at this level, would seek to agree on a coherent package of investments and disinvestments, coordinated *ex ante*, that would best meet their interests. Thus, the social owners with respect to investment decisions would embrace a wider set of interests than the social owners with respect to existing assets. At the level of the firm, both those who work within it and those outside it who have an interest in its activities constitute the social owners. Representation on the Board of Directors of these internal and external interests enables generalised participation in the determination of strategic objectives and the monitoring of the firm's senior managers and performance. Whether the senior management is appointed by the workforce, on the principle of worker self-management, or by the Board, may be considered a secondary issue, since the concept of generalised participation could be interpreted either way. The process of generating, mobilising and articulating the tacit, social, pathdependent knowledge that gives rise to potential entrepreneurial and innovative activities within the firm takes place in this participatory context. The output of the firm's entrepreneurial and innovative activity is then offered for sale in the market. Since the knowledge base or competence of firms is pathdependent, each firm is unique. The internal processes of each unique firm therefore generate variety in the products, both final and intermediate goods that are offered for sale. In the course of market exchange selection occurs and information is generated, in the form of the degree of capacity utilization and relative profitability, about which products users prefer. capitalist society (Hutton, 1994; Kelly, Kelly & Gamble, 1997). We have elsewhere drawn an analogy with the M-firm corporate structure in which the divisions engage in market exchange and the headquarters deals with investment and disinvestment (Adaman & Devine, 2001). One of us has elsewhere argued for internal worker self-management (Devine, 1988).

What happens then? In a capitalist economic system market forces, despite imperfections, in general allocate capital to the firms that are or are expected to be the most profitable. Other firms seek to imitate them, incremental innovation takes place, diffusion occurs and from time to time new non-incremental innovations and general purpose technologies emerge.

Schumpeter's gale of creative destruction proceeds, sometimes in the form of firm bankruptcies or takeovers, more generally in the form of new products, technologies and production units replacing old, frequently accompanied by a geographical redistribution of economic activity, both within countries and globally. What is evident about the operation of market forces is that it allows no scope for generalized participation, indeed for any real participation, in the determination of the overall allocation and reallocation of economic activity. Instead of the process of economic change being consciously shaped in accordance with people's explicit and tacit knowledge as to how they might be affected by it, the outcome is what no one willed.

Of course, for the Austrian's this creation of 'spontaneous order' is the real attraction of the market process. In the context of the objective of generalised participation, however, a model of democratic planning through negotiated coordination provides an alternative to the operation of market forces as a process for consciously selecting across the entrepreneurial and innovative output of firms and allocating capital for future entrepreneurial and innovative activities according to socially agreed criteria. The process of negotiated coordination is envisaged as being mediated through an interlocking set of institutions extending beyond the firm and constituted at differing levels, e.g. industry or sector, locality, national region, nation, international region, global. The composition of the social owners at each level, indeed the specification of the different levels, would depend on the nature of the economic activities involved and would be expected to change as technology or markets change, much like the constant redrawing of boundaries discussed in recent theories of the firm, and as social values and priorities change, for instance in favour of more local and less global production. The outcome of the negotiations would be an allocation of capital constituting a coordinated programme of investments that balanced considerations of revealed productive efficiency and entrepreneurial competence, the consequences for the communities involved, and the judgments of the social owners as to their priorities for future entrepreneurial and innovative activities.

An Evaluation of Participatory Entrepreneurship

This organisational context seems to us to incorporate both the efficiency and the criteria arguments set out at the beginning of the previous section. Our claim is, first, that the process of mobilising knowledge, tacit and explicit, is likely to be more efficient in a participatory system based on social ownership than in a system made up of privately owned capitalist firms; and, second, that the criteria used for allocating the firm's internal resources and selecting across the entrepreneurial and innovative activities of firms are able to embrace a wider set of social concerns than capitalism's single overriding criterion of expected or realised profitability.

The Austrian school claims that the market process is the most, indeed the only, efficient way to mobilise social knowledge and that this process depends on private ownership. Since we have already argued at the beginning of Section 3.1 that the alleged necessity of private ownership is mere assertion and has never been theorised, we concentrate here on the case for the market process. The Austrian argument is that the tacit knowledge of individual entrepreneurs can only be drawn upon by the individuals themselves, who then discover whether their judgements are correct by engaging in market competition.

Our evaluation of the literature on entrepreneurship concluded, *inter alia*, that 'tacit knowledge arises in relation to both individuals and organisations and that such knowledge is not only tacit but also social and path-dependent'. Thus, it is the characteristics of the enterprise that are relevant when considering the efficiency with which knowledge is generated and mobilised within the firm. The socially owned firm is a more inclusive and participatory community than the capitalist firm, able to draw on the wider knowledge base of the tacit knowledge of all its social owners, rather than just that of the individual Austrian entrepreneur or the top management of the capitalist corporation or state enterprise. The essential element of trial and error, given the inherent uncertainty associated with entrepreneurial and innovative activity, is present in the competition between firms as they engage in market exchange and discover whether their judgements are well-founded. Would-be entrepreneurs and innovators, whether individuals or existing enterprises, need access to capital. The socially owned extra-firm institutions that allocate capital across firms in our model are more inclusive and participatory communities than capitalist financial institutions, with again a wider knowledge base. These institutions would have available as a basis for their decisions the two forms of knowledge that have been conceptualised in the literature on entrepreneurship and innovation—explicit and tacit. Explicit knowledge would include the relevant firm-based data on degrees of capacity utilisation and profitability, reflecting the choices made by potential users when selecting across the output of different firms in the course of engaging in market exchange. Tacit knowledge would be mobilised in the process of negotiation within the socially owned financial institution. The representatives of the social owners would seek to articulate and evaluate the reasons for the differential performance of firms, the ways in which they would be affected by alternative responses to that differential performance, the characteristics of the innovation programme proposed and the likelihood of future success. Just as the decision-making processes of firms, which incorporate tacit social knowledge, are revised in the light of experience, thus constituting the firm as a learning organisation, so the same is true of financial institutions, whether they are privately or socially owned. The difference is that socially owned financial institutions, like socially owned firms, are able to draw on a wider set of information inputs when reaching their decisions. This is the fundamental reason, in our view, why a system of negotiated coordination has clear advantages over market forces as an allocative and evolutionary selection mechanism. It would be more efficient, since firms and financial institutions are able to draw on the knowledge of all those involved in productive and innovative activities. The selection of the future activities for which capital would be made available would be on the basis of a wider set of criteria than the single criterion of expected private profitability. The criteria would be arrived at and agreed upon by those who would be affected by the outcome of these activities, rather than being imposed by the coercion of market forces, or by the authority of the state or any other agency acting on behalf of some presumed, known-from-above, general interest.

The difference can be illustrated in the context of a judgement in relation to how much of society's limited resources should be allocated to similar innovative projects. If too many parallel projects are financed, the result will be unnecessary duplication and waste; if too few, the necessarily experimental nature of innovative activity, in conditions of radical uncertainty, will be stifled. Dasgupta & Maskin (1987), working within a neoclassical game theoretic framework, conclude that capitalist rivalry results in social inefficiency, with too many resources being devoted to parallel projects; Metcalfe (1997), from within an evolutionary framework, argues that parallel projects are a necessary part of technological competition as a trial and error process of discovery and selection.

While we agree with Metcalfe that the uncertainty inherent in innovation means that parallel projects are likely to be necessary, the resources devoted to innovation in capitalist economies reflect not only uncertainty but also oligopolistic rivalry. From the standpoint of the criteria that might emerge from a participatory process of deliberative democracy, the resources allocated to innovation might well be judged excessive. Negotiated coordination based on social ownership would make it possible for competition to be combined with cooperation, with the risk associated with radical uncertainty being borne collectively, the outcome of innovative activity resulting in public rather than private knowledge, and the decision on how much resources to allocate to which inherently uncertain activities being made by the community that bears the risk and benefits from the outcome. A further advantage of negotiated coordination is that, although in the case of innovative entrepreneurial activity the irreducible element of radical uncertainty is likely to be relatively large, some forms of uncertainty present in a capitalist economic system can be reduced significantly through the conscious coordination of interrelated activities. As Demsetz (1997, p. 28) has observed, commenting on recent developments in neoclassical theory, 'the focus in this effort has led to the neglect of information problems that do not involve agency relationships. These are associated with planning in a world in which the future is highly uncertain, and they include problems of product choice, investment and marketing policies, and scope of operations.' Although Demsetz's comment is in the context of planning in relation to interdependent privately owned firms, social ownership makes it all the more possible to coordinate the interrelated activities of firms through negotiation and cooperation. Indeed, the process of negotiated coordination makes it possible to combine the *ex ante* adjustment classically associated with economic planning (Dobb, 1955, 1960) and the *ex post* adjustment classically associated with market forces and the invisible hand. Extra-firm institutions allocate capital according to the criteria they have evolved, taking account of known interdependencies, but they are path-dependent learning organisations able to revise the criteria they use and improve their competence in applying them (Adaman & Devine, 1997).

This discussion of a new perspective on entrepreneurship, that of participatory entrepreneurship, has embraced both the firm, as the institution within which entrepreneurial activity results in innovative output, and the extra-firm processes and institutions that select across firms and allocate capital for future entrepreneurial activity. The perspective is one of an evolutionary process, based on trial and error and selection, that fully recognises the inherent uncertainty associated with entrepreneurial and innovative activity. We have sought to examine both the ways in which generalized participation might be achieved and the advantages of generalised participation in both parts of the evolutionary process. In our view, it is important to emphasise that firm and extra-firm processes are inseparably linked. Participation at the level of the firm alone, with selection and allocation left to market forces, is inevitably subject to the coercion of expected profitability as the sole criterion for decision-making. This is the fallacy of market socialism (Adaman & Devine, 1996, 1997; Devine, 1992).

The central concept of our system of participatory entrepreneurship is that of decision-making through a process of negotiated coordination between those who will be affected by the outcome, the social owners. However, innovation disrupts existing patterns, has differential effects on different groups. Is it not likely that those who will be *prima facie* adversely affected by potential innovations will seek to block them, thus imparting a conservative bias to the system? More generally, what if negotiation fails to result in agreement? Furthermore, are there not likely to be power imbalances, enabling some groups, perhaps the more forceful and articulate, to impose their interests on the rest? These are real issues, to which we have sought to respond elsewhere (e.g. Devine, 1988, Adaman & Devine, 2001).

The classic distinction is between uncertainty that is due to unpredictable events or outcomes, including innovative attempts to do something that has not been done before, and uncertainty due to a form of economic organisation based on atomistic decision-making, so that decision makers are unaware of decisions made simultaneously but which affect the outcome of their own decision (Devine, 1988; Dobb, 1960; Koopmans, 1957). We are grateful to an anonymous referee for reminding us of these issues.

In summary, we have argued that social owners should be represented on decision-making bodies in proportion to the degree to which they are affected and we have suggested ways in which this might be determined. We believe that a process of negotiated coordination has a dynamic that makes for agreement, since it encourages people to be aware of the interests of others as well as of their own interests. However, although we favour consensual decision-making, if agreement cannot be reached decisions would be made through an agreed formal voting procedure. We are fully conscious of the fact that the personal resources available to people when participating in social life differ and are shaped by their lifetime experience. It is for this reason that we have argued for the abolition of the social (not the functional) division of labour, so that everyone has access to the different types of selfdevelopmental experience necessary to enable real as opposed to merely formal participation. We envisage movement towards a participatory society as a slow process involving continuous struggle over the distribution of ownership, power and life experiences. However, while aware of these problems, we are equally aware of the far greater problems and injustices in capitalist societies that arise from the unequal distribution of power and the fact that conflicts of interest are resolved by the privileged position of privately owned capital and the coercion of market forces. There remains the question of motivation. Within a capitalist economic system it is perhaps not unreasonable to assume that people in their economic lives act primarily in the expectation of financial gain. However, there is a substantial body of theoretical and empirical work which suggests that even in capitalist economies human motivation cannot be reduced to the single dimension of financial gain (see e.g. Bowles, 1998; Hodgson, 1998b; Margolis, 1982; Sen, 1977; Solow, 1994). Furthermore, the motivation of financial gain is not at all obviously the prime mover in relation to entrepreneurial activity in the capitalist firm. The desire for achievement, or self-realisation, or even the concept of 'selfcompetition' (Khalil, 1997) may be sufficient motivation. Of course, if access to capital, to the means for engaging in entrepreneurial activity and therefore to the opportunity to seek achievement or selfrealisation from such activity, is allocated according to the sole criterion of the expected profitability of the activity, then a bias is imparted to the type of entrepreneurial activity that will be undertaken. As we have seen, Baumol has argued that the allocation of entrepreneurial effort across different activities will depend on the structure of rewards attached to those activities. In an economic system based on social ownership, generalised participation and negotiated coordination, with a reward system structured accordingly, the desire for achievement and self-realisation would be directed towards those activities that were judged by the communities affected to be socially productive, based on the criteria that they had themselves established. Furthermore, the motivations not associated with personal financial gain already present in capitalist economic systems are likely to be greatly strengthened in a participatory economic system. Finally, generalised participation would create a framework and an ethos, a moral community, in which responsibility and accountability to others is part of the generally accepted underlying assumptions on the basis of which people engage in social, including economic, life.

To sum up, it is argued that entrepreneurial and innovative activity cannot only thrive in a participatory economic system based on social ownership and negotiated coordination, but can contribute more effectively to human well-being in such a system than in a capitalist economic system based on private property. The criteria for success would be defined by the pluralistic interests constituting the relevant community, and entrepreneurial activity would be embedded in the activities of those who would be affected by it. Much experience has been gained and much research has been undertaken on various. 'It is often assumed that an economy of private enterprise has an automatic bias towards innovation, but this is not so. It has a bias only towards profit' (Hobsbawm, 1969, p. 40). Participatory schemes at different levels. This has recently been primarily at the micro level (see e.g.Levine & Tyson, 1990; Winther & Marens, 1997), but earlier experience at the macro level should not be forgotten (Crouch & Dore, 1990; Schmitter & Lehmbruch, 1979). In a sense these studies represent tentative acknowledgements of the interrelationship between participatory cooperation and participation in defining the criteria of success. What has been missing in these approaches, in our view, has been a clear recognition that participation at the micro and the macro levels must be seen as part of a single participatory process if their full potential is to be realised. The further exploration of these issues constitutes a rich agenda for future research.

Categorisation of Theories of Entrepreneurship

There is a categorisation, the different writers on entrepreneurship in terms of the following dimensions of the theory of entrepreneurship:

- Market Discussed.
- What is forecasted by the Entrepreneur.
- Number of Forecasts made by the Entrepreneur.
- Action Taken by Entrepreneur.
- Entrepreneur's Perception of Risk.
- Cause of Entrepreneurial Profit.
- Effect of Entrepreneurship on Equilibration of Economy.

5

Forms of Business Enterprises

Legal Forms of Business Organisation

Business undertakings can be organised as public or private form of ownership. From the point of view of private organisation or ownership, there are four forms of organisations for a business unit. It may be organised by an individual as sole proprietorship, by mutual agreement of two or more persons as partnership or by an association of persons who form a cooperative society for specific purpose, or else it may be organised by a number of persons as Joint Stock Company or corporation. The law prescribes a variety of forms of business ownerships the choice of which depends upon size, type and objectives of individual functions and goals critical to the success of the organisation formed.

For business purpose, the chief forms of private ownership or organisations are:

1. Sole proprietorship (ownership by one individual)
2. Partnership (ownership by two or more people)
3. Corporation (ownership by the shareholders)
4. Cooperative (by, for and of the members)

Characteristics of an Ideal Form of Organisation

In choosing a particular form of organisation, an entrepreneurship will try to find out how far his requirements will be met by a particular form of organisation. He/she will generally consider the following factors while making this type of assessment:

1. *Ease of Formation:* An ideal form of organisation is one, which can be brought into existence with the least difficulty. A good form of

organisation, as judged from the point of view of ease of formation, is one that involves the least expense in formation and minimum legal formalities.

2. ***Ease of raising capital:*** Where a large amount of capital is needed, it is desirable to ensure that investors in the business concerned are assure of safety of investment, fair return on investment and the transferability of investment.
3. ***Limited Liability***: From the point of view of risk, the entrepreneur will naturally prefer limited liability. This means that in case of insolvency or winding up, the owner or owners will be held responsible only up to the amount of capital agreed to be contributed by them.
4. ***Direct relationship between ownership control and management:*** The right of an individual or a group of individuals represents ownership of a business. As a rule, the control should lie where the ownership lies. This will ensure that the management will take active interest in the efficient running of the enterprise.
5. ***Flexibility of operation:*** A good form of organisation offers the maximum flexibility and adaptability to situations.
6. ***Continuity or stability:*** An ideal form of organisation enjoys uninterrupted existence over a long period of time.
7. ***Retention of business secrets:*** The entrepreneur will also have to be careful to ensure that the form of organisation chosen by him will allow the vital business secrets to be retained without being leaked out top the competitors.
8. ***Freedom from state regulation:*** Various forms of organisations are exposed to varying degrees of control and regulations by the state. Where the extent of regulations by the government is considerable, the enterprise may have to spend considerable amount of time, money and energy in complying with legal formalities and instruction.
9. ***Low tax burden:*** Various forms of organisations are assessed to income tax on different bases. Obviously other things being equal, the ideal form of organisation will be that which will attract the minimum amount of tax liability.

It will be naïve to expect all the above features in any one form of organisation. No single form can be called ideal for each lacks in one criteria or the other.

Sole Proprietorship

It is a form of business ownership in which a single individual assumes all the risk of operating the business, owns its assets, controls and uses any profit that is made. This form is known also as individual or single proprietorship, sole ownership or individual enterprise.

The individual may run the business alone or take the help of the members of the family or may obtain the assistance of employees. The owner drives the total benefit and assumes the risk to which the business is exposed. In the eyes of the law there is no distinction between the business and individual private affair, meaning that the law recognizes the individual and the business as being one and the same. This business is very common form of ownership carried out in different areas where the capital required is small and the risk is not quite heavy.

Salient Features

The salient features of this form of business organisation are as follows:

1. *Single ownership:* The business is owned by a single individual who finances, controls and manages the business and consequently enjoys the profits or suffers losses solely and exclusively.
2. *Owner- manager:* Ownership and management of the business concern rests in the hands of the sole proprietor who enjoys full control over the business.
3. *No separate legal entity:* The sole proprietorship firm has any separate legal identity of its own as distinct from its owner. Both are treated as one and the same in the eyes of the law.
4. *Undivided risk:* The question of sharing the profits or losses of the business by another person other than the sole owner does not arise and the proprietor bears the risks all by himself/ herself.
5. *Unlimited liability:* In case of losses the liability of the sole owner is unlimited and his personal property may also be attached, if needed, to discharge the debts incurred in running the business.
6. *Freedom from government control:* Except for the permission required to be obtained from the legal authorities, this form of organisation has virtually no government control and is free from government regulation.

Advantages of Sole Proprietorship:

1. *Ease and low cost of formation and dissolution:* It is easy to form a sole proprietorship because the legal formalities or other complicated procedures required are less and if all debts of the business are paid and the businessman is not willing to carry on or wants to change it to other form, it is easy to dissolve as was to form it.
2. *Direct motivation and personal care:* In this form of organisation, all the profits of the business belong to one person and he faces every loss. This gives greater incentive to the owner to take personal interest in his business and manage it most efficiently.
3. *Freedom and promptness in action:* In matters of business dealing, the sole proprietor can take his own decisions and there is no question to his authority. This type of freedom of action promotes initiatives and

self reliance. As there is no need to consult other person, the sole proprietor can take prompt decisions.

4. ***Business secrecy:*** In this type of business organisation, it is easy to maintain the secrecy of business. Since confidential information is the key to success for a competitive business, it is unlikely that owner will leak the information vital to the business.
5. ***Social desirability:*** From the social point of view, the sole proprietorship is desirable as it ensures that too much wealth does not concentrate in hands of few. It may be one of the ways in which equitable distribution of the wealth is ensured.
6. ***Absolute control:*** The sole proprietor has direct and absolute control over his business affairs and he is free to act or manage the business in his own chosen way. His control on all business operations is complete which minimizes outside interference or influence.
7. ***Flexibility in operations:*** Since the sole proprietor does not need to consult any one or is not obliged to discuss with anybody in regard to his business operations there is greater scope for flexibility. This form of ownership allows for maximum flexibility as the sole owner can, at his will, change the business operations to suit the changing business conditions.
8. ***Minimum government control:*** Any central or state law, except the general laws of contract and sale of goods, does not regulate this form of business ownership. Consequently, there is little interference or control by government in day to day business affairs. The sole trader is not required to submit any profit and loss account to the government.
9. ***Personal touch:*** Customer satisfaction and worker's motivation are two most important factors that contribute to the success of business. By paying personal attention to the customers and by maintaining an intimate personal touch with the workers, the sole proprietor will boost the business prospect as well as his own personal image which helps to make him flourish beyond his own expectations.

Disadvantages of Sole Proprietorship:

1. ***Limited resources and size:*** In this type of concerns, the resources (capital, human, material, informational) are limited. As only one person is responsible for the business these resources are limited to his capacity.
2. ***Unlimited liability:*** The sole proprietorship will be liable for all debts of the business. At times of loss and bankruptcy, if the business assets are not sufficient to satisfy the obligations or debts of creditors, his personal and real property may be required to pay off. This indicates how the owner is committing his personal assets for the business failure.
3. ***Limited managerial skills:*** A sole proprietor may not be expected in performing every function like purchasing, selling, accounting, hiring

and other necessary functions which may lead to business suffer from not being managed properly. Due to limited financial capability he may not be able to afford to employ trained and professional managers thus depriving the business specialization and expertise in field of balanced management.

4. *Uncertain future:* This kind of business suffers from uncertain future that means there is no stability or lack of continuity. This business may come to an end if the owner cannot continue the business due to death, insanity, imprisonment or bankruptcy.

Partnership

This form of organisation represents the second in the evolution of the forms of business organisation. It grew essentially to meet the requirements of expanding business which calls for more capital, increased risk, and more managerial ability that were considered as limitations of the individual proprietorship.

In Ethiopian as per the commercial code of 1960, Article 211, reads as, "A partnership agreement is defined as a contract whereby two or more persons who intend to join together, make contribution for the purpose of carrying out activities of an economic nature and of participating in the profit and loses arising out there of if any."

Characteristics of Partnership

From the above definition of partnership, which is almost similar in all countries' regulations, the following general characteristics can be indicated:

1. *Plurality of persons:* This form of business requires the existence of two or more persons entering into contract which is an agreement between parties known as Memorandum of Association or Article of Partnership deed.
2. *Contractual relationship:* Partnership comes into existence by mutual agreement which stipulates the contractual relationship between the partners. The memorandum lays down the terms and conditions of partnership and the rights, duties and obligations of partners.
3. *Capital contribution:* In this form of business, every partner shall make a contribution which may be in money, debts, other property or skills. The contribution that is to be made for the business shall be equal unless otherwise agreed.
4. *Management:* Every partner has the right to take an active part in the management of the firm's affairs. But the partnership agreement may provide the pattern of managing indicating how the management activity is shared among the different partners according to experience and knowledge.

5. ***Duration:*** The partnership firm legally comes to an end if any of the partners withdraws or dies or is no longer able under the law to be partner or declared bankrupt.
6. ***Unlimited liability:*** The liability of each partner of the firm is unlimited in respect of the firm's debts. The liability of the partner is joint, in the sense that the creditors can recover their dues from the property of any or all partners in case the firm's assets are insufficient.
7. ***Agency relationship:*** The partner will be liable for the faults and wrongful acts of a co-partner in the course of the firm's business while acting for the business. Since every partner has the right to take part in the management activity, when acting on his given specified areas, every partner has the authority to act on behalf of his fellow partners and the firm in the ordinary course of business. Thus, he is an agent of the firm and other partners.
8. ***Utmost good faith & trust:*** There must be highest standards of honesty among the partners. Partnership agreement is based on mutual confidence and trust of the partners. The partner must, therefore, be just and honest to other partners.
9. ***No separate legal entity:*** The partnership firm has any independent legal existence apart from the persons who constitute it. In the eyes of the law, like that of sole proprietorship, there is no distinction between the partners and the firm.
10. ***Restriction on transfer of interest:*** A partner cannot transfer his share or give his ownership to outsiders without the consent of other partners. In other words, no partner is entitled to bring in another person as partner without the permission of existing partners.
11. ***Unanimity of consent:*** No changes may be made in the nature of business and no partner can act out of the specified way or any partner cannot make any decisions without the consent or agreement of all the partners.

Types of Partnership

There are two types of partnership, namely:

1. General partnership; and
2. Special partnership.

The basic difference between the two is that while the former has unlimited liability and the latter type allow for a limited liability to its partners. Under each category there are other types of partnership as well, which are as under:

General Partnership

1. ***Partnership-at-will***: In this form, no stipulation is made as to when and how the partnership will come to an end. In the absence of any specific

provision in partnership deed about the duration of the partnership, a partner can pull out of the firm after giving certain number of days notice to the firm withdrawing from the partnership or terminating the Deed of Agreement.

2. ***Particular partnership:*** This type of partnership specifies a fixed period of time for completion of a particular business venture and after achieving the objective or after expiry of stipulated period, it automatically becomes dissolved.
3. ***Ordinary joint Venture:*** This in fact is a temporary partnership arrangement between two or more persons to carry out a particular business venture. After accomplishing the tasks, the joint venture comes to an end. In joint venture, generally the right of management is delegated to one of the partners who are accountable to other members. While in a general partnership, all the partners are entitled to carry out the business; in a joint venture all the members do not enjoy the right of implied agency.

Special Partnership

(a) ***Limited partnership:*** In this form there is at least one partner whose liability is unlimited and one or more partners whose liability is limited to the extent of capital contributed. The duties and obligations of the limited partner are:
    1. The limited partner is not entitled to take an active part in the management of the business and as such cannot bind by his acts.
    2. He cannot withdraw any part of his capital nor can he transfer his interest to others without the consent of the general partner.
    3. The general partner who has unlimited liability need not take the consent of the limited partner to admit a new partner into the business.
    4. The death or insolvency of the limited partner does not affect the business or the limited partnership.

(b) ***Special joint ventures:*** In this form, the partners have limited liability and they will terminate after accomplishing the task for which they are created.

Kinds of Partners

Partner of a firm may be classified into the following categories:

1. ***Active Partner:*** A person who takes an active part in the conduct of business and manages its affairs is called an active partner or working partner.
2. ***Sleeping partner or dormant partner:*** He who does not take any part or active interest in the conduct of business is called sleeping or dormant partner. He only contributes a limited capital and his liability is also limited to that extent.

3. *Nominal or Ostensible partner:* A nominal partner is one who does not invest any money nor takes any share in the profits but he only lends his name to the firm. He does not take any active part in the business.

Ideal Partnership

A partnership survives and succeeds on the strength of its members in terms of morality, good faith and mutual trust. In order to be called an ideal partnership it must have the following essential characteristics:

1. *Mutual trust and good faith:* There must be proper understanding and mutual trust between the partners.
2. *Common approach:* The partners must have a like-minded common approach to all the business problems. There must be cooperation and coordination among the partners for smooth running of business.
3. *Adequate capital:* Both the long-term and short-term capital requirements must be met by the partners alleviating the need for borrowing from outsiders.
4. *Written agreement:* In order to avoid disputes and misunderstandings among the partners at a later stage, the partnership agreement must be reduced to writing.
5. *Registration:* Although registration is not compulsory, an ideal form of partnership must get itself registered as otherwise it cannot enforce its rights against outsiders in the courts.

Advantage of Partnership:

1. *Ease of organisation:* Except some formalities like that of proprietorship, the partnership is quite easily formed. All that is required is an agreement among partners. The initial expenses are less and legal formalities are simple.
2. *Large financial and managerial resources:* In this form of organisation compared to sole proprietorship, the capital to be raised will be more because the financial resources of the two or more persons will be available and this will make the business to enjoy high credit standing and get more credit.
3. *Personal supervision:* Partners look after the business personally and guard against the wastage and other inefficiencies because they are initially interested in the success of the business and also known if there is any failure on their part they may put even their private property in jeopardy.
4. *Reduced risk:* The losses incurred by the firm be shared by all partners and hence the share of loss of each partner will be less than in case of sole proprietorship.
5. *Flexibility:* The partnership firm is not subjected to government interference or regulation in the day-to-day functioning. Hence, partners are free to change the line of business or the place of business at their will.

6. *Democratic functioning:* In a partnership firm every partner has a right to participate in the decision making process or management of the firm irrespective of his status based on capital contribution.
7. *Better public relations:* The reputation of a sole proprietor rests on one person whereas all the partners of a partnership firm can pool in their resourcefulness and goodwill to boost up the image and business prospects of the firm.
8. *Tax liability:* A partnership firm is not subjected to double taxation. Either it is assessed for tax as individual or its income is taxable in the hands of the partners.

Disadvantage of Partnership:

1. *Unlimited liability:* If the assets of the partnership are not sufficient to meet the obligations, the creditors may choose to sue any or all to satisfy the debts.
2. *Risk of implied agency:* A dishonest or incompetent partner may make, by his acts, misjudgments or faults, the firm in difficulties because his acts would bind the firm and the remaining partners.
3. *Lack of harmony:* As every partner has equal voice in the management, everyone would try to assert his position and try to promote his personal interest and this may lead to internal frictions and misunderstandings.
4. *Lack of continuity:* The business can come to an end due to death, retirement or withdrawal of a partner for any reasons like dissatisfaction, bankruptcy or any serious disagreements.
5. *Non transferability of interest:* Yet, another disadvantage in a partnership firm is that no partner can transfer his interest or get back his investment in business by selling off to outsiders whenever he wants without the consent of the other partners.
6. *Lack of public confidence:* a partnership firm is not legally bound to disclose its affairs and statements of accounts to general public. Since, even registration is not compulsory the firm is virtually free from government control or regulations. In absence of public scrutiny of its affairs or auditing of its accounts, public can have little confidence in the soundness of the firm and hence hesitate to deal with the firm in any way.

Joint Stock Company (Corporation)

A joint stock company is essentially a group of persons coming together voluntarily to carry on certain business by organising themselves into a single entity with a view to function as an artificial person in the eyes of the law.

Corporation as defined by Chief Justice Marshal, "an artificial being, invisible, intangible and existing only in contemplation of law being the mere creature of law, it possesses only those properties, which the character/certificate of incorporation of its creation confers upon it."

Features of Corporation:

1. *Separate legal entity:* The right and privileges are given to it by its character, which is granted by the state in which it is incorporated, gives privileges to it. Thus, the corporation becomes the legal entity and is granted the right to manage its own affairs, the right to sue and be sued, and the right to own and dispose property.
2. *Limited Liability:* Since the company has a separate legal entity, its debts are its own.
3. Transferability of shares: The shareholder of the business can transfer to others without consulting other shareholders.
4. *Perpetual existence:* The corporation can be dissolved in only three ways: a. by court order: b. by the approval of majority of the shareholders or: c. by expiration of the corporate charter.
5. *Common seal:* A company, not being a natural person, cannot sign document for itself. The common seal with the name of the company engraved on it is, therefore, used as a substitute for its signature.
6. *Separation of ownership from management:* Here all the owners, large in number, do not have the opportunity of managing the day-to-day working of the company.

Corporate Structure:

There are three groups that comprise the corporate structure:

1. The stockholders;
2. The board of Directors; and
3. The officers of the corporation.

The stockholders are known as the owners of the corporation. They are the individuals who bought shares of stock that show the proof of ownership.

Group Rights of Shareholders:

1. The right to elect directors;
2. The right to vote and amend the by-laws;
3. The right to change the charter;
4. The right to vote on the disposal of corporate assets;
5. The right to dissolve the corporation.

Individual Rights of Shareholders:

1. The right to buy, sell and transfer his/her stock;
2. The right to receive dividends in proportion to the number of shares owned;
3. The right to inspect and review the company's records;
4. The right to vote at stockholder's meeting;
5. The right to receive evidence of ownership (stock certificates);

6. The right to sue officers and director for fraud;
7. The right to share in distribution of assets in event of dissolution.

Advantage of Corporation

1. ***Financial Strength:*** The Company can raise a large amount of capital by issuing shares. It can also attract capital from thousands of varying incomes. It can also expand as long as investors are willing to purchase additional shares of stock
2. ***Limited Liability:*** The shareholders liability is limited to the extent of the face value of the shares held by him and his personal properties are not affected. The creditors cannot look beyond the assets of the corporation to settle their debts.
3. ***Scope of expansion:*** As large capital is invested, it would be possible to use up-to-date equipments and expensive machinery and carryout operations at large scale which leads to economies of scales, leading to higher profits.
4. ***Stability:*** The Company enjoys perpetual succession, which means that bankruptcy, insanity or death of a shareholder, change in management or owners; etc cannot affect the continuity of the company.
5. ***Efficient & bolder management:*** There is availability of managerial talent because the most efficient persons may be chosen as directors and if found unsatisfactory they can be fired. Since the persons who manage the company have relatively smaller financial stakes, they will have an adventurous spirit and can undertake big risks needed to infuse innovation and success in the business.
6. ***Diffused Risk:*** The risk is spread over several members of the company and is reduced for each member, which helps the business in attracting more investors and to venture in new opportunities.
7. ***Public confidence:*** No company can keep its affairs or accounts secret because its existence, activities and even dissolution are governed by statutory laws. In fact by advertising its records and business secrets it wins the confidence of the public.

Disadvantage of Corporation

1. ***Difficulty of Formation:*** Before a company can start functioning, though vary from country to country there are numerous requirements of the law to be complied with. This form of organisation requires huge amount of money and thus a large number of people have to be approached for raising the required capital.
2. ***Lack of owner's personal interest:*** These forms of organisations are managed directors and paid officials and employees who may not be expected to have such an intense interest in the success of the business. Even the owners may be having only a small percentage of the total equity so they also do not put forth their maximum efforts.

3. ***Delay in decision making:*** Decisions, especially on key issues, require consent of the general meting of the shareholders which may be then delayed because of the time interval between the meetings, difficulty of getting the required numbers of the members to pass the decision.
4. ***Fraudulent management:*** Though democratic in nature, but actually the management is concentrated in few hands who if consist of dishonest persons may resort to fraudulent practices and window dressing of accounts.
5. ***Taxation:*** These forms of organisations attract quite a large amount of taxation nearing to 35 per cent of the total profits.
6. ***Lack of secrecy:*** The publication of the financial reports of a corporation becomes a matter of public record. Therefore, the large corporation is unable to keep confidentiality in certain areas that they may not wish to reveal allowing competitors to alter their plans based on data disclosed.
7. ***Expensive management:*** A company is huge corporate body that has to necessarily employ a team of competent and professional managers to organise and manage its affairs. This increases the cost of expenses incurred.

6

Fundamentals Steps to Entrepreneurial Venture

Project Identification and Classification

Meaning of Project

In the precise sense, a project presupposes commitment to tasks to be performed with well defined objectives, schedules and budget.

It can be defined as *a scientifically evolved work plan devised to achieve a specific objective within a specified period of time.*

Project Identification

Meaning: Project identification is concerned with the collection, compilation and analysis of economic data for the eventual purpose of locating possible opportunities for investment and with the development of the characteristics of such opportunities.

Opportunities, according of Drucker (1955), are of three kinds: additive, complementary and break-through.

- Additive opportunities are those opportunities which enable the decision maker to better utilise the existing resources without in any way involving a change in the character of business.
- Complementary opportunities involve the introduction of new ideas and as such do lead to a certain amount of change in the existing structure.
- Break-through opportunities, on the other hand, involve fundamental changes in both the structure and character of business.

Factors to be considered for Project Identification

Input Output and Social Costs and Benefits

Project identification can not be complete without identifying the characteristics of a project. Every project has three basic dimensions – inputs, outputs and social costs and benefits.

The *input characteristics* define what the project will consume in terms of raw materials, energy, manpower, finance and organisational set up. The nature and magnitude of these inputs must be determined in order to make the input characteristics explicit.

The *output characteristics* of a project define what the project will generate in the form of goods and services, employment, revenue etc. The quantity and quality of all these outputs should be clearly specified.

In addition to inputs and outputs, *every project has an impact on the society.* It inevitably affects the current equilibriums of the demand and supply in the economy. It is necessary to evaluate carefully the sacrifice which the society will be required to make and the benefits that will accrue to the society from a given project.

Internal constraints: Internal constraints arise on account of the limitations of the management system which will eventually be responsible for the implementation of a project. The internal constraints for the entrepreneurs while venturing the projects comprise inputs, resources and outputs. These are narrated as under:

- Entrepreneurs, while implementing the projects, rely more on outside consultants for preparation of feasibility reports in the formulation of their projects. The limitation on the part of entrepreneurs to provide inbuilt project services in the form of preparing feasibility reports is an important internal constraint in the early implementation of the project.
- For early implementation of projects within the budgeted cost and time schedule, all the entrepreneurs cannot develop independent project management systems, organisation structure, network analysis and other elements. In such a situation, the entrepreneur's inherent internal constraints are developing well equipped project management strategies and tools which implementing them.
- Project goals and objectives lay down the main purpose for which an organisation exists. Practically, project management team is not much involved with the determination of project objectives. Certainly, this will be another internal constraint for the project team to achieve the unrealistic objective which is decided by the top management personnel of the business.
- The availability of the necessary internal project elements and resources are physical and non-physical resources. The physical resources include finance, personnel, inventories and facilities. The non-physical resources are patents, secret processes, unique experiences and skills. Both physical

and non-physical resources are the important constraints for the entrepreneurs to make available at a time the project implementation is in progress.

External Constraints: The external constraints are also another important constraint for the entrepreneurs who venture into project implementation. The important external constraints are the project environments comprising things, people and situations outside a project constitute the environment of the project. The other tangible environment factors are namely social taboos, government policies and the state of capital market. These are described as under:

- The external environment factors like nature, size, location and the extent of project are the important limiting factors for the entrepreneurs when the project does not conform to the socio-economic objectives of the country.
- Government policies and regulations are another major hurdle for the entrepreneurs while implementing the projects. They are mainly in the form of delay in giving approval to the entrepreneurs in the medium of industrial licensing, foreign collaboration approval, CCI clearance, environmental clearance, foreign exchange permit, capital goods approval and import goods clearance.
- Financial institutions, banks are the important financial source for the entrepreneurs while financing their projects. The financial institution's and commercial bank's cumbersome procedures and documentation system are important external constraints for the entrepreneurs in the form of delay in financing the projects.

Project Objectives: Project objective is an important element in the project planning cycle. Project objectives are concerned with defining in a precise manner what the project is expected to be achieved and to provide a measure of performance for the project as a whole. The essential requirements for project objectives are:

- Specific, not general
- Not overly complex
- Measurable, tangible and verifiable
- Realistic and attainable
- Established within resource bounds
- Consistent with resource available or anticipated
- Consistent with organisational plans, policies and procedures.

Project objectives are divided into two categories, namely, 'retentive' objectives and 'acquisitive' objectives. Retentive objectives are concerned with the retention and preservation of resources like money, time, energy, equipment, and skills. Acquisitive objectives, on the other hand, involve acquisition of resources or attaining status that the organisation or its managers do not have.

Project objectives are also economical and social in nature. The economical objectives of the project are in the form of profit-oriented. The social project objectives are service-oriented.

Desk Research and Techno-Economic Survey: Desk research and techno-economic survey are two important techniques of project identification. Desk research implies the collection and use of information from published sources like journals, magazines, reports, etc. Techno-economic survey is an investigation conducted by a team of experts for identifying the industrial development potential of an area.

Data and product identification may be obtained from the following sources:

- Industrial potential surveys
- Lead bank survey reports
- New process/product development in research laboratories
- Literature on industries within the country and abroad
- Import/Export statistics
- Profitability studies of selected industries
- Studies on price and shortage of certain commodities

Project Life Cycle

Like human beings, projects also have a life cycle. Project life cycle consists of three main stages.

1. **The pre-investment Phase:** This is the first phase in the life of a project. It is primarily concerned wioth objective formulation, demand forecasting, selection of optimal strategy, evaluation of input characteristics, projections of the financial profile, and if necessary cost benefit analysis and ultimately the pre-investment appraisal. The project idea is developed into an investment proposition during this phase.
2. **The Construction Phase:** This phase begins after the investment decision is taken. Resources are invested during this phase in building the basic assets of the project, which can in due course be utilised to achieve the project objectives. The assets may in the nature of land and buildings, plant and machinery, ancillary accommodation, communication services, control systems and marketing organisation. In projects not involving the use of plant and machinery, the construction phase may merely consist of developing necessary manpower resources. Thus, the construction phase consists mainly of developing the infrastructure for the project. It is one time effort.
3. **The Normalization Phase:** This phase starts after the trial run of the project framework developed during the construction phase. It involves routine procedures which are performed in a cyclic order. The primary objective of this phase is to produce the goods and services for which

the project was established. For this purpose, a provision has to be made for raw materials and other consumables. These can be determined by analyzing the process cycle identifying the sequence of process operations. Projects which do not involve production of goods do not require raw materials but only supplies or supporting goods needed to sustain the project process. Thus, the assets created during the construction phase are utilised during the normalization phase.

Project Classification

The project classifications are explained below.

1. ***Quantifiable and Non-quantifiable projects:*** Quantifiable projects are those in which a plausible quantitative assessment of benefits can be made. Non-quantifiable projects are those where such an assessment is not possible. Projects concerned with industrial development, power generation, and mineral development are forming part of quantifiable projects. The non-quantifiable projects category comprises health, education and defense.
2. ***Sectoral Projects:*** A project may fall in the following sectors.
   - Agriculture and Allied Sector
   - Irrigation and Power Sector
   - Industry and Mining Sector
   - Transport and Communication Sector
   - Social Services Sector
   - Miscellaneous Sector

The sector classification of projects is quite useful for resource allocation at macro levels.

3. ***Techno-Economic Projects:*** Techno-economic projects classification includes factors intensity-oriented classification, causation-oriented classification and magnitude-oriented classification.
   (a) ***Factor intensity oriented classification:*** The factor intensity is used as base for classification of projects such as capital-intensive or labour-intensive which depends upon the large scale investments in plant and machinery or human resources.
   (b) ***Causation oriented classification:*** The causation oriented projects are determined based on its causes namely demand based or raw material based projects. The non-availability of certain goods or services and consequent demand for such goods or services or the availability of certain raw materials, skills or other inputs is the dominant reason for starting the project.
   (c) ***Magnitude oriented Classification:*** The size of investments forms the basis for magnitude oriented projects. Projects may thus be classified based on the investment such as large scale, medium scale and small scale projects.

United Nations and its specialized agencies use the International Standard Industrial Classification of all economic activities (ISIC) in collection and compilation of economic data. Economic activities are under this classification grouped into ten divisions, which are sub divided into ninety sub-divisions. The divisions are:

- Division 0 - Agriculture, Forestry, Hunting and Fishing
- Division 1 - Mining and Quarrying
- Division 2 & 3 - Manufacturing
- Division 4 - Construction
- Division 5 - Electricity, Gas, Water and Sanitary Services
- Division 6 - Commerce
- Division 7 - Transport, Storage and Communication
- Division 8 - Services
- Division 9 - Activities not adequately described

4. ***Financial Institutions Classification:*** Financial Institutions classify the projects according to their age and experience and the purpose for which the project is being taken up. They are as follows:
   - New Projects
   - Expansion Projects
   - Modernization Projects
   - Diversification Projects

The projects listed above are generally profit-oriented and the services oriented projects are classified as under:

- Welfare Projects
- Service Projects
- Research and Development Projects
- Educational Projects.

Strategic Decision Making Process for Entrepreneurial Venture

The strategic decision making process for undertaking entrepreneurial venture is comprised of the following fundamental steps.

Step 1: Develop a Basic Business Idea

This step calls for identifying the broadest needs and wants of customers that will be a base for the development of product lines and product ranges. The basics of this step is that it is based on the prevailing needs and wants of customers and it consists of the following three sub steps.

1. Creating business ideas
2. Study & process the ideas
3. Select the best idea

Creating Business Idea

It is mainly concerned with generating product ideas that would be profitable if capitalized. It is like identifying opportunities based on the wants and needs of consumers or else it is searching for markets that arise for new products and services. The ideas are generated from various sources and put for preliminary evaluation and testing.

Idea Generation Methods

Methods to generate new ideas include:

1. ***Focus groups***: A group of individuals discuss and provide information in a structured format to arrive at new business ideas. Here a group that is made up of individuals is created as a structured part of the overall organisational hierarchy to obtain new ideas.
2. ***Brainstorming:*** Is a group method for obtaining new ides and business solutions. This method is extensively used for generating ideas for new product packing and distribution. The groups are organised for sitting together and stimulate greater creativity by exchange of mutual experiences and participating in the discussions. Different group of stakeholders will be organised and think hard to generate ideas. What makes this method different from the former is it may include informal groups that are not part of the organisational structure
3. ***Check list:*** The new ideas for the business are developed based on discussions on list of related issues. A specific area of discussions is listed by entrepreneur and a list of questions, suggestions and statements are developed for in-depth discussions and arrive at a business idea. For instance if a burning issue in a given time interval turns out to be environmental protection, entrepreneurs may look towards producing a new product that is an eco friendly. An issue that is meant for discussion can take many forms.
4. ***Problem inventory analysis***: It is a method of obtaining new ideas and solutions for business by focusing on the problems. In this case the individual are used similar to focus groups for generating new business ideas. The group discusses category of products. The group is given the problems that are commonly felt by consumers, dealers, transporters and general public and based on the identified problems, product ideas that provide solutions are hallucinated.

Study and Process Idea

Once the business ideas are lacerated, study, screening, and testing of these ideas are done based on the entrepreneur's own experience or with the help of experts in the field.

While evaluating the points to be considered are:

1. ***Technical feasibility*** that is the possibility of production with the available skill & technology.
2. ***Commercial viability*** of the idea based on cost and profitability. It evaluates the tradeoff between cost and income to judge the attractiveness of a business idea.

Selecting the Best Idea

After the technical feasibility and commercial viability of a given business idea has been proved, not every business idea represents the best opportunity. Therefore, the prospective entrepreneur performs selection based on the following criterions:

1. Product where the entrepreneur has firsthand manufacturing experience.
2. Product where the entrepreneur has the marketing work experience with the particular product.
3. Product which is perceived as highly profitable.
4. Product where government has banned imports
5. Product where the export demand is high and with good margins.
6. The raw material requirement of an existing nearby big unit.
7. Products on which government declares sub sides incentives, other industrial/financial benefits.
8. Products where there is demand growth.
9. Products that are easy to distribute

Step 2: Analysis of Internal and External Environment (SWOT Analysis)

Entrepreneurial environments are critical to the creation of favorable atmosphere to the development of entrepreneurs. Entrepreneurship environment refers to the various facets within which enterprises have to operate in. These entrepreneurial environments are most rationally divided into two major parts: internal and external environment. Analysis of internal and external environment follows after the selection the best business idea. The major objective of this step is to identify the threats and opportunities faced by the prospective entrepreneur in the light of the strengths and weaknesses that are apparent, hence the name SWOT analysis. The two major parts of this step are:

- Scanning the External Environment
- Assessing the Internal Environment

Scanning the External Environment

By and large, entrepreneurship is influenced by environments created by the external forces. These external forces are demarcated as macro and micro environmental forces.

1. Macro-Environment

Macro environment is the type of environment that is not specific to a given entrepreneur or company. It has universal application to all the entrepreneurs in a given country irrespective of the type of entrepreneurs. Macro environmental force more or less include the following environments:

(a) ***Economic environment:*** related to factors of production & distribution like economic staged, economic system, economic policies economic indices (per capital income), infrastructural factors, living standards, etc.

(b) ***Socio-cultural environment:*** related to social attitude & cultural factors. Demographic factors, social concern & attitude, education level, aspirations and values, consumer motives etc

(c) ***Political- legal environment:*** related to government regulation & consumer protection-like political system, consumer protection, taxation laws, quality leadership, etc.

(d) ***Technological environment:*** It relates to the knowledge applied and equipments used-like source of technology, communication & infrastructure facilities, and patent protection.

2. Micro-Environment

Micro environmental forces on the other side are forces that are specific to companies or entrepreneurs. It includes forces like customers, suppliers, competitors, intermediaries, etc

Sources of Environmental Scanning

- Formal Sources: research studies, consultants.
- Secondary Sources: publications, magazines, books.
- Internal Sources: MIS records, co- employees.
- External Sources: marketing intermediaries, customers, suppliers etc.
- Spy

Assessing the Internal Environment

This is the second part of SWOT analysis. It identifies the weaknesses and strengths that are internal in nature. In sensible terms it is assessing the expertise, resources, abilities, skills, costs, organisational structure and culture, manufacturing techniques etc.

Step 3: Developing Feasibility study (DECIDE GO/NO GO)

After weaknesses and strengths have been identified in terms of the prevailing opportunities and threats, feasibility study can be undertaken.

It the basic business idea appears to be a feasible business opportunity, the process should be continued.

Feasibility study should focus on the following:

- *Marketing feasibility:* total demand size, growth rate of market.
- *Technical feasibility:* Technical know how of production, cost of acquisition.
- *Physical resource feasibility:* availability of raw materials & suppliers.
- *Financial feasibility:* availability of adequate capital, and cost of funds.
- *Time feasibility:* duration required to operationalize the business & make expected profit.

If feasibility fails, no go is the option.

If feasibility test results positive, go is the option.

Step 4: Generating Business Plan

After testing the feasibility of business idea, a business plan is prepared. A business plan transforms the idea in to how it will be applied and projects the likely results to be attained. It leads the transformation of idea into reality. It is used to convince the shareholders & creditors for raising capital.

To be successful, the business plan must begin with the real foundation of any business - the customers. Too often, entrepreneurs fall victim to marketing myopia, concentrating solely on their product or service & waiting for the world to beat a pate to their doors to buy it. Linking the purposeful action of strategic planning to an entrepreneur's little ideas can produce results that will shape the future.

Specifically, a business plan performs the following activities:

(a) Develops the proposed mission, objectives, Strategies and policies
(b) Defines the proposed enterprise in terms of its product or service, market characteristics, the entrepreneurial team, the likely BOD
(c) Specify the market plan, manufacturing plan, financial plan
(d) Develop performance projections (month wise for at least 3 years)

Let's capitalise on strategies. In business planning, the strategies to be followed in order to overtake the competitors are outlined by entrepreneurs. In this spirit, entrepreneurs may adopt one of the following competitive strategies. There are three types of competitive strategies:

(a) Cost leadership: being cost efficient
(b) Differentiation: making your product different, i.e. superior products
(c) Focus: being sensitive to customers than your competitors

Step 5: Developing Action Plans

No strategic plan is complete until it is put in to action. To make the plan workable, the business owner should divide the plan into projects, carefully defining each one of the following:

1. *Purpose:* What is the project designed to accomplish?
2. *Scope:* Which areas of the company will be involved in the project?
3. *Contribution:* How does the project relate to other projects & to the overall strategic plan?
4. *Resource requirements*: What human & financial resources are needed to complete the project successfully?
5. *Timing:* Which schedules & deadlines will ensure project completion?

Under this particular step, how strategies are going to be undertaken is specified. Who does it? Why it is done? When it is done? How it is going to done? Is answered. For instance in answering the how and who questions, an entrepreneur tries to focus on the ways of obtaining finances, licenses, raw materials, equipments, recruiting staff, distribution network, construction of plant etc.

Step 6: Implementation and Evaluation

Now it is the time of reality. When action plans are materialised, business plans are considered to be implemented. Evaluation follows after implementation. Evaluation is mainly concerning towards making sure the achievement of mission, objectives etc

Deciding on Development Approach

After an entrepreneur establishes him/herself, he/she looks for how to develop further. In general, there are three approaches for the expansion of business activity.

Approach 1: Start up venture (New set-up):

It is a new venture established from the scratch as per the dreams and plan of entrepreneur.

Advantage

1. The business is created as per entrepreneurs planning and being a new venture; there is no compromise on entrepreneurial dreams or plans.
2. Owner (entrepreneur) doesn't inherit the ill will of previous organisation.
3. If a business idea is unique, this is the only viable option

Disadvantage

1. High cost of equipment & organisation
2. Lack of source of genuine advice since there is no past records
3. It may saturate the existing market
4. Lack of recognition.

Approach 2: Buying an existing business (Buyout firms):

It is the second approach of launching a new venture when the entrepreneurs feel that they can quickly change direction of existing firm as per his own plans & dreams in a fairly substantial way. The following steps are recommended as a checklist before buying an existing firm.

Do the product/service fit to the entrepreneur's interest/need?

Yes

Is it an appropriate business is for sale (profitability/Legality)? Accountants may be consulted to prove profitability, while lawyers may be consulted in terms of legality.

Yes

Is Business condition good? (Financial health)

Yes

Purchase price reasonable

Yes. Buy the firm

Advantages

1. A successful firm can provide immediate returns
2. Existing firm comes with an advantage of good location, working staff, established supplied of raw materials, distribution network installed machineries and inventories etc.

3. Advice can be sought from previous owners on the strength and weaknesses of the firm.
4. Low cost of organisation when it is specially compared to starting a new venture.

Disadvantages

1. Ill reputation of previous owner may be faced if the previous entrepreneur is not well established or don't posses a good will.
2. Poor staff, obsolete machineries and layout can trouble entrepreneur.
3. Buyout costs are usually high.

Approach 3: Purchasing a license (Franchising/Licensing)

It is the third major approach to develop a business. A new venture is not something obtained in this approach. The key terms of this development approach include:

Franchise: It is the right and license to sell a product or service and possibly the entire business system developed by another company in return of a royalty and conformity to a standard operating procedure. It is an intellectual property which is sold in return of royalty.

Franchisor: is usually the manufacturer or sole distributor of a trademarked product or service who has a considerable experience in that business. Eg owners of Kodak, Pepsi, etc

Franchisee: is an individual entrepreneur who purchases the franchise in return for royalty and conformance to standard operation and who in the process gets the opportunity to enter an established entrepreneur.

Types of Franchising

1. *Trade name franchising:* franchisee gets only the right to use trade name of franchiser.
2. *Product distribution franchising:* Right to use name as well as selected products of franchiser.
3. *Pure/Comprehending franchising:* Right to use entire business of the franchiser.

Advantages for Franchiser

1. Expanding the existing business network at low investment or limited capital.
2. Company growth with minimum risk without expanding the HR and other facilities.
3. Regular income from royalty (5%)

Advantages for Franchisee

1. Gets advantage already established brand name.
2. Easy to establish business using well developed system.
3. Initial financial assistance.

4. Opportunity to marketing training and counseling.
5. Greater chance of success.

Disadvantages to the Franchiser

- Absolute control cannot be exercised.
- Physical separation.

Disadvantages to the Franchisee

- Sharing profits in terms of royalty is mandatory.
- Strict adherence to standard operating procedures or limited freedom.
- Restriction on buying other's product.

Business Plan

Business Plan Preparation: Scope & Elements

Business plan is a written summary of the entrepreneur's proposed venture, its operational and financial details, its marketing opportunities & strategy, and its manager's skills and abilities.

The plan describes the direction the company is going in, what its goals are, where it wants to be, and how it's going to get there. The plan serves two essential functions:

1. It guides the company's operation by charting its future course and devising a strategy for following it.
2. It attracts lenders and investors. The best way to secure the necessary capital is to prepare a sound business plan.

Purpose of Business plan

Well conceived business plan can thus serve:

(i) When

- *At star-up stage:* after conception of idea & feasibility study, detailed planning stage follows so as it develop operation guidelines.
- *Buyout stage:* Risk is benefit undertaken
- *On going review stage:* Review start up, buyout performance, matching against relatives changes due to environment.

(ii) Who

- *Managers:* Developing strategies, establish standards & attracting capitals.

- *Owners:* evacuating enterprise's elements and enhance of success.
- *Lenders:* Determining principles, risk involves in business.

(iii) Why (Purpose)

- *Managers:* Clarifying ideas and finding strength, weariness, opportunity & threats.
  - Building a team of committed people
  - Assist in raising capital
- *Owners:* Assessing feasibility & viability of business
  - Setting objective & budgets.
  - Calculating capital investments.
- *Lenders:* Evaluate risk us benefits.
  - Appraise quality of managements

Scope of Business Plan

Business plan includes information on the following aspects:

(a) *Economic aspects:* Economic justification like market size, market growth, market share.

(b) *Technical aspects:* Details on technology needed, equipment and match their sources.

(c) *Financial aspects:* Total investment, cost of capital, ROI, source of capital, enterprise contribution.

(d) *Production aspects:* product, its design, standard of quality, usage, production aspect like production process, schedule, technology.

(e) *Managerial aspects:* Qualification & experience, commitment & planning.

Elements of Business Plan

1. *Executive summary:* it should be concise and should summarize all of the relevant points of proposed deal. It is designed to capture the reader's attention
2. *Company History:* A brief history of the operation, highlighting the significant financial and operational events in the company's life. This section should concentrate on the accomplishment of past objectives & should convey the firm's image.
3. *Business Profile:* This section should begin with a statement of the company's general business goals and a narrower definition of its immediate objectives. Together they should spell out what the business plans to accomplish, how, when and who will do it.
4. *Business Strategy:* This segment of business plan should outline the methods the company can use to meet the requirements for success cited earlier Game-plan to compete with competitors like cost leadership, innovation, strong sales force.

5. *Description of the firm's product:* describe company's overall product line, giving an overview of how the goods/services are used. Besides, a statement of thc goods' position in the product life cycle may also be helpful. This section should include also a summary of any patents, trademarks, or copy-rights protecting the product from infringement by competitors. Finally, it should describe the production process, strategic raw materials required & sources of supply used.
6. *Marketing strategy:* The plan must discuss the company's target market and its characteristics. It must show how the entrepreneur plans to turn the idea into a product that customers will want to buy. Proving that a profitable market exists takes two steps:
   (a) Showing market place interest
   (b) Documenting market claims: target market, market size & trends, pricing, advertising & distribution.
7. *Competitors Analysis:* Demonstrate that the entrepreneur's company has an advantage over its competitors. What distinguishes ones product form others already on the market, and how will these differences produce a competitive edge?
8. *Officers' owners' Resumes:* The resumes of business offices, key directors, & any person with at last 20 percent ownership in the company.
9. *Plan of operation:* organisational chart identifying the business's key positions & the personnel occupying them; the steps taken to encourage important officers to remain with the company; and form of ownership and description of any leases contracts other relevant agreements.
10. *Financial data:* A detailed outline of the loan or investment package. The owner should supply copies of the firm's major financial statements from the past three years audited by certified public accountant; monthly projected financial statement for the operation for the next two to three years, which includes income statement, balance sheet, cash budget, and schedule of planned capital expenditures.
11. *Loan Proposal:* the purpose of the Loan, the amount requested, and the plans for payment.

Common Mistakes Committed during Business Plan Preparation

Raymond Loen offers the following list of the ten most common mistakes that business owners make in using their plans- and the remedies for them.

1. *Single-Purpose use:* Entrepreneurs typically prepare a plan to raise money and seldom give thought to actually using it.
   - *Remedy:* stress implementation. The plan must include specific objectives for managers and plan to accomplish them.
2. *One- person commitment:* if one person writes the entire plan mangers are unlikely to be fully committed to it.
   - *Remedy:* Involve all members of management.

3. *Benign neglect:* Once completed, the business plan sits on the shelf and collects dust. Out of sight, out of mind.
    - *Remedy:* Make following up the plan easy, schedule regular meetings to discuss the plan & the progress made in accomplishing the goals & objectives established.
4. *Unworkable document:* Managers create a plan that is so huge & complex that it discourages every one from actually using it.
    - *Remedy:* Give the plan life by supplying one-page action summaries for each department.
5. *Unbalanced application:* Sometimes managers give a disproportionate amount of attention to one portion of the plan.
    - *Remedy:* Get balanced participation from managers & employees in all areas of the company, and also focus 90 per cent of management's attention within the next year.
6. *Disillusionment:* Managers become disillusioned when the scenario laid out in the plan fail to develop.
    - *Remedy:* Develop contingency plan-both positive and negative
7. *Too- action Oriented:* Action oriented managers tend to forget about the plan once it is completed. They want get back to the real world of business.
    - *Remedy:* use these mangers' action orientation to encourage them to develop plans for their areas of responsibility.
8. *No Performance Standard:* Too often, managers fail to establish measurable standards in the plan.
    - *Remedy:* Encourage managers to establish specific, measurable objectives in their respective areas.
9. *Poor progress Control:* Implementing the plan is without control because progress reports are lost in the jumble of everyday business.
10. *Remedy:* Hold regular meetings to discuss progress on the plan & nothing else.
11. *Early consumption:* The plan becomes outdated because no one bothers to update it.
    - *Remedy:* Update the plan every six months.

Five "Cs" that Bankers look in Business Plan

Most bankers consider a loan acceptable if it conforms to the five Cs of credit: capital, capacity, collateral, character, and conditions.

(a) *Capital:* a small business must have a stable capital base before a bank will grant it a loan.

(b) *Capacity:* a synonym for capacity is cash flow. Venture should have ability to meet its regular financial obligation & repay bank loan.

(c) *Collateral:* includes any assets the owner pledges to the bank as security for repayment of the loan.

(d) *Character:* The evaluation of character frequently is based on intangible factors like honesty, competence, determination, intelligence, and ability.

(e) *Conditions:* Bankers consider factors relating to the business operation such as potential growth in the market, competition, location form of ownership, and loan purpose.

Business Plan Template

I. Description of the Organisation

Under the title description of the organisation, we have to discuss the nature of the business, location of the business, the competitors, competencies,, etc.

A. Nature of the Business

1. The type of products and services to be dealt with (milk, milk products, vegetables, fruits, processed foods, etc.)
2. Organisational description of the organisation (how to organise, when to organise, composition of the members, etc.)

B. Location of the Business

1. Name the proposed head quarters for the organisation.
2. Examine the transport, communication facilities available to the members.
3. The number of households in the proposed area of operation.
4. Approximate households to be absorbed as members and their background, and economic potential.
5. The sustainability of the membership – target to increase the membership every year.
6. The number of dairy animals owned and the expected supply of milk to the organisation.
7. The type of vegetables/fruits grown and the expected supply.

C. The competitors

1. Examine the type of competition that may come once the organisation is started.
2. Form strategies to face the competition.
3. Examine the role and stake of the prospective members and directors to face the competition.
4. How far the price mechanism can be used as an instrument to resist the competition.

D. Competencies

1. Geographic location – Ideal location for the vast majority of the members in terms of transport, communication, accessibility, all season mobility, etc.
2. Superior customer satisfaction - to attend to the needs of the consumers and the grievances of the consumers.

3. Form a mechanism to attend the daily problems and grievances of the customers.
4. Try to enlist as much institutional customers as possible.
5. Dedicated personnel – Recruiting the talents locally available.

II. Organisational Analysis

The organisational analysis consists of selection/election of competent and dedicated committee members/board of directors, manager, and staff.

A. Committee members

1. Even during the preliminary stage, locate educated, dedicated and competent committee members.
2. Short training programme can be arranged for them as well as for the prospective members about the business plan.
3. The committee members must be educated about the competitive nature of the business, using of price and dividend mechanism to enlist the permanent loyalty of the members.
4. To work for the viability and sustainability of the organisation by means of enrolling more and more members on a time frame basis.
5. To conduct the committee meeting and general assembly meetings periodically and to introduce transparency in the operations of the organisation.
6. Exposure visits to the committee members can be arranged at frequent intervals.

B. Manager and Staff

1. To go for a qualified manager, if available in and around the particular location
2. From the beginning he must be paid reasonable salary with adequate perquisites (fringe benefits).
3. Select adequate staff to work for the services of the members and for the faster growth of the organisation.
4. Selfless service must be expected from the employees.
5. Training programme for the manager and the staff must be made a continuous process.
6. Exposure visits to the staff can be arranged at frequent intervals.

III. Marketing and Sales Analysis

A. Overall marketing strategy

1. Marketing penetrating strategy
2. Growth strategy (monthwar and yearwar)

B. Procurement Strategy

1. Procurement timings every day.
2. Fixation of procurement responsibility to each staff.

3. Purchasing/procurement target
4. Storage facility
5. Preservation facility
6. Steps to avoid wastage, pilferage during procurement stage and storage stage.

C. Pricing Strategy
1. Study the market price for the intended produces.
2. Try to fix a price slightly above the market price.
3. If possible, from the beginning create a *price fluctuation fund*, from out of the net profit, to offset the down fall in market price.

D. Sales Strategy
1. Identify institutional customers (Institutional customers are bulk purchasers and payment will not be a problem).
2. Timeliness and speed of the sales very important.
3. The sales force (employees) must be motivated to take care of the quality, timeliness, cleanliness, etc., of providing supplies.

E. Transport and Communication Services
1. To start with higher private transport services.
2. The transport system must cover nearest cities, and institutional and individual customers.
3. Alternative arrangements to be made if regular transport service is disrupted.
4. Any transport dislocation should be communicated to the customers immediately.
5. The sales staff must be provided with communication facilities.
6. The head office and manager must be provided with round the clock communication facilities (mobile phone).

IV. Financial Analysis

The organisation needs two types of capital viz., block capital (long term capital) and working capital. Block capital is needed to construct office buildings, purchase equipment, etc. Working capital is needed to meet the day-to-day expenses and monthly establishment.

A. Members Stake
1. To start with members may contribute very little amount as share capital. But minimum shares to be taken and value of each share can be fixed.
2. From out of the business dealings, members can be asked to contribute compulsory savings.
3. Voluntary savings can also be opened to the members.

B. Voluntary Agencies

1. Voluntary agencies like the SHDI can be approached to contribute towards the funds by way of revolving fund, etc.
2. Voluntary agencies can be approached to provide equipment and furniture.

C. Government

1. Government can be approached to provide block capital (repayable long-term loan, as being practiced in many developing countries).
2. Government can provide subsidies for the purchase of equipment.
3. Government can provide tax exemptions and duty exemptions while import of equipment.

D. Commercial Banks

1. Commercial banks can be approached for raising block capital and working capital.

V. Cost and Profitability Analysis

A. *Break-even Analysis* – The proposed organisation must be able to earn a profit at the end of third year. Strategies must be worked out.

B. *Cost Analysis* – Cost must be worked out in terms of fixed cost and variable cost. Flexibility must be allowed in the case of variable cost to attain profitability at the end of third year. To keep the cost to the minimum, the organisation can go for rented building, hired vehicles, etc during the beginning years.

C. *Profit Analysis* – The proposed organisation should give a reasonable dividend and not a high dividend. A ceiling of 25 per cent can be fixed.

D. *Reserves and retained earnings* – Every year from the net profit reserves must be created. A percentage of retained earnings (eg. 25%) must be created to plough back the profit money to the business.

8

Managing the Enterprise

Marketing Management

Meaning

The decade of this millennium is one of great promise & great uncertainty. Already sea change have been taking place in global economy: the rising power of Far East in the global markets: development of ECM; the mass privatization of state run enterprises worldwide; the giant advances in technology and so on. Companies today are learning that it is hard to build a reputation & easy to lose it. In the end, the companies that best satisfy their customers will be the winners. Today, smart companies are not merely looking for sales; they are investing in long term mutually satisfying customer relationship based on delivery quality, service and value. Authentic marketing is not the art of selling what you make but knowing what to make!

Marketing is the business function that identifies unfulfilled needs and wants, defines and measures their magnitude, determine which target market the organisation can best serve decides on appropriate products, services and programmes to serve these markets and calls upon everyone in the organisation to " think & serve the customer".

According to Philip Kotler, "Marketing is a social and managerial process by which individual and groups obtain what they need and want through creating, offering and exchanging products of value with others."

Marketing management takes place when at least one party to a potential exchange thinks about the means of achieving desired responses from other parties.

"Marketing management is the process of planning and executing the conception, pricing, promotion, and distribution of ideas, goods and services to create exchange that satisfies individual and organisational goals".

Importance of Marketing

Marketing is extremely important to the consumers, producers and other intermediaries in the economy of the country. Marketing completes the basic mission of the economic system. Broadly, the importance of marketing can be summarized in to two categories, namely:

1. Discovering what goods and services consumers need and want.
2. Providing these items for the customers in the places where they are, at the times they want, and at prices that they are able and willing to pay.

In other words, marketing creates certain form utility, place utility, time utility and possession utility or marketing utilities.

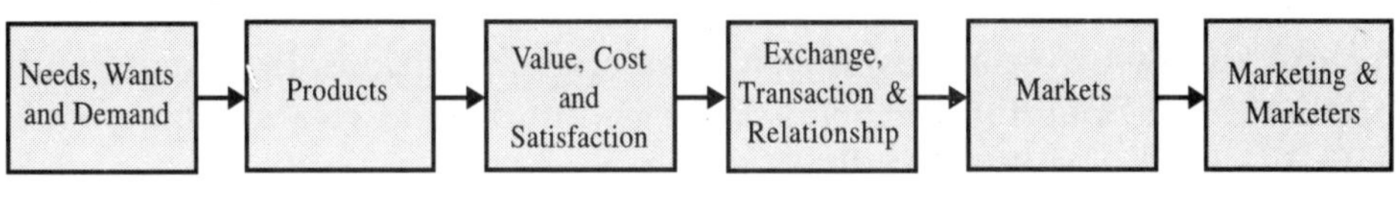

Fig. 8.1

Core Concepts of Marketing

Need: A human need is a state of felt deprivation of some basic satisfaction. People require food, clothing, shelter, safety, belongingness, esteem, etc. These needs are not created by the society or the marketer but exist in the very texture of human biology and the human conditions.

Wants: Wants are desires for specific satisfiers of needs. It differs from society to society. An Ethiopian needs foods and may want "injera", "wat" and a "tej" for satisfying it, while it may differ for a European who may be wanting "Burger", "Pizza",etc.

Demands: Demands are wants for specific products that are backed ability to and willingness to buy them. Wants become demands when they are supported by purchasing power. Many people want a Mercedes; only few are able to buy. Companies must therefore measure not only how many would actually be willing and able to buy it.

Products: People satisfy their needs and wants with products. A product is anything that can be offered to satisfy a need or want. Physical products are really vehicles that deliver services to us. Services can also be supplied by other vehicles, such as persons, places, activities, organisations and ideas.

The marketer's job is to sell the benefits or services built into physical products rather than just describe their physical features.

Value: Customer value is the difference between the benefits that the customer gains from owning and using a product and the costs of obtaining the product.

Cost: The investment incurred in the acquisition of the product or the services.

Satisfaction: The extent to which a product's performance falls short of the customer's expectations, the buyer is dissatisfied. If performance exceeds expectations, the buyer is delighted. If performance matches exceptions, the buyer is satisfied.

Exchange: Exchange is the act of obtaining a desired product from someone by offering something in return. Exchange must be seen as a process rather than as an event. Two parties are engaged in exchange if they are negotiating and moving toward an agreement. When an agreement is reached, we say that a transaction takes place.

Transaction: A transaction consists of a trade of values between two parties. Transactions are basic units of exchange.

Relationship Marketing: A marketing effort sought to build up long term, trusting "win-win" relationship with customers, distributors, dealers and suppliers. The operating principle here is, build good relationships, and profitable transactions will follow.

Markets: The concept of exchange leads to the concept of a market. A market consists of all the potential and actual customers sharing a particular need or want who might willing and able to engage in exchange to satisfy that need or want. Thus the size of the market depends on the number of people who exhibit the need or want, have resources that interest others, and are willing and able to offer these resources in exchange for what they want.

Marketing: Marketing means working with the markets to actualize potential exchange for purpose of satisfying human needs and wants.

Marketer: A marketer is someone seeking a resource from someone else and willing offer something of value in exchange.

Classification of Markets

Markets may be classified in various ways based on different characteristics:

(a) Classification of markets on the basis of free intercourse:

Markets have been classified as perfect and imperfect markets on the basis of free intercourse. A market is said to be perfect market when all potential buyers and sellers are promptly aware of the prices at which transactions take place and all the offers made by other sellers and buyers and where any buyer can purchase from any seller. Under such conditions, the price of commodity would be the same all over the market. A market is in perfect when some buyers and sellers or both are not aware of the offers being made by others.

(b) Markets on the basis of time classification:

1. *Very short period market:* Time is insufficient to make any adjustment between the demand and supply. This is applicable to highly perishable articles like vegetables, milk and fruits.
2. *Short period market:* Time is given to adjust the supply to meet the demand. The time given is not enough and influence of demand is greater than that of supply.
3. *Long period markets:* Sufficient time is given for the changes in supply to adjust them to the change in demand. Under these circumstances supply influences demand.

(c) Classification the basis of the position of sellers:

1. Primary markets: In this market all farm products are sold to wholesaler in the village itself by the primary producers. This market deals in sales of fruits, vegetables etc.
2. Secondary Market: Here wholesalers supply their goods to the retailers for selling them to consumers.
3. Terminal Markets: The goods are finally disposed of directly to consumers.

(d) Classification on the basis of the characteristics of the consumer:

Markets are broadly classified as consumer or industrial markets. Consumer markets consist of purchasers and/or individual household members who intend to consume or benefit from the purchased products and who do not buy products to make profits. Industrial markets, also called business-to-business markets, are grouped broadly into producer, reseller, governmental, and institutional categories. These markets purchase specific kinds of products for use in making other products, for day to day operations.

Marketing Philosophies

We have defined marketing management as the conscious effort to achieve desired exchange outcomes with target markets. But what philosophy should guide marketing efforts? What relative weight should be given to the interest of the organisation, the customers, and society? Very often these interest conflict.

There are five competing concepts under which organisations can choose to conduct their marketing activities: the production concept, the product concept, the selling/sales concept, the marketing concept, and the societal marketing concept.

1. The Production concept

The production concept is one of the oldest concepts in business.

- The production concept holds that consumers will favor those products that are widely available and low in cost. Managers of production oriented origination concentrate on achieving high production efficiency and wide distribution.

The assumption that consumers are primarily interested in product availability and low price holds in at least two situations. The first is where that demand for a product exceeds supply; the second situation is where the product's cost is high and has to be decreased to expand the market.

2. The Product concept

- The product concept holds that consumers will favor those products that offer that most quality, performance, or innovative features. Managers in product-oriented organisations focus their energy on making superior products and improving them over time.

The managers assume that the buyers admire well made products and can appraise the product quality and performance. The product concept leads to "marketing myopia" an undue concentration on the product rather than the need.

3. The Selling concept/Sales concept

- The selling concept holds that consumers, if left alone, will ordinarily not buy enough of the organisation's products. The organisation must therefore undertake an aggressive selling and promotion effort.

The selling concept is practiced most aggressively with unsought goods, those goods that that buyers normally do not think of buying. Most companies practice selling concept when they have overcapacity. Their aim is to sell what they make rather than make what they can sell. The selling concept is also practiced in the non profit area by fund - raisers, college admissions officers, and political parties.

4. The Marketing concept

- The marketing concept holds that the key to achieving organisational goals consists of being more effective than competitors in integrating marketing activities toward determining and satisfying the needs and wants of target markets.

The marketing concept rests on four pillars namely a market focus, customer orientation, coordinated marketing and profitability.

(a) *Market focus:* No company can operate in every market and satisfy every need. Nor can it even do a good job within one market. Company do best when they define their target markets and prepare a marketing programme for each target market.

(b) *Customer orientation:* Even after defining market carefully, company orientated marketing requires defining customer need from customer's point of view and not from its own point of view.

(c) *Coordinated Marketing:* It means that on one hand, various marketing functions (sales, advertising) must be coordinated among themselves while on other hand; marketing must be well coordinated with departments of company.

(d) *Profitability:* The purpose of marketing concept is to help organisation achieve its goals where the key is not to aim for profits alone but to achieve them as byproduct of doing the job well.

5. The Societal Marketing concept

- The societal marketing concept holds that the organisation's task is to determine the needs, wants and interests of target markets and to deliver the desired satisfaction more effectively efficiently than competitors in a way that preserves or enhances the customer's and society's well being.

The Societal marketing concept calls upon the marketer to balance three considerations in setting their marketing policies namely consumer want satisfaction, public interest and company's profits.

Market Segmentation

A company that decides to operate in a broad market recognizes that it normally cannot serve all customers in that market. The customers are too numerous and diverse in their buying requirements. Instead of competing every where, the company needs to identify the market segments that it serves most effectively.

To choose its markets and serve them well, many companies are embracing target marketing. In target marketing sellers distinguish the major market segments, target one or more of these segments and develop products and marketing programmes tailored to each segment. Instead of scattering their marketing effort, they can focus on the buyers whom they have the greatest chance of satisfying.

Target marketing requires marketers to take following major steps:

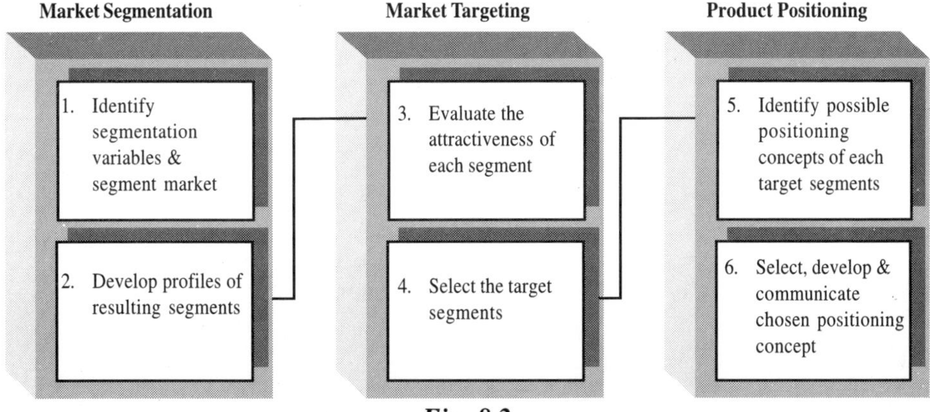

Fig. 8.2

- Market Segmentation: Identifying and develop profile of distinct groups of buyers who might require separate products and/or marketing mixes.

Market segmentation is dividing a market into distinct groups of buyers with different needs, characteristics, or behaivior who might require separate products of marketing mixes.

Basis for Segmenting Consumers Market

There are four commonly used bases for segmenting consumers markets. These are:

(a) *Geographic Segmentation:* Geographic segmentation is the dividing of an overall market into homogeneous groups on the basis of population location. This is the earliest form that served a base for segmenting markets. It considers current population location and residence (urban or rural) and future expected shifts. Geographic segmentation is used in order to know regional variation in customer taste and also determine and supply good appropriate to climate changes.

(b) *Demographic Segmentation:* Demographic segmentation is dividing and over all market into homogeneous group based upon population characteristics such as age, sex and income level. It is now the most common approach used for market segmentation. This method uses such variables as sex, age, income, occupation, education, household size and stage in the family life cycle. These variables are often used because variables are often used because:

1. They are easy to identify
2. They are associated with the sale of many products and services
3. They are typically referred to describing the audiences of advertising media.

(c) Psychographics: Psychographic segmentation utilizes behavioural profiles developed from analyses of the activities, opinions, interest and life styles of consumers. The life-styles of potential consumers may prove important in order to determine their preferences; life style refers to the mode of lives. Consumer's life-styles are regarded as a composite of their individual psychological make-ups their needs, motives perceptions and attitudes.

(d) Behavioural Segmentation: Benefit segmentation focuses on product usage rates. This focuses on such attributes as product usage rates and the benefits derived from the product. Potential segments may be divided into two categories. Users and non-users. Users may be further divided into heavy, moderate and light users.

The summary of common segmentation bases is as shown in following table:

Common Basis of Markets Segmentation

Demographic	Psycho graphic	Geographic	Behavioural
Age	Personality	Region	Volume usage
Gender	Attributes	Urban, Suburban	End use
Ethnicity	Motives	Rural	User Expectations
Income	Lifestyle	Market density	Brand loyalty
Education		Climate	Price sensitivity
Occupation		Terrain	Benefits derived
Family size		City size	Occasion
Family life cycle		Country size	User status
Religion		State size	Buyer readiness stage
Social class			

In psychological segmentation, buyers are divided into different groups on the basis of VALS (Value and Life Style).

- Market Targeting: For market targeting sellers first evaluate the profile of and profit potential of each segment. The seller decides how many segments to cover based upon the size and growth of the segment, its structural attractiveness and company's objectives & resources.
- Product Positioning: Positioning is an act of designing company's offer and image so that target market understands and appreciates what company stands for in relation to its competitors.

Marketing Mix

Marketing mix is the set of controllable tactical marketing tools that the firm blends to produce the response it wants in the target market. The marketing mix consists of everything the firm can do to influence the demand for its product the marketing mix is the blending of the four P's strategic elements of marketing decision making that satisfies chosen consumer segments.

According to McCarthy, the four P's are product, price, place and promotion.

- Product means the goods-and –service combination the company offers to the target market.
- Price is the amounts of money customers have to pay to obtain the product.
- Place includes company activities that make the product available to target consumers.
- Promotion means activities that communicate the merits of the product and persuade larger consumers to buy it.

Product

Product: Product is the first & most important element of marketing mix. A product is anything that can be offered to a market for attention, acquisition, use or consumption that might satisfy a want or need. Product strategy calls for making coordinated decisions on product mixes, brand packaging & labeling.

A product mix is the set of all product lines and items that a particular seller offers for sale to the buyers. It includes breadth, length, depth and consistency.

A brand is a name, symbol or some combination used to identify the products of one firm and to differentiate them from competitive offerings.

A trademark is a brand that has been given legal protection. It is granted totally to the brand's owner.

Product Classifications: Products can be classified in three groups according to their durability or tangibility.

(a) Non-durable goods: Non-durable goods are tangible goods that normally are consumed in one or few users e.g. beer, soap, salt, etc.

(b) Durable goods: Durable goods are those tangible goods that usually survive many users e.g. Refrigerator, TV, clothing, etc.

(c) Services: Services are activities, benefits or satisfactions that are offered for sale eg. Haircut, repairing, etc.

Consumer Products: Consumer products are those bought by final consumers for personal consumption. Marketers usually classify these goods further based on how consumers go about buying them. Consumer products include convenience products, shopping products, special products and unsought products. These products differ in the ways consumer buy them and therefore in how they are marketed.

- Convenience products are consumer products that the consumer usually buys frequently, immediately, and with a minimum of comparison and buying effort.
- Shopping products are less-frequently purchases consumer products that customers compare carefully on suitability, quality, price, and style. When buying shopping products and services, consumers spend much time and effort, ingathering information and making comparisons. Examples include furniture, clothing, hotel services and etc.
- Special products are consumer products with unique characteristics or brand identification for which a significant group of buyers is willing to make a special purchase effort.
- Unsought products are consumer products that the consumer either does not know about but does not normally think of buying, most major new innovations are unsought until the consumer becomes a ware of them through advertising.

Product Life Cycles Strategies (PLC)

What is product? A product is a bundle of physical, service and symbolic attributes designed to produce consumer want satisfaction. An important feature of many products is the product warranty. Warranty is the guarantee to the buyer that the manufacturer will replace the product or refund its purchase price if it proves defectives during a specified period of time.

Product Life Cycle

Product like individuals passes through a series of stages. Successful products progress through four stages, namely: introduction, growth maturity and decline as shown in figure:

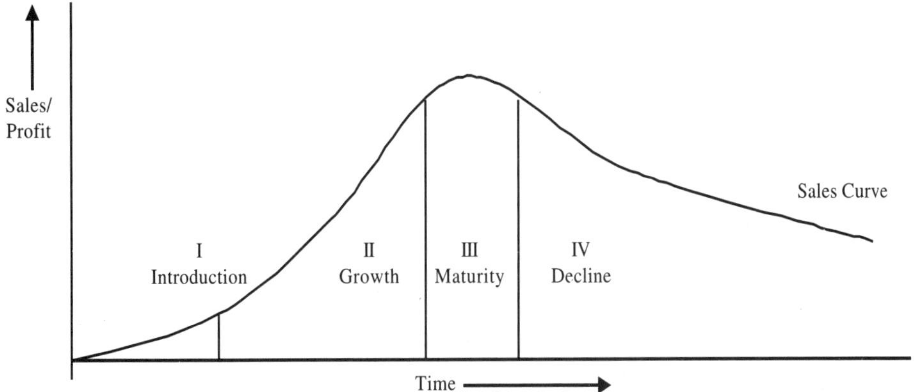

Fig. 8.3: **Product Life Cycle**

Stage I: Introduction - The firm's objective in the early stage of the product life cycle is to stimulate demand for the new product. Since product is not familiar to the public, promotional campaign stresses information about its features. The basic features are as listed below:

- Customers are hesitant in buying the product
- Productivity is low since demand is low
- Sales volume is low
- High amount of money is placed in advertisement
- Expenses are high
- Therefore it is the least profitable stage.

Stage II: Growth - Sales volume raises rapidly during the growth stages as new customers make initial purchases. The basic characteristics of the growth stage are listed below:

- This stage has the highest growth rate
- Customers are now familiar with the merits and demerits of the product
- Accordingly, sales volume increases very rapidly

- A proportional rise in profits occurs
- In this stages, competitors enter the market bringing about imitation of the product
- Promotional campaign is still very high.

Stage III: Maturity - Sales continue to grow during the early part of the maturity stage. This stage can be summarized as:

- Large number of competitors have entered market
- Available products exceed customer demand
- Sales increase levels out into a plateau reaching its highest peak.
- Reduction in prices may occur in this stage.

Stage IV: Decline - In the final stage, shifting consumer preferences brings about decline in sales. Important trends that follow are:

- Sales show downward trends.
- Profits decline, in some cases actually becoming negative.
- It necessitates product differentiation, that is having different uses for the same product.
- Or a totally new product may have to be introduced.

Product life cycle predicts that profits assume and go through certain pattern. The length of the life cycle is considerably different from one product to another. A new fashion may have a total life span of one calendar year, with an introductory stage of two months. But the automobile has been in maturity stage for more than twenty years.

Price

It is the amount of money charged for a product or service, or the sum of the values that consumers exchange for the benefits of having or using the product or service.

It is the only element in marketing mix that produces revenues, the other elements produce costs.

Prices are determined by the cost & supply conditions and the demand & competitive conditions. The cost and supply conditions dictate the minimum price that producer can charge while demand and competitive conditions determine the maximum price he can charge.

Types of Costs in Marketing

There are broadly two types of costs in marketing in marketing namely:

- Production costs (i.e. fixed costs & variable costs)
- Selling and delivery costs.

Factors considered when setting prices:

A company's pricing decisions are affected both by internal company factors and external environmental factors.

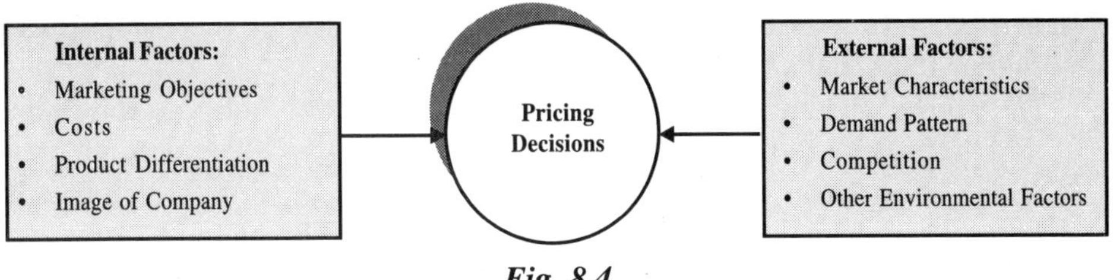

Fig. 8.4

Steps in Pricing:

Step I: Defining Pricing Objectives: Pricing objectives (as market penetration, market share, market skimming, fighting competition, optimum capacity utilization, profit maximization, etc.) are to be determined at the onset of price determination.

Step II: Analyzing Market Characteristics: There are several market characteristics like demand pattern, consumer income level, trade characteristics, competitive environment, etc. about which information have to be collected to establish prices of the product.

Step III: Calculating Costs: The main elements that should be covered in a calculation of costs are:

1. Direct Production Costs
2. Production Overheads
3. Marketing and Distribution Costs

Step IV: Establishing target Price and ascertaining feasibility: The next step is to establish a target price based on the analysis of the market characteristics and to ascertain whether it will be possible to sell at that price. There after any one of the pricing methods is adopted which best meets the company's objectives.

Pricing Methods:

1. ***Cost- plus Pricing:*** Cost based pricing, also known as cost plus pricing, and includes a certain percentage of profit margins on the sum total of the full cost of production, marketing costs and an allocation of overheads.

   Price = [Fixed cost + Variable Cost + Overheads + marketing Costs] + Specified Percentage of Total Costs
2. ***Market Oriented Pricing:*** This is a very flexible policy in the sense that it allows the prices to be changed in accordance with the changes in the market conditions. The product may be priced higher when demand conditions are very good and the prices may be lowered when the market is sluggish provided it helps in increasing sales.
3. ***Following Competitors***: Many firms follow the dominant competitors, particularly the price leader, in setting the price. The various alternatives

can be setting price at the same level; below that of the competitor; higher than that of the competitor.

4. ***Negotiated Prices:*** Deciding the price by negotiation between the seller and the buyer is very common in government and institutional purchases.
5. ***Break-even Price:*** The firm tries to determine the price at which it will break even or make the target profit it is seeking. Break even point is a point in a graph or mathematical model where cost equals revenue.

   Break- even Price = [Fixed Costs + Variable Costs]/Quantity

   Break- even Price for pre-determined profits = [FC +VC +Required profits]/Quantity
6. ***Creative Pricing:*** Creative pricing means taking advantage of the flexibility between the lower limit of break even pricing and the upper limit of the competitor's price for similar product.

Distribution (Place)

Place i.e. Placing the product refers to distribution of products, covering both channel of distribution (which includes direct & indirect transfer of title to a product) and physical distribution (which includes management of movement of raw materials, parts and supplies into & through firm and management of movement of finished products to consumers).

There are a number of channels for the distribution of goods. The one adopted depends upon numerous factors. The common channels of distribution are stated below:

Channels to Consumer

1. *Producer to Consumer:* This channel, often called the direct channel, includes no marketing intermediaries.
2. *Producer to retailer to consumer:* A retailer is a middleman that buys from producers or other middlemen and sells to consumers. This channel is most often used for products that are bulky and perishable.
3. *Producer to wholesaler to retailer to consumer:* This channel is known as the traditional channel because many consumer goods pass through the wholesalers to retailers.
4. Producer to agent to wholesaler to retailer to consumer. Agents are functional middlemen that do not take title to products and that are compensated by commissions paid by producers.

This channel is used for highly seasonal products and by producers that do not have their own sales force.

Channels for Consumer Products

Channels for industrial products:

Producers of industrial products generally tend to are short channels. We will obtain the two that are most commonly used.

1. Producer to industrial user: In this direct channel, the manufacturer's own sales force sells directly to industrial user. Heavy machinery, airplanes and major equipment are usually distributed in this way.
2. Producer to agent middlemen to industrial user. Manufacturers use this channel to distribute such items as operating supplier, accessory equipment. Small tools and standardized parts. The agent and independent intermediary between the producer and the user. Generally, agents represent sellers.

Promotion

Marketing communication or promotion means the transmission of a message to the buyers/consumers/channel of distribution in which the supplying company aims to tell each one of these receivers why they should buy or handle the product. The company must blend the major promotion tools advertising, personal selling, sales promotion, and public relations.

1. ***Advertising:*** Refers to any paid form of non-personal presentation and promotion of ideas, goods or services by an identified sponsor.
   - The many forms of advertising contribute uniquely to the overall promotion mix.
   - Advertising can reach masses of geographically dispersed buyers at a low cost per exposure.
   - It enables the seller to repeat a message many times, and it lets the buyers receive and compare the messages of various competitors.
   - Advertising also has some shortcomings. Although it reaches many people quickly, advertising is impersonal and cannot be as persuasive as company sales people in addition, advertising can be very costly.
2. ***Personal Selling:*** It is a personal presentation by the firm's sales forces for the purpose of making sales and building customer relationships.
   - Personal selling is the most effective tool at certain stages of the buying process, particularly in building up buyer's preferences, convictions, and actions.
   - Compared to advertising, personal selling has several unique qualities.
     - It involves personal interaction
     - It allows all kinds of relationships
     - The buyer usually feels a greater need to listen and respond
   - These unique qualities come at a cost. A sale force requires a longer-term commitment than does advertising – advertising can be turned on and off, but sales forces size is harder to change. Personal selling is also the company's most expensive promotion tool.

3. Sales promotion
   - It consists of a diverse collection of incentive tools, mostly short term, designed to stimulate quicker and /or greater purchase of particular products/ services by consumers or the trade.
   - Where advertising offers a reason to buy, sales promotion offers an incentive to buy.
   - Sales promotion includes tools for consumer promotion (samples, coupons, premiums, warranties, prices off and etc.
   - Sales - promotion effects are usually short lines, however, and are not effective in building long-run brand preference
4. Public Relations

   Public relations offer several unique qualities. It is very believable news stories, features, and events seem more real and believable to readers than advertisement do. Public relation departments perform the following:

   Press relations: Presenting news and information about organisation in he most positive light.

   Product publicity: Sponsoring various efforts to publicize specific products
   - *Corporate communication:* Promoting understanding of the organisation with internal and external
   - *Lobbying:* Dealing with legislators and government officials to promote or defeat legislation and regulation.
   - *Counseling:* Advising management about public issues and company positions and image.

Steps in developing Marketing Communication:

Step I: Identifying target audience: Even for same product, the target audience may be different in different markets because the decision making roles of different categories of people are not the same in all the markets.

Step II: Determining communication objective: The communication objectives may also be different in some cases. For example, when the product is in the introduction stage in a market, the emphasis is on consumer education and creation of primary demand while in other stages of PLC, the communication objectives could be fighting the competition, increasing market share, product differentiation, etc.

Step III: Determining message: This involves the decisions regarding the message content, message structure, message format, message source.

Step IV: Budget decisions: the size of total promotional expenditure and apportioning of this amount to the different elements of promotional mix are very important. The common methods used are namely; affordable method, percentage of sales method, objective & task method and competitive parity method.

Step V: Communication mix decision: Differing in marketing environment may necessitate variations in the communication mix because a channel or medium that is very effective in one market may not be so effective in other market.

Promotional Strategy: Promotion includes all the activities the company undertakes to communicate and promote its products to the target market

Promotion Mix Strategies

Marketers can choose from two basic promotion mix strategies- push promotion or pull promotion.

(a) ***Push Strategy***: involves "Pushing" the product through distribution channels to final consumers. The producer directs its marketing activities (Primarily personal selling and trade promotion) to ward channel members to induce them to carry the product and to promote it to final consumers.

Producer marketing activities (Personal selling, trade Promotion, others)

Reseller marketing activities (personal selling, advertising, sales)

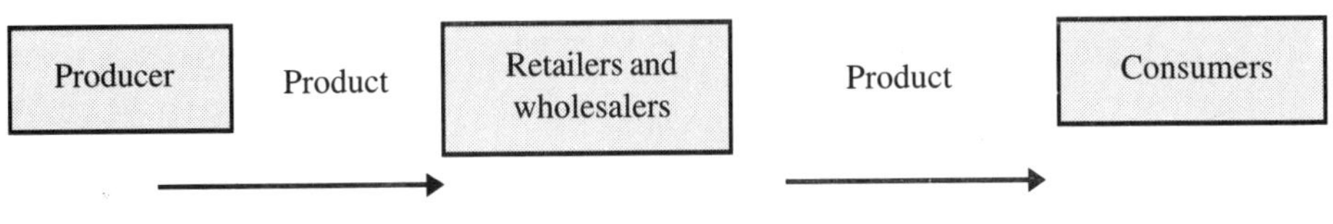

Fig. 8.5

(b) **Pull Strategy**: the producer directs its marketing activities (Primarily advertising and consumer promotion) toward final consumers to induce them to buy the product. It the pull strategy is effective, consumers will then demand the product from channel members, who will in turn demand it form producers.

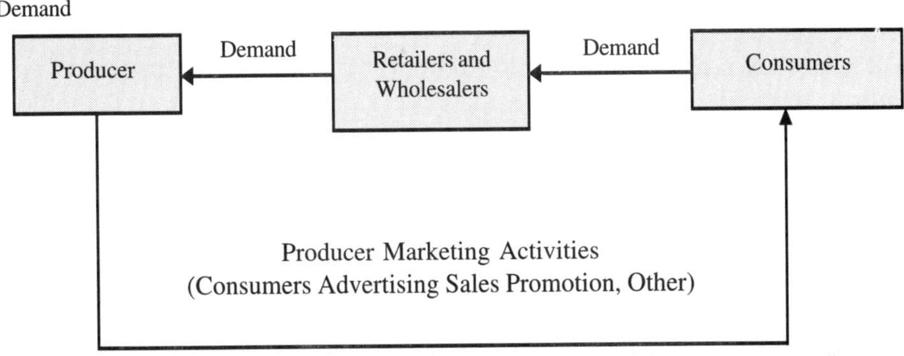

Fig. 8.6

Production and Operations Management

Meaning

Production is the transformation of resources into goods and services that have value to the customers. In businesses, this transformation takes the form of production processes, which have following components:

1. *Inputs:* Inputs are the four factors of production as land, labor, capital and entrepreneurship.
2. *Activities that add value:* These activities include engineering, design, manufacturing, and similar activities that add value for the customers.
3. *Outputs:* These are in the form of finished goods, services, idea.

There is also an additional component in the form of option of being repeated.

The Production Process

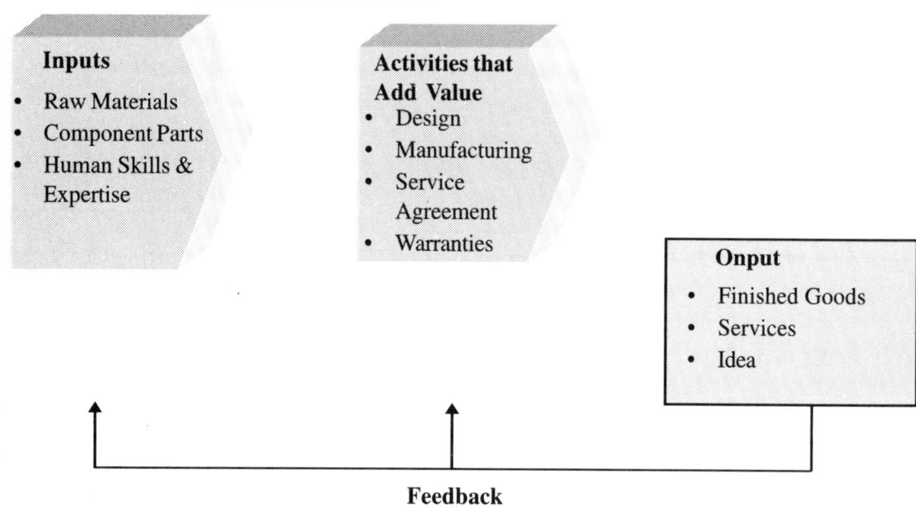

Fig. 8.7: **Production and Transformation Process**

As shown above, the transformation process of the inputs produces an output that will take the form of goods, services or information. It should be noted that although the process is easier to visualize in relation to production of goods, the concept of formation of inputs in to an output can also be applied to the service sector (where the term operations might be considered more appropriate than word production).The feed back loop reflects the in formation gained during the entire process. This information makes it possible to decide whether changes are required.

Definition

Productions and Operations Management is the coordination of an organisation's resources to produce finished goods or services.

More conservatively called as production management, now operations has been incorporated into that term to emphasize that production processes also apply to services.

The objective of production & operations management in a business firm is to maximize the value created. Briefly the difference between the value of inputs & the value of output represent the value created through production activities, i.e. profit & customer satisfaction.

Examples:

	Inputs	Processing	Output	Feedback
Hospital	Doctors, Nurses, Medical Supplies, Healthcare - Equipments	Healthcare treatment	Treated patients	Hospital costs, No. of treated patients, Quality of care
Farm	Land, Labour, Farmer, Tractor, Seeds	Ploughing, Harvesting, fattening	Grain, Beef, Milk, Fruits	Prices received, Turnover, Crop condition

Criteria for Plant Location/Site Selection

With rare exceptions, production facilities are expensive and permanent and cannot be easily moved. As a result, site selection is an important decision that can increase or decrease the costs and affect the future profits of a business. In general, production sites are chosen on the basis of five main criteria:

1. *Labour Issues:* Companies that produce services or goods are dependent on the location of skilled labor. A company may want to go where the most productive or technically skilled workers can easily be found. Besides, companies also choose to avoid those areas for labor related reasons such as high union activity and the higher wage and benefits packages sometimes associated with union labor.
2. *Government receptiveness:* Government receptiveness influences site selection because many towns, states and foreign countries offer tax breaks or favorable regulatory environments to attract business.
3. *Condition of infrastructure:* Infrastructure, from road and railways to electricity and water systems, can be a critical factor in site selection. Examples are locations of automobile industry.
4. *Proximity to suppliers:* Production facilities must be convenient to suppliers. To avoid costly transportation expenses, facilities are built around the sources that are used as necessary inputs in the production processes. Examples are those like cotton textile industries.
5. *Convenience for customers:* Many services must be produced where they are consumed, so some businesses place multiple production facilities within easy reach of their customer markets. Examples are those of consumer non durable and fast food industry.

Basic Kinds of Production System

Conversion System or methods of production can broadly be categorized as:

1. ***Intermittent Production System:*** These systems produce a variety of products either one at a time or finite number of different products in batches. Therefore they can be classified as:
   (a) *Job Production:* A job is a one-off product; if it is repeated there will be considerable interval between the similar jobs. Job production is a method of production found mainly in the civil engineering and construction industries.
   (b) *Batch Production:* Batch production involves a group of products of the same design passing through the production process together. It is mainly found in production of a batch of cases of wine of same type, construction of estate of twenty houses of same design, manufacture of rolls of wall paper, etc.

   Intermittent manufacturing is conversion with production characteristics of low product volume, special purpose machine equipment, labor intensive operations, etc

2. ***Continuous/Flow/Process/Mass Production System:*** Continuous conversion operations are featured by large volume deliveries of materials, highly automated equipment, highly specialized workforce, products of standard design and construction.

   Basic comparisons between the two production systems are as follows:
   (a) Continuous processing system usually yields a lower unit cost of products due to economies of scale, specialization of labor, and the likes while in comparison the unit cost is higher in intermittent production system due to the unique nature of production.
   (b) Storage costs per unit are usually lower in continuous processing system because of low inventories.
   (c) In Continuous processing system, fixed path material handling equipments are used while in intermittent production system variable path material handling equipments are used.
   (d) Time required for production is usually shorter in continuous processing system.
   (e) Continuous processing system requires larger investments because it uses special purpose machine, fixed path material handling equipment and larger scope.
   (f) In Continuous processing system marketing efforts are directed towards developing distribution channel for high volume while for intermittent production system all efforts are directed towards satisfaction of individual taste of the customers.

Plant Layout

1. *The Process Layout:* Methods of arranging equipment so that production tasks are carried out in discrete locations containing specialized equipment & personnel. A process layout is arranged according to the specialized equipment, workers & materials involved in the various phases of the production process.
2. *Product Layout:* Resources such as equipment, personnel, materials & supporting resources are arranged according to the functions being performed to produce a certain product. Factories such as chemical, cement, sugar, & textile factories are full under the product layout systems.
3. *Assembly-Line Layout:* Methods of arranging equipment in which production is in a flow of work processing along with a line of work stations. Systems such as automobile & personal computer manufacturing follow assembly-line layout.
4. *Fixed Position Layout:* Methods of arranging equipment in which the product is stationary, equipment & personnel are brought to it. Examples are airplane assembly, road, building, and bridge construction.

Production Planning and Control

In the planning stage, it is necessary to analyze the business plan and long range productions plans of the company and then create a working plan that specifies how these will be carried out. Production control involves determining whether current performance meets the standards set out in the plans. Production planning takes place in three steps. Then control processes give managers or employees the feedback necessary to track and control performances and if necessary, to revise plans in order to meet goals.

Production planning and control takes place in four basic steps as follows:

Step I: Analyzing overall business plan: Before making specific plans, the production manager analyses the organisation's overall business plan to ensure that the business will have an adequate supply of products to reach this goal which may be increasing sales or profits, launching a new product, entering a foreign market, collaboration with another company and the likes. This helps in determining what needs to be produced, how when and where.

Step II: Create a Long Range Production plan: Creation of long range production plan includes decisions concerning capacity needs and how additional capacity should be added. Increasing output means increasing capacity which a production manager can do by increasing the efficiency of current production processes, increasing the size or number of production processes or subcontracting with other companies to use their production processes.

Step III: Develop Working Plans: Working plans for running the production process specifies who does what, when and where. Here, working plans are drawn up for the production process and production facilities. Working plan generally takes place in two forms: a master production plan and a facilities plan. The master production schedule lists products, the facilities where they will be made and when they will be made. The facilities plan specifies the location and layout of facilities that will be needed. Detailed schedules state what employees and suppliers will need to do to meet the master schedule, the parts that will be needed and the number of workers who will be needed.

Step IV: Production Control: It includes the development of control and the tracking and correction of performance. There are five steps in production control:

1. *Production planning:* Estimating material and resources that will be needed and stating where and when they will be used.
2. *Routing:* Deciding what value-adding activities should take place, where, and when. It is the task of specifying the sequence of operations & the path through the facility that work will take. The way production is routed depends on the type of the product & the layout of the plant.
3. *Scheduling:* Preparing a detailed timetable for labor, materials, and production activities. It is the process of ensuring that materials are at the right place at the right time. In any production process, the production manager must incorporate a time element in to the routing plan, setting up a time for each operation to begin & to end. Some of the most widely used scheduling tools are Gantt charts, Critical Path Method (CPM) & Programme Evaluation & Review Technique (PERT).
4. *Dispatching:* Sending people, materials, and equipments to where they are needed. It is the issuing of work orders & the distribution of papers to department-supervisors. These orders specify the work to be done & the schedule for its completion. The production manager would dispatch orders to the appropriate departments, which are responsible for delivery of the needed materials & machines before the schedule starting time.
5. *Follow-up:* Activities by managers or employees to compare actual work performed with plans and schedules for that work. Once the schedule has been set up & the orders dispatched, a production manager cannot just sit back & assume that the work will automatically get done correctly & on time. Accident, mechanical-breakdown or suppliers' failures can delay production. Thus the production manager must have a system for handling delays & preventing a minor disruption from growing in to chaos.

The production manager must also develop a system of production control that will help to make sure the company's products meet quality standards, through physical inspection, testing & quality control.

Quality control is the process of ensuring that goods & services are produced in accordance with the design specifications. The major objective of quality control is to see that the organisation lives up to the standard it has set for itself on quality.

Financial Management

Finance: A Company's Lifeblood

Financial Management can be defined as an effective acquisition and use of money.

The Process of Financial Management:

Developing a financial plan for a company is done with two objectives in mind: achieving positive cash flow and effectively investing excess cash flow to make the company grow. The process consists of five basic steps:

Step 1: Estimating month-by-month flow of funds into the business from all the sources, including gains on external investments.

Step 2: Estimating month-by-month flow of funds out of the business, including both operating expenses and capital investments.

Step 3: Compare inflows and outflows. If cash flow is negative, determine how to make it positive, either by reducing the outflows or increasing the inflows. If cash flow is positive, determine how to invest excess funds most productively.

Step 4: Choose which capital investments should be made for continued growth. Determine the most cost effective combination of inside and outside sources of financing.

Step 5: Establish a system for tracking flow of funds and measuring the return on investment.

Fig. 8.8: **The Process of Financial Management**

Sources and Uses of Funds

From where the can a firm obtain the money it needs? The most obvious source would be revenues, or suppliers who may extend credit, or loans from financial institutions, or through stocks and bonds. Generally speaking, the goal of a company is to obtain money at the least cost and risk, whereas the goal of lenders and investors is to receive the highest possible returns on their investments at the least risk. Therefore, a company's cost of capital, the price it pays to raise the money, depends on the risk associated with the company (the quality of venture and time), the prevailing level of interest rates and management's selection of funding vehicles (internal vs. external; short vs. long term funding; debt vs. equity).

Initial capital consists of ownership equity (owner capital) & debt capital (credit capital) obtained from internal & external sources respectively.

1. ***Individual investor as sources of funds*:** This includes sources as personal savings, funds from friends, relatives & local investors and the sale of capital stock as major sources of funds.
2. ***Short-term financing:*** Short-term debt is any debt that will be repaid within one year. The three primary categories of short term debt are:
   (a) *Trade credit:* Trade credit is the most widely used source of short term financing for business in which the supplier finances the purchase by giving the buyer 30 days or more to pay. In effect, the buyer obtains financing from supplier rather than from a bank. Two of the most common forms of trade credit are open-book credit (open account) and promissory notes.
      - *Open-book credit:* It is an informal credit agreement that a buyer makes purchases & pays for them later. It is "open" because the buyer is not required to sign a written repayment agreement in advance.
      - *Promissory notes:* It is a signed "promissory to pay". The note indicates in writing the amount of money owed by the buyer & the repayment date. It is drawn by the buyer in advance of the purchase.

   (b) *Loans:* As important as trade credit may be to a business, a time may come when other sources of short term funding are require. The real business of most banks is lending money to commercial borrowers. The interest on a short term loan may be either fixed (constant-rate) or floating (variable-rate).
      - *Secured Loans:* Secured loans are those that are backed by something of value, known as collateral, which may be seized by the lender should the borrower fail to repay the loan. The three main types of collateral are accounts receivable, inventories, and other property. When a business loan is secured with accounts receivable, its customers' outstanding balances on open book accounts are used as collateral. A less attractive alternative, known as factoring, for most business is to sell accounts receivable to a finance company instead of

using them for collateral. Another form called as chattel mortgage, is an agreement where the movable property purchased through the loan belongs to the borrower, although the lender has a legal right to the property if payments are not made as specified in the loan agreement.

- *Unsecured Loans:* An unsecured loan is one that requires no collateral. Instead the lender relies on the general credit record and the earning power of the borrower. To increase their returns on such loans and to obtain some protection in case of default, most lenders insist that the borrower maintain some minimum amount of the money in the bank, known as compensating balance, while the loan is outstanding. Although the borrower pays interest on full amount of the loan, a substantial portion of it remains on deposit in the bank. Another important type of unsecured loan that eliminates the negotiation with the bank each time the business needs to borrow, is called the line of credit. However the line of credit does not guarantee that loan will be available. If a firm commitment is required, a revolving line of credit is agreed upon which guarantees that the bank will honor the line of credit up to the stated amount, for an extra fee.

(c) *Commercial paper:* A short-term financing option that has become increasingly popular is to borrow from other business and investors. The company borrowing money issues commercial paper, which represents a promise to pay back a stated amount of money within the stated number of days (legally, 1 to 270 days). The business or investor generally buys commercial paper at a price lower than the face value; then at the end of the period, the buyer receives the face value, the difference of which is the equivalent of the interest on the loan.

3. ***Long-term financing:*** One of the basic principles of finance is that long-lived assets are purchased with long terms funds. To finance long term projects such as major construction, acquisition of other companies, research & development, most companies rely on a combination of internal & external funding resources. The four main sources of external funding are loans, leases, bonds & equity.

1. **Debt Capital:**

   (a) *Long-term loans:* Long term loans are repaid over a period of one year or more and can be either secured or unsecured. Most common type of secured loan is a mortgage, in which a piece of property is used as collateral.

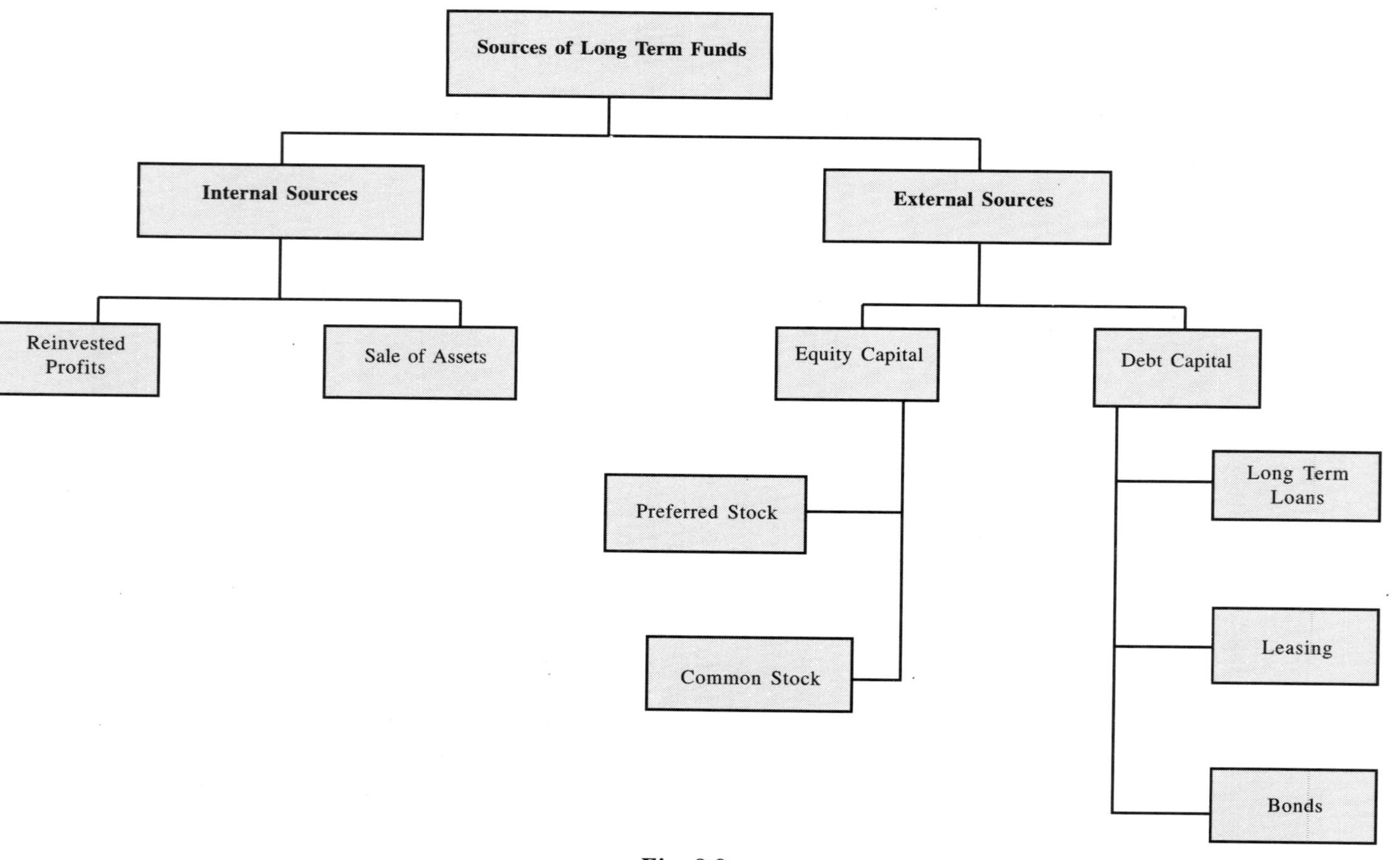
Sources of Long Term Funds
Internal Sources
External Sources
Reinvested Profits
Sale of Assets
Equity Capital
Debt Capital
Preferred Stock
Common Stock
Long Term Loans
Leasing
Bonds

Fig. 8.9

(b) *Lease:* A firm may enter in to a lease agreement rather than borrowing from a commercial lender to buy a piece of equipment or property. In a lease agreement, the owner of an item allows another party to use it in exchange for regular payments.

(c) *Bonds:* When a company needs to borrow a large sum of money, it may not be able to get the entire amount from a single source. Under such circumstances, it may borrow from many individual investors by issuing bonds. A bond is a certificate of indebtedness that is sold to raise funds, and the company is obliged to repay the sum plus interest to the bondholder. Each bond has a denomination, amount of loan represented by one bond. Bonds typically have maturity dates of 10 years or more. Like loans, bonds may be either secured bond (backed by specific property of one kind or another) or unsecured bond also called debentures (backed not by collateral but by the general good name of the issuing company).

2. ***Equity Capital:*** Unlike debts, which must be repaid, equity represents a "piece of action". When a company raises capital by increasing equity, it expands the ownership of the business. Stocks can be sold to many individual investors on the open market. A company may issue two types of stocks:

   (a) *Preferred stock:* Preferred stock gives its holders certain privileges that holders of common stock do not have. They are preferred as to dividends. They are preferred as to assets. It has some of the features of a bond & some of a common stock. Like a bond, preferred stock carries a fixed income payment or dividend. But the dividend represents a distribution of corporate profits, not payment of interest on debt. Like ownership of common stock, ownership of preferred stock represents ownership of the issuing company (corporation). Preferred stock doesn't have a maturity date. In the event of liquidation of the firm, the claims of preferred stock come before those of common stock holders but after those of the bondholders.

   (b) *Common stock:* Common stock holders are owners of corporation. By purchasing a share of stock, an investor is buying a "share" of the ownership pie. The total number of shares held by all investors represents the total ownership of the corporation. Common stock is less predictable but potentially more valuable.

3. ***Retained Earnings:*** Retained earnings are the amount of money left at year end after all expenses, interest payments, taxes & dividends have been paid. They are just about the only source of capital for smaller companies.

4. *Sale of Assets:* A company may also decide to sell its unutilized or non performing assets to maintain its liquidity or reinvest that amount in some productive areas that could fetch it higher returns or help it repay its outstanding or market debts.

Personnel (Human Resource) Management

Managing Human Resource in today's Business Environment

As national economies are getting integrated with the global economy, the businesses are forced to develop strategies that help them compete by cutting costs and permitting flexibility, so that they can respond to customers' changing needs. But necessary as these strategies are, they can bump headfirst into another important organisational need- finding, hiring, training and motivating employees who can function as empowered members of teams, pursuing organisational goals at a level of high productivity. Add to this the dynamics of an increasingly diverse workforce and managing human resource becomes a constant challenge.

Human Resource is the sum of activities required to attract, select, develop and retain people with knowledge and skills needed to achieve an organisational objective.

The Changing Workforce

Here are some of the predicted changes and some current findings for the next decade:

1. *Many more women will work outside the home*: It is predicted that more and more working-age women will join the workforce. They will also join that segment of jobs that were hereby held exclusively by males.
2. *Minority and immigrant workers will be a larger portion of workforce:* The number of immigrants joining the workplace across major service locations throughout the world is going to increase as major economies around the world are integrating the global economy.
3. *Percentage of workers in the contingent workforce will increase:* Part-time, temporary and self employed workers will be found in increasing share as more and more people opt for being entrepreneur and companies too focus on cost cutting.
4. *Labor shortages will occur:* The rate of growth in labor force will fall sharply, as per year lesser numbers of people join the workforce and more start up their own enterprises.
5. *Jobs will require developed skills:* As increased number of jobs will be service, technical or managerial positions, employers will increasingly demand more skilled and trained employees.

Human Resource Process/Functions

1. ***Human Resource Planning:*** It is a process of determining future manpower requirements and the means for meeting these requirements in order to carry out integrated plans of the organisation.
2. ***Job Analysis:*** It is a systematic collection; evaluation and organisation of information about a job i.e. job duties, qualifications required, working environment, and evaluation of worth of a job.
3. ***Recruitment:*** It is a process of finding and attracting capable applicants for employment. It can be done either through the internal or external procedure.
4. ***Selection:*** It is the process by which an enterprise chooses from a pool of applicants those persons who best meet the organisational criteria for positions available in given environmental conditions.
5. ***Training & Development:*** Training is a process of increasing the knowledge and skills of an employee for doing a particular job. It is usually applied on current job applications of non-managerial staff. Development is a programme designed to improve existing capacities of a manager to meet future organisational requirements. Various on-the-job as well as off-the-job methods are available for imparting training and development to the employees.
6. ***Performance Appraisal:*** It is a formal system of periodical review of and evaluation of an individual job performance. There are various formal and informal methods for performance appraisal.
7. ***Compensation:*** It refers to every type of reward that an individual receives in return of his labor. It can be either in financial terms or non-financial terms.
8. ***Movement of personnel:*** It refers to the displacement of the personnel within the organisation. It is done through promotion, transfer or initiating disciplinary action.

Factors that Influence EDP

Need for/Benefits of Entrepreneurship

Entrepreneurship has social and economic benefits to the individual and to the nation. The following are the benefits of EDP:

1. *Economic growth:* EDP encourages fast economic growth and new employment opportunities are created. EDP also encourages the growth of multi-national organisations and large scale industries.
2. *Productivity:* Productivity denotes the ability to produce more goods and services with less labour and other inputs. Higher productivity is guaranteed by EDP, through improved production techniques. Research and development and investment in new plant are ensuring productivity.
3. *New technologies, products, and services:* Through innovative techniques, products and services entrepreneurs bring new knowledge and techniques of production.
4. *Market change:* Market change and expansion of markets take place by the entrepreneurs. They act as agents of change in a market economy. The international markets also provide entrepreneurial opportunity.

Factors that Influence EDP

The factors that influence entrepreneurship development can be classified as internal factors and external factors.

I. Internal Factors

Internal factors are relating to the personality of an individual and they are psychological in nature and motivate an individual to become an entrepreneur. Family plays an important role as an internal factor for entrepreneurship. The internal factors are categorized as follows:

Demographic Factors	Personal Characteristics	Social Factors
• Age • Gender • Birth order • Education • Ethnic background • Nationality	• Technical expertise • Managerial expertise • Entrepreneurial expertise • Leadership skills • Personal values	• Parental role models • Cultural role models • Family support • Community
Personality Traits	**Cultural Factors**	**Environmental Factors**
• Achievement motive • Focus of control • Risk taking • Tolerance of ambiguity • Need for independence	• Individualism/ Collectivism • Uncertainty avoidance • Materialism • Dynamism	• Lack of employment • Little opportunity for advancement • Economic resources • Political climate

II. External Factors

External factors lay outside the environment and they influence internal factors. They also motivate and encourage a person to take decisions to become an entrepreneur.

1. *Political environment:* The political environment within a country influences government policies, which in turn influences entrepreneurship. Political stability, stable governments, stable policies, encouraging taxation policies, foreign investment opportunities, etc come under political environment.
2. *Social and cultural environment:* This factor is an extended version of family environment. The encouragement of certain societies and communities towards entrepreneurship could be a factor in certain countries for entrepreneurship. Some cultures encourage entrepreneurship, some encourages government jobs, and some encourages private sector jobs.
3. *Economic environment:* The economic environment denotes the ancestral property or property earned by an individual, current income status, standard of living, financial status he enjoys, etc. These factors influence the size of business and capacity to take risk. At the macro level, factors like market structure, competition, availability of capital, raw material, etc have influence on entrepreneurship.
4. *Legal environment:* Business has to operate basically in a legal environment. There are various laws that prevail in a country relating to license,

permit, tax, labour laws, etc which encourage or discourage entrepreneurship.

5. *Technological environment:* A new entrepreneur must have sound knowledge on latest technology and new product development. The best example is computer-based industries.

Business Success and Failure of Entrepreneurship

Business Success – Factors

In running a business or small-scale industry, there are number of social, economic, political and environmental factors that may lead to the business success. Here below, find some of the important factors for business success.

1. *Hard work:* Hard work of the entrepreneur during the initial stages of the enterprise as well as hard work in due course will lead to the success of the business. An entrepreneur should give continuity in his hard work.
2. *Time/Speed:* In undertaking a business, an entrepreneur must do the stages of work in time. For example, conducting feasibility studies, project preparation, and project appraisal must be done in time. Speed is also essential for the success of a business. Punctuality and timeliness are also relative factors of time and speed.
3. *Self-reliance:* Self-reliance denotes the dependability of the entrepreneur in taking risks on his own. He cannot depend on others to take risk.
4. *Communication:* An entrepreneur has to communicate with the customers, marketers, financiers, and other people involved in his business frequently.
5. *Motivator:* A successful entrepreneur motivates others around him and gets himself motivated. He has to motivate his workers as well as his distributors and customers to make his venture success.
6. *Initiative:* In organizing the business as well as running the business, he himself undertakes the initiative. He will not depend on others to take initiative, but he may consult others for improving his business.
7. *Discipline:* A successful entrepreneur is disciplined one in organizing the business, running the business, spending the resources, and keeping punctuality. His whole concentration is to make the business success.
8. *Willpower:* Willpower is the determination one should have to complete a work successfully. Willpower goes with hard work and facing so many challenges in running a business.

Leadership

A leader is one who is taking initiative to organise a business and run the business successfully. He performs himself as an example to others and spearheads the business for success. Some of the leadership qualities in business are as follows:

1. Selfless nature
2. Dedication
3. Example for others
4. Clean and uncorrupt nature
5. Creating followers
6. Achievement motivation
7. Impress people around him

The Need for Leadership in Business

The following are the factors, which explain the need for leadership in business.

(a) *To run a business successfully:* To run a business successfully, an entrepreneur must act as a leader. He must plan the programmes properly and must take steps to implement the programme stage by stage.

(b) *To face competition:* In any business or industry, stiff competition is there. The success of an entrepreneur lies in the facing the competition and come out successfully. For this purpose, leadership quality is necessary.

(c) *Sustainability:* Sustainability denotes the running of business successfully from the beginning to the end. There should not be any leniency in the middle in running the business.

(d) *Expansion:* A business leader after the initial success would like to expand his business. Through this process, many famous industrial houses have come up in various countries.

(e) *Team building:* Leadership is necessary to provide team spirit in the particular organisation. Team spirit is necessary especially among the employees who are working in the organisation.

(f) *To face external environment:* External environments like social, economic, and political situations affect the success of a business organisation. To face them, leadership is necessary.

Critical Elements of Entrepreneurship

Entrepreneurship has lot of characteristics, which have been explained in the introduction chapters. Here, we can discuss the critical elements apart from the characteristics of an entrepreneur, which are needed for an enterprise.

1. *Risk taking:* This is the basic element needed for an individual to undertake an enterprise. There are various types of risks that may come across in a business like organisational risk, financial risk, marketing risk, environmental risk, etc.
2. *Negotiating skill:* To make the enterprise a success, an entrepreneur must have negotiating skill. He must come in to contact with officials, customers, distributors, financiers, partners, etc. He should have the

bargaining skill to achieve his objectives successfully. His manners and activities should please the above group.

3. *Time management skill:* To start a business and to run the business, time management is one of the critical elements needed. All activities must be completed punctually as per the time schedule planned.
4. *Motivating and leading:* An entrepreneur should motivate his colleagues and workers and take the lead in running the business successfully.

Barriers to Entrepreneurship

While undertaking a business, the following difficulties may have to be encountered by the entrepreneurs.

1. *Government regulations:* An entrepreneur has to follow government regulations and such regulations may be changing very often.
2. *Competition:* This is the most important challenge an entrepreneur has to face.
3. *Unsteady market:* Many times, the market situations may fluctuate and may put lot of difficulties for an entrepreneur.
4. *Change in consumer behaviour:* Due to change in fashion and taste, the consumers may change their consumer behaviour, which may affect the marketing of the product of an entrepreneur. So, he has to watch closely the consumer behaviour.

Factors for Failure

The following are the factors, which may lead to the failure of enterprises:

1. *Delay:* Delay in starting the venture and delay in getting infrastructure facilities like license, power, water, etc may lead to the failure.
2. *Coordination:* Coordination between various financial agencies, distributors, etc is needed to make a venture successful. Lack of coordination may lead to failure.
3. *Suppliers:* Raw material suppliers must supply the materials in time and with prescribed quality to the organisation. Their failure may lead to total failure.
4. *Following the rules and regulations:* An entrepreneur has to follow the government rules and regulations relating to tax payment, labour laws, etc. Any failure to follow the rules may lead to action by the government and failure of the business.
5. *Labour turnover:* Labour turnover denotes shifting of the job by a worker from one industry to other industry frequently. This may affect the working condition of a firm.
6. *Raw material:* Raw materials must be available cheaply and nearer to the production center. Otherwise, this may lead to failure.
7. *Cost escalation:* The cost of erecting machineries, the cost of labour, etc are high, which may lead to the failure of the firm.

8. *Training:* Lack of training for the workers and the manager may lead to the failure of the enterprise.
9. *Technology updating:* If a firm is not updating its technology, production may come down, quality may be affected, and ultimately lead to the failure.
10. *Competition:* Any industry will have competition. If a firm is not surviving in the competition, it may lead to the failure.

Small Scale and Rural Industries

Meaning of Small Scale and Rural Industries

A Small Scale Industry or a small business is defined by USA's Small Business Association as "is one that does not dominate its industry".

1. A small scale industry is one which is organised with low capital.
2. It is labour intensive in nature.
3. A small beginning is made to start with.
4. Entire risk is taken by the promoter.

Classification of small scale industries

1. Manufacturing industries.
2. Feeder industries – Casting, welding etc.
3. Service industries – Repair, etc.
4. Mining or quarrying.
5. Ancillary or spare parts.

Rural or village or cottage industries

1. Located in rural areas.
2. Using locally available raw material.
3. Traditional technology applied.
4. Dependence on local market.
5. Entire family members are involved.

Objectives of small scale industries

1. Provide employment opportunities to the local population.
2. Promoting the production of large variety of goods – labour intensive methods.

3. Encouraging the adoption of modern techniques without causing technological unemployment.
4. Facilitating the mobilisation of capital and skill which are remained unused.
5. Integrating small sector with large scale industries.
6. Encouraging and supporting local talents using local resources.
7. Avoiding the problems of unplanned industrialisation.
8. Equitable distribution of national income and balanced growth of industries and avoiding regional imbalances.
9. Creating a cadre of small entrepreneurs, professionals and self employed experts.
10. Dispersal of industries throughout the country.

Advantages of Small Scale & Rural Industries

1. They are mainly located in rural areas.
2. They are the main sources of employment opportunities in countries where the density of population is high.
3. They remove the drawbacks of large scale industries like monopoly, abnormal profit, concentration of wealth and economic power.
4. They avoid the concentration of industries in a particular area.
5. New but simple techniques of production can be adopted with less capital.
6. They foster individual skill and initiative and promote self employment particularly among educated youth.
7. They pave the way for decentralized industrial growth.
8. Small industries result in higher national income, higher purchasing power in rural areas and high standard of living.
9. They reduce the rural urban gap.
10. Reduction in urban pollution.
11. Encouragement of even development of industries and encouragement of traditional industries.

Agencies for Entrepreneurship Development Programme (EDP)

Role of Government and Non-Government Agencies in EDP

In the entrepreneurial development government as well as non-government agencies are engaged in their promotion. There are three types of roles that are played by government and non-government agencies. Such roles are as follows:

1. *Promotional Role:* In this role both government and non-governmental agencies try to promote entrepreneurship by awareness building, encouragement, motivation, and guidance. The entrepreneurial spirit is encouraged by publicity and promotional efforts. Various EDP measures fall under this category. The objective of the role of these agencies is to attract people to start new ventures on their own. Identification of potential entrepreneurs through research and scientific methods has to be done. The efforts for the promotion of entrepreneurship are of three types:
   (a) *Awareness creation programme* – Through such programmes efforts are taken by agencies to create awareness among prospective entrepreneurs about various schemes, financial arrangements, marketing channels, etc.
   (b) *Programme on creation of new entrepreneurs* – Under this promotional role, training arrangements are made for the prospective entrepreneurs.
   (c) *Programme for current entrepreneurs* – Under this programme, the existing entrepreneurs are given managerial training and related programmes on marketing, new technology, etc.

The above programmes can be grouped again under three categories:

(a) *Target group oriented* – Under this category, promotional role is given to specific groups like youth, women, rural, technical entrepreneurs.

(b) *Products specific* – Under this category product base promotional role are given to entrepreneurs. Example, food products, engineering units, mechanical units, etc.

(c) *Location specific* – Promotional role is given to entrepreneurs on region wise or particular industrial area wise.

2. *Supportive Role:* Various agencies lend support in establishing and managing enterprises. Supportive role helps in promotional, maintenance, and development of entrepreneurship. Supportive role includes setting up of industries in exclusive areas like industrial estates and giving infrastructural facilities (road, water, power, etc). Financial support in the form concessional rate of interest, tax holidays, etc are also given. Institutions providing supportive role are established at regional levels and national level.

3. *Regulatory Role:* After the promotion and supportive role, the need for regulation and control emerges. Through various laws, government tries to regulate and control entrepreneurs. The regulatory institutions give clearance for the construction of factories, supply of power, tax relief, concessions, etc. All regulatory institutions have their policies and programmes to provide necessary support to entrepreneurs. The rules and regulations relating to the regulatory role should be simple and positive for the promotion of entrepreneurship.

The promotional and development activities for entrepreneurs are undertaken under two categories, namely entrepreneurship development programmes and entrepreneurial training.

Phases of EDP

An EDP involves three phases.

1. *Initial Phase (Pre-Training Phase):* Through publicity and training programmes awareness is created about the entrepreneurial opportunities.
2. *Development Phase (Training Phase):* Under training two types of training are given to the entrepreneurs, the first one is general training, which imparts need for entrepreneurship, factors affecting entrepreneurship, benefits of entrepreneurship, etc. Under the second type of training, motivation training is given to the entrepreneurs. Factors that motivate people to become entrepreneurs are taught to the prospective entrepreneurs.
3. *Support Phase (Post-Training Phase):* Under this category, counseling, encouragement, infrastructural, financial support are provided for establishing and running a new enterprise.

An EDP can be promoted in different phases. It is not necessary that all EDPs have to go through all phases. Some EDPs can be developed to take care of only one phase. First, the pre-training phase, where the programme is to be advertised, trainees have to be selected and arrangement of venue, infrastructure, framing of syllabus, etc is to be organised. In the second phase training is given, which is the training phase. After the programme is over, feedback should be collected and it is the post-phase training or follow-up phase.

EDPs should develop programmes on the latest issues and train the entrepreneurs to face challenges, for example in the case of WTO. It paves the way for the free exchange of goods and services across countries, resulting in free imports, which would have a direct impact on the small-scale industries. As quantitative restrictions on as many as 800 items are to be lifted as per the agreement of WTO, training on such programmes can be organised.

Some of the criticisms relating to EDP are as follows.

1. Poor quality of training.
2. Lack of commitment from the organisers.
3. Lack of focus.
4. Lack of follow-up.
5. Lack of support.
6. Emphasis on quantity but not on quality.

Maslow's Need Hierarchy Theory

In order to understand what motivates people to become entrepreneurs, Maslow's Theory would be helpful. His theory is based on human needs. He classified human needs into five different categories in order of priority from lower to higher needs. He called them hierarchy of needs. The reason why they are called so is because certain needs have to be fulfilled before human beings seek the next higher level need. If one is hungry, he will first demand food, before seeking prestige or status. Thus, when the lower needs are satisfied a new and higher need emerges and the process continues.

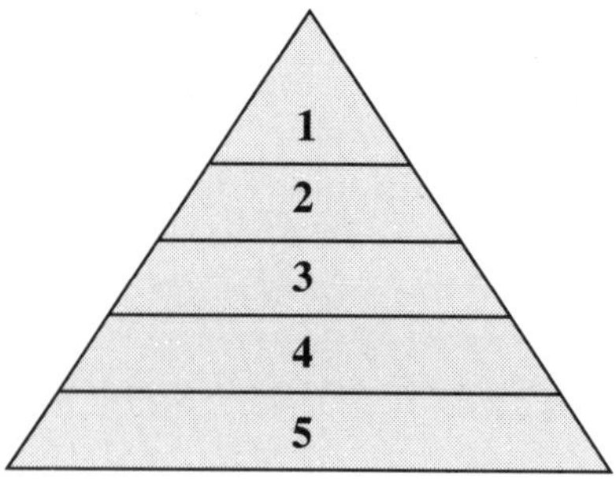

Fig. 11.1

1. *Physiological Needs:* Needs like food, clothing, shelter, air, and other necessities of life.
2. *Safety and Security Needs:* such as economic security and protection from physical dangers.
3. *Social Needs:* refer to a sense of belonging, recognition, acceptance, interaction, etc.
4. *Esteem Needs:* which are in terms of self-esteem, self-respect, self-confidence, achievement, reputation, etc.
5. *Self-Actualization Need:* which aims at self-fulfillment. Once this need is satisfied, human needs cease to be a motivating factor.

For entrepreneurs mainly the social, esteem and self-actualization needs motivate them to work more and more. Different types of motivating factors could be:

(a) ambition, compelling or facilitating;
(b) economic or non-economic;
(c) intrinsic or extrinsic.

Some of the factors, which prompt one to become entrepreneurs, are enterprising attitude, training and education, previous experience which are intrinsic factors and extrinsic factors like shortages, government assistance, taking over the running units, made available at a cheap price, etc.

12

Schemes and Incentives for Women and Unemployed Youth

Problems of Women Entrepreneurs

Women entrepreneurs may be defined as "woman or a group of women who initiate, organise, and run a business enterprise". According to another definition, a woman-run enterprise is defined as "an enterprise owned and controlled by a woman having a minimum financial interest of 51 per cent of the capital and giving at least 51 per cent of the employment generated in the enterprise to women". The following are the major problems of women entrepreneurs.

1. *Lack of education:* Compared to men, the rate of literacy among women is low. In the competitive world, women also lag behind men in getting technical and professional education, which are needed to manage an enterprise. Having little education and less experience, it is not possible to run an enterprise in today's context.
2. *Male dominated society:* Our society is still dominated by men. In very many societies women are not allowed to take jobs or organise their own enterprises. Such seclusion makes women not to venture in organising business or small scale industries.
3. *Limited mobility:* Due to primary household responsibilities towards her family, her time gets divided between two worlds. She has restricted timings for work due to which, she is not in a position to travel frequently and be away for longer periods. Thus, her mobility is restricted, which will have its impact on business.
4. *Problem of finance:* To raise finance from banking organisations and other sources, property is necessary. In many societies, property is in the name

of male members and this restricts them to raise funds. They have to manage funds through other ways of raising money from friends and relatives. Under restricted financial conditions, an enterprise cannot be run on a successful line.

5. *Low risk bearing ability:* Women by nature are unable to take risks which are very high in organising and running business organisations. The protected nature of bringing the girl child from the childhood also makes her inability to take risks.
6. *Social recognition:* In many conservative societies, women are not given due recognition to undertake business enterprises. They are looked down as small and weak. Even in advanced societies, women take lot of time to get recognition for their achievements in their enterprises.
7. *Management and control:* In managing business organisations as well as controlling such organisations, she has to depend on the men folk or her husband or family members. Even in Europe, it has been pointed out only 3 per cent of the CEOs consist of women.
8. *Continuity in enterprises:* An enterprise can be successful if it is taken care from its inception to the final successful stage. Continuity is needed. But women due to their family and related commitments are not in a position to give continuity. This can be endorsed by the failure of enterprises started by women.

The following problems are encountered for women entrepreneurs:

1. Shortage of working and investment capital resulted from gender inequalities

   Due to deep rooted social norms and values, women in most of the communities in Ethiopia lack equal rights in passing decisions on properties or resources. This condition puts women in a most difficult situation to raise sufficient money for investment either from their own savings or credit, as they cannot meet collateral requirements of lending institutions.
2. Work burden of women

   Women in Ethiopia are entrusted with wide range of responsibilities that include contributing labor to production activities, up keeping home, rearing children, and others. In this regard, they face shortage of time in carrying out the business activities.
3. Lack of basic business skills and technical knowledge

   In Ethiopia, in many parts of the country, women do not have equal access to education and training with men. As there are general shortages of such services, men seize the existing limited opportunities. Therefore, women remain losers and consequent lack of proper skill and knowledge to undertake business activities.

4. Other cultural barriers

   Women are not encouraged or motivated to own and run income generating activities that could improve their economic conditions. Although women significantly participate in all economic and production activities, they are not accorded proper recognition for their contribution due to the cultural barriers, which consider women as weak, less reliable, and inefficient.

Scope/Steps to Encourage Women and Unemployed Youth

Encouragement of Women: The following steps are advocated to encourage women to undertake enterprises.

1. *Access to capital, infrastructure, and markets:* Government and related organisations like banking institutions must come forward to provide liberal capital to organise enterprises by women. Infrastructure facilities in the form of industrial estates exclusively for women can be established. Marketing facilities for the products of women entrepreneurs can also be arranged by governments.
2. *Development of managerial and production capacities:* Training and development activities can be developed especially for women entrepreneurs and such training could be given to selected target groups. Training should be made a continuous process for such women entrepreneurs.
3. *Identifying investment opportunities:* Government and NGOs must come forward to identify investment opportunities and production venture suited to women. In all regions of the country selected areas can be located and such investment opportunities can be initiated and it can be extended to other areas in future.
4. *Promotional measures:* Promotional measures like sponsoring, delegating, participation in trade fairs, exhibitions, arranging buyer-seller meets and specialized conferences, etc can help the promotion of women entrepreneurs.
5. *Seminars and workshops:* Organizing seminars, workshops, and training programmes for giving wider exposure to women entrepreneurs will be useful to develop their entrepreneurial capabilities.
6. *Tie up arrangement:* Women enterprises can be tied to medium and large scale industries for marketing their products and to make a permanent development for their enterprises.

Unemployed Youth: The following are the measures considered to develop unemployed youth in organising their enterprises.

1. *Identification of enterprises:* The government and the promotional agencies must identify suitable areas for developing the enterprises for unemployed youth. Areas like computer, engineering, technology, etc can be identified and can be addressed to the youth.

2. *Banking institutions:* The banking institutions must come forward to finance the unemployed youth liberally. Only banking institutions can initiate the enterprise revolution among the unemployed youth.
3. *Training:* At the national level various types of technical and managerial institutions must be promoted by government to promote the entrepreneurial interest of unemployed youth. Various types of training on a continuous basis must be given to them.
4. *Marketing:* The products and services, which are the outcome of the unemployed youth and their enterprises, must be helped in the form of marketing. Marketing is an important area for the success of the ventures promoted by unemployed youth.
5. *Seminars and conferences:* Seminars and conferences relating to self-employment and new ventures must be arranged by the government, chamber of commerce, industrial associations, etc.

Problems Relating to Youth

1. *Poor entrepreneurial qualities:* The educational system that the country pursued in the past years did not prepare the youth technically and psychologically for self-employment. This developed negative attitude towards self-employment.
2. *Lack of basic managerial and technical skills:* The school system, which the students underwent, did not equip them with adequate technical and managerial skills that would enable them to harness the existing and potential resources for enterprise development.
3. *Shortage of capital and working premises:* These are also the major pressing problems that hindered the entrance of unemployed youth to the small scale sector.

13

Procedures and Steps Involved in Establishing Small Scale and Village Industries

Before a venture is started, certain preliminary steps must be taken as a logical step. An entrepreneur starts with business idea generation and identification of business opportunities. Then, marketing, financial, and technical feasibilities are undertaken. The last stage is the preparation of project report by the entrepreneur and the project appraisal by the banking institutions and promotional agencies.

Business Idea Generation Techniques and Identification of Business Opportunities

A business idea is a business seed, which expands and grows into a business tree. A business idea can emerge from two sources, namely, technical source and market source.

A. Technical Source (within the company)

Technical source emerges within the company. Technicians, managers, supervisors, and workers think over new products and new ideas. New ideas are generated as follows:

1. By the scientist working in the Research and Development department of the organisation.
2. By the engineers working in the production department.
3. By the field staff who may get new ideas while solving problems. These new ideas are relating to:
   (a) New methods to be adopted for production
   (b) New product design
   (c) New machinery, etc.

B. Market Source (outside the company)

There are various methods of generating ideas from market sources. They are:

1. *Focus groups:* In this method, group of consumers are interviewed. A moderator leads the group through an in-depth discussion. A group consisting of 8 to 14 members is stimulated for developing a new product.
2. *Brain storming:* In this method also a group of consumers are selected. Brain storming tends to generate lot of ideas. In this method, the group is encouraged to combine various ideas and improvement of these ideas leads to new ideas.
3. *Problem inventory analysis:* This method uses individuals rather than a group to generate new product ideas. Instead of generating new ideas themselves, participants are provided with a list of problems for a product category. They are then asked to identify and discuss products in this category.
4. *Checklist method:* In this method a new idea is developed through a list of related issues or suggestions. An entrepreneur can use a list of questions to guide the direction of developing entirely new ideas. The checklist may take any form at any length.
5. *Free association:* This technique is used in developing entirely a new idea. First, a word or phrase related to a problem is written, and then it is developed, thereby creating a chain of ideas with a new product.
6. *Value analysis:* This technique develops methods for maximizing value to the entrepreneur. In value analysis procedure, regularly scheduled times are established to develop, evaluate, and refine ideas.

Identification of Business Opportunities

After the generation of various business ideas, the next step would be to screen them for identifying the business opportunities. An entrepreneur should have an ability to spot a business opportunity among the various business ideas. An opportunity has the qualities of being attractive, durable, and timely and is anchored in a product or service, which creates or adds value for its buyer or end-user.

Various Sources Business Identification Opportunity

There are three sources through which we can identify a business opportunity

1. *Systematic innovation:* According to Peter Drucker, systematic innovation means monitoring the seven sources innovative opportunities. The first four sources of innovative opportunities lie within the enterprise. The other three sources refer to changes outside the company.

A. Internal sources of innovating opportunities

   1. Unexpected success and unexpected failure – No other area offers rich opportunities for successful innovation than an unexpected

success. Unexpected successes are totally neglected. On the other hand, unexpected failures cannot be rejected and rarely go unnoticed.

2. Incongruity (Inconsistency) – This is a symptom of an opportunity to innovate. It creates an instability in which minor efforts can move large masses and bring about a re-structuring of the economic or social conditions.
3. Process need – It is task-focused rather than situation-focused. It perfects a process that already exists and sometimes it makes possible a process by supplying the missing link.
4. Industry and market structure – A change in the industry's structure and market structure offers exceptional opportunities.

B. External sources of innovating opportunities
  1. Demography – Change in population provides innovative opportunities.
  2. A change in perception – A critical problem in perception-based innovation is timing. Timing is the essence of exploiting change in perception.
  3. New knowledge – They are based on the convergence of different kinds of knowledge. Knowledge-based innovation requires careful analysis of all the new factors, whether knowledge itself, or social, economic, or perceptual factors.

2. *Trade Fairs and Exhibitions:* They are conducted at local level, regional level, national level, and international level. They provide greater opportunities for identifying business opportunities.
3. *Positioning:* Positioning is the position of the product or brand in the minds of the consumers. With the help of marketing research, it is possible to quantify and see the perceptual map, which shows the gap in the market. Positioning can be undertaken by means of promotional and advertising measures.

Marketing, Financial, and Technical Feasibilities

A feasibility study is the evaluation of a business idea. A feasibility study can be undertaken by the entrepreneur himself or through professional bodies.

Marketing Feasibility

The success of any product depends on the capturing of the market. A market should be captured by facing competition. When new products are introduced, to make it a success, marketing efforts are very much needed. The stages in new product development are as follows.

1. Idea generation
2. Screening
3. Concept development and evaluation

4. Business analysis
5. Product development and evaluation
6. Development and evaluation of marketing mix
7. Test marketing
8. Commercialisation of the product

The marketing feasibility also includes the market structure, the competitors, market share estimation, market growth, and price feasibility.

Financial Feasibility

After ascertaining the marketing feasibility, financial feasibility is ascertained. Here, the income and expenses are estimated on the basis of cost and price. Marketing feasibility tests the business idea for marketing, whereas, in financial feasibility, the financial soundness of the idea is tested. Finance is the most important pre-requisite to establish a business.

Methods of evaluating financial feasibility

1. Cost of production and marketing
2. Break-even analysis
3. Assessment of fixed and working capital requirements
4. Capitalisation
5. Sources of finance
6. Cost of capital

Technical Feasibility

Technical feasibility is also known as techno-economic feasibility. In a technical feasibility study we can ascertain whether a business idea is feasible, whether it can be transformed into a product, and whether a business opportunity really exists. *The technical study evaluates the choice of technology, production process and the location of the business*. The technical analysis has the following items.

1. Technology analysis (labour intensive or capital intensive)
2. Raw material analysis
3. Make or buy decision
4. Plant size and location
5. Market oriented location or material oriented location
6. Cost benefit analysis

Apart from these three analysis (marketing, finance, and technical feasibilities), there are other related feasibilities like managerial feasibility, legal feasibility, and location feasibility.

Project Report and Project Appraisal

Project Report

Project identification is done first. Then on the basis of feasibility studies selection is made. The preparation of the project report is the next stage.

Project report is the presentation of detailed business plan in writing. The project reports are used primarily for raising the capital. It is a blueprint of a business plan. The objective of the business plan is to attract investors and lenders. A project report contains the following items.

1. Introduction
2. Details of the promoters
3. Details about the proposed structure and operations of the business
4. Proposed project location
5. Project cost
6. Foreign exchange required
7. Sources of project funding
8. Technology and manufacturing process
9. Raw material, power, and water
10. Human resources
11. Market
12. Environment impact
13. Financial projection of the project

Project Appraisal

Assessing the viability or feasibility of a project by the lending institution is called project appraisal. The difference between feasibility and appraisal is that, the feasibility is done by the entrepreneur, while appraisal is done by the investors and lending institutions.

There are different methods followed by lending institutions to evaluate a project proposal. Marketing, economic, financial, management, and other feasibilities are studied by lenders. Various methods of profitability appraisal are used, they are pay back period method, return on investment method, discounted cash flow method, internal rate of return, net present value method, and profitability index method.

Part – II

Cooperative Entrepreneurship

14

Cooperative Entrepreneurship

Economic development originates and fosters in relation to the strength and health of the local entrepreneurship and depends on the rate of its generation and equally to the intensity of its sense of social responsibility, its innovation quotient and its index of management capabilities. Entrepreneurial density, innovative propensity and management capability in the society in a particular period determine the character and future of economic development.

Entrepreneurs are rarely mentioned in connection with cooperative development, which reflects the state of entrepreneurship in conventional economic thinking, where entrepreneurs are more often than not a missing category.

Meaning

Cooperative entrepreneurship denotes the application of entrepreneurship talents and outcome to the cooperative institutions. Unlike the independent, individual entrepreneurs, cooperative entrepreneurs vary in nature and component.

Cooperative Entrepreneurship – Frame work

Cooperative entrepreneurship refers to a role or a set of roles whose influences are conditioned by characteristics of group members. The personalities of the entrepreneurs are influenced by the situation. But the true entrepreneurship though individual oriented has got a collective group foundation in cooperatives. Cooperative entrepreneurs collectively engage in the enterprise activity for the economic interest of themselves.

Cooperative entrepreneurship should function collectively and should have courage to stand up when something wrong is done and should be capable of owning a mistake openly. Such cooperative entrepreneurs will not only succeed but will also make the cooperatives a succeed story in the world.

Definition of Cooperative Entrepreneurship

Cooperative Entrepreneur "Cooperative Entrepreneur is one who undertakes and assumes the responsibility to discovery innovate cooperative opportunity, on the basis of collective effort, which has the cooperative effect for the socio-economic development of the member entrepreneurs simultaneously with the cooperative values".

(M. Karthikeyan 2004)

Principles of Cooperative Entrepreneurship

1. **Principle of Innovation**

   Innovation is the basic principle of an entrepreneur. Through innovative process an entrepreneur can solve problems in a cooperative set up and he/she can achieve new levels of performance, return, etc.

2. **Principle of Cooperation**

   Cooperative entrepreneurship is the property of the group and does not reside in any individual entrepreneur. As it is a group approach this principle of cooperation states that the cooperation among the entrepreneurs of a cooperative in itself and with the entrepreneurs of other cooperatives.

3. **Principle of Active Participation**

   Entrepreneurs contribute equitably to, and democratically control the capital of their cooperative enterprise. They allocate surplus towards various funds as per cooperative law. The surplus is also allocated for benefiting member entrepreneurs in proportion to their participation with the cooperative enterprise. This principle emphasizes the active participation of the cooperative entrepreneurs in all dimensions of a cooperative enterprise ie., in constitution, management & administration, and business.

4. **Principle of Democratic Management**

   Cooperatives are democratic enterprises controlled by their member entrepreneurs, who actively participate in setting their policies and making decisions. In all cooperatives "men and women entrepreneurs serving as elected representatives are accountable to the membership ie., entrepreneurship".

5. **Principle of Information**

   Cooperative entrepreneurs inform the public particularly youth and opinion leaders about the values and socio-economic, democratic benefits of cooperative enterprises. Cooperative information can be passed/communicated through cooperative education and training. Cooperative information plays an important role in the decision making process and helps the cooperative entrepreneurs to take right decision at the right time.

6. **Principle of Collective Decision making**

   In cooperative enterprises member entrepreneurs have equal voting rights (one member; one vote). Decisions are made collectively considering views and ideas given by all member entrepreneurs.

7. **Principle of Self Confidence**

   Confidence and self effort alone bring success in life. In cooperative entrepreneurship honesty and courage are important. A cooperative entrepreneur should be a person of self-confident and must have belief in themselves and the ability to achieve their goals. An honest entrepreneur automatically becomes a courageous entrepreneur.

8. **Principle Cooperative Development**

   Entrepreneurial development leads to cooperative development. It can be achieved through cooperative education, proper training at all levels, and extension. Cooperative Entepreneurship Development Porgrammes may be organised for the purpose.

9. **Principle of Social Responsibility**

   Cooperative entrepreneurship is a social entrepreneurship. Cooperative entrepreneurs have to exercise social responsibility for the sustainable development of their cooperative enterprise and the entire community through policies approved by the general body.

10. **Principle of Time Management**

    Timely identification of weaknesses, information retrieval and dissemination at the right time, and initiation of corrective measures are related to time management. Decision making process needs time management to take proper decisions for the success of the cooperative enterprises. Entrepreneurs must keep in mind this principle for their success.

Cooperative Entrepreneurship Ladder

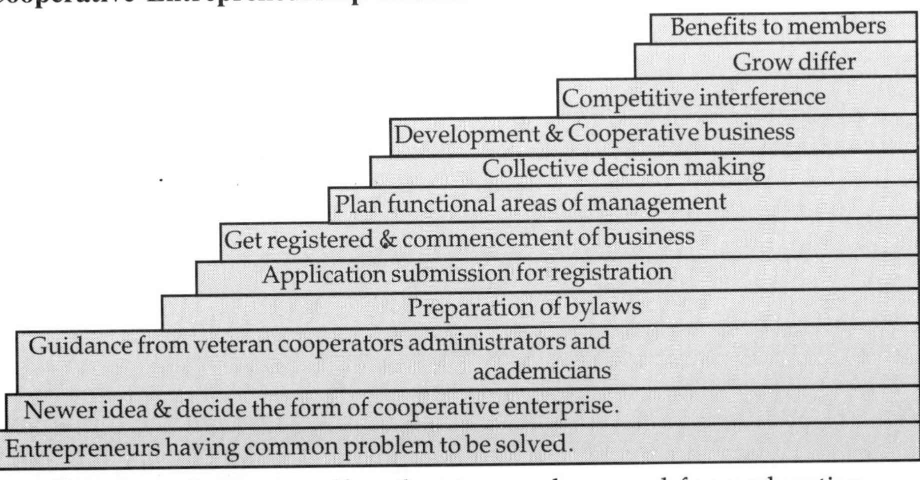

The above ladder is self explanatory and no need for explanation.

15

Pattern of Cooperative Entrepreneurship

Pattern of Cooperative Entrepreneurship

The pattern of cooperative entrepreneurship may be classified into the following categories:

1. Cooperative entrepreneurs are part of the class of members (*Member Entrepreneur*)
2. cooperative entrepreneurs are managers of the cooperative enterprise (*Executive Entrepreneur*)
3. *Director Entrepreneurs* are elected from among the members as representatives to administer the cooperative enterprise.
4. Cooperative entrepreneurs are part of a governmental or parastatal administration bureaucratic entrepreneurs. (*Bureaucratic Entrepreneur*)
5. Cooperative entrepreneurs are members of other non-cooperative orgainsation (such as schools , universities, donor/aid and sponsoring agencies, churches) who provide career possibilities and incentives independent from or in addition to cooperative entrepreneurship. (*Catalytic entrepreneur*)

From these five patterns of cooperative entrepreneurship, the first three can be characterized as effort taking, the other two as external, promoting entrepreneurs. In ffort taking cooperative entrepreneurship, the vital entrepreneurial decisions are made by person with function within a cooperative society.

In addition cooperatives can be established through the initiative of external agents: functionaries from administrations which very often have been set up especially to organise and assist cooperatives are responsible for the establishment of cooperative organisation: bureaucratic entrepreneur. Usually, but not necessarily, this type of entrepreneurship implies the "officialisation" of the cooperative movement.

But cooperative can be promoted by outsiders in another way: person who specialize in local institutional development are endowed with responsibilities for getting mutual self help processes stared. These catalysts can be paid professionals of volunteers, employed by the government or non –government organisation.

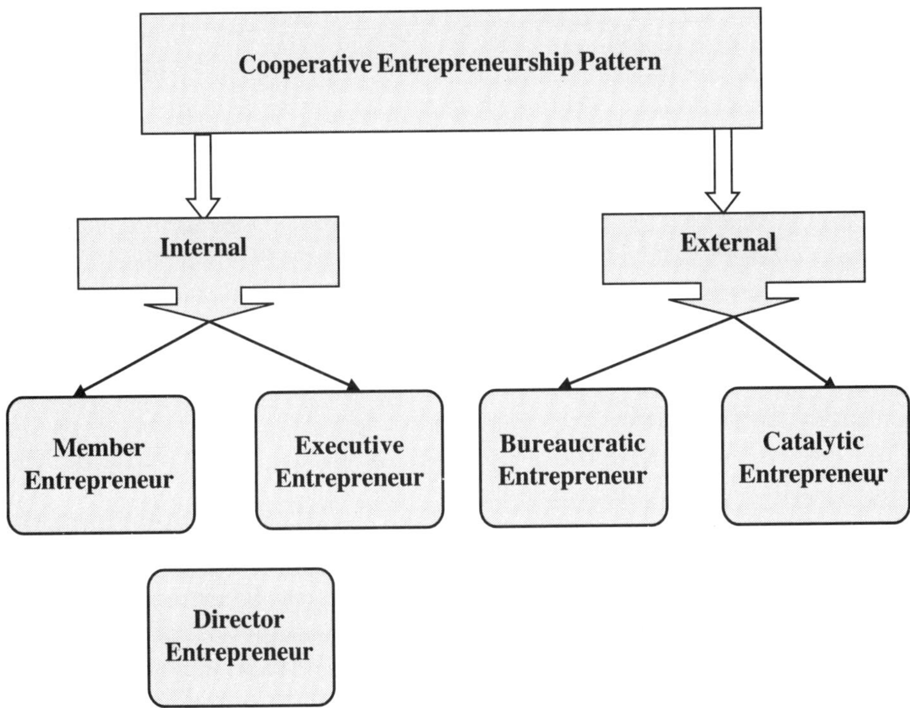

Fig. 15.1: **Cooperative Entrepreneurship Pattern**

Member Entrepreneurs

This kind of entrepreneurial pattern normally assumes, in order to be successful, a high level of member-heterogeneity, and may result in a quite unequal distribution of the wealth created.

But again, these outcomes of members entrepreneurship should not surprise us, given the difficulties and peculiarities of cooperatives action, the unequal appropriation of cooperative wealth is one of the few realistic avenues open for spontaneous cooperative entrepreneurship and hence for spontaneous cooperative evolution.

The member entrepreneur in cooperation corresponds to the intrapreneurs is a public corporation (public limited company) who own equity (or options for the acquisition of equity) as holders of corporate equity or shares they are (as other-non managerial/entrepreneurial owners/ shareholders) residual claimants of the variability in the operation of the firm.

Member entrepreneurs are the basic ingredients for the cooperative entrepreneurship. Individual talents, merits, risk bearing abilities, innovative nature, etc of members are pooled and consolidated for the betterment of the cooperative entrepreneurship. So a member can contribute to the development of the cooperative, as an entrepreneur in the form of contributing share capital, member patronage, participation in democratic associations, providing leadership and acting as the watchdog for the wrongs of his cooperative.

Professor K.K. Taimni, ILO COOPNET Director, views that:

> *"...individual members take to entrepreneurship, i.e., scan the environment, identify and seize opportunities, assume risks, deploy their own capital and derive benefits. The role of the cooperative is confined here to provide support services, including essential advisory services so that risk-related losses are minimized and links between a member's enterprise and external agents and markets are effectively established".*

Executive Entrepreneurs

It is observed that those individuals creating and implementing cooperative opportunities will not necessarily be identical with those who manage the ongoing cooperative. This will be the case especially during the initiating or founding phase of a cooperative venture.

Managers do not necessarily share the objectives of the members owners. They have some choice in the direction, pace, quality, and duration of their efforts, depending, among other factors on the effectiveness of members participation and the cooperative's external environment. Managerial discretion has to be recognized as a fact commercial life also in cooperatives.

(a) Manager Entrepreneurs include chief executives of cooperatives with various denominations (general manager, manager, secretary, etc.), deputy managers, line supervisors, and heads of various sections. Manager entrepreneurs implement the policies and programmes assigned by the board. Hence, they must be well-qualified, hard working, must have integrity, and work for the success of the cooperative. They have to look after the day-to-day working of their cooperatives and provide feedback to the board about the problems and challenges of the cooperative. The special competencies required by managers to promote cooperative entrepreneurship are as follows:

    1. Knowledge of cooperative principles and practices.
    2. Knowledge of cooperative laws and bylaws.

3. Devotion to the cooperative ideal.
4. Sensitivity and responsiveness to members' interests and wishes.
5. Community orientation.
6. Close watching of the market conditions and the acts of competitors.

Peter Davis, the British cooperator views that:

> *"...we desperately need who have the qualities to take responsibility for leading and building the whole community of members and employees into a social and value-based business seeking the fulfillment of the cooperative purpose".*

Director Entrepreneurs

The board members are responsible for the administration of a cooperative where they have the board membership. They are the internal administrative entrepreneurs to look after the affairs of the cooperative enterprise. Board members elect the president and vice-president in order to delegate authority and responsible. The president is the head of a cooperative enterprise in all respects.

Bureaucrat Entrepreneurs

One prominent and very often also empirically attempted solution to the problems of incentive failure in cooperative has been the take over of entrepreneurial functions by the government: government officials in open of disgusted form try to act as cooperative entrepreneur.

The blue print, up-down or synoptic approach may indeed succeed in establishing cooperatives: by bureaucratic command or force, officials are required to set up cooperative societies. Following the colonial model, the government works at the local level, and often through local leaders.

Hierarchical control, or supervision, become indispensable and hierarchical incentives (power, prestige, rank and status) the main motivators for entrepreneurial action. These are the people who are mostly government officials engaged in the promotion of cooperatives on behalf of their government. In many developing countries cooperatives have been introduced as a state subject by their respective governments. During colonial periods the colonial governments introduced cooperation to eradicate poverty and improving agricultural development. Such countries were not having a level of education to organise and run the cooperatives. So government officials attached to the department of cooperative had to take the responsibility of organising the cooperatives, giving guidelines and counseling to the cooperative leaders. The success and failure of cooperatives in many countries depended on the nature and outlook of these bureaucrats. In due course, when the voluntary movement (cooperatives) developed, the necessity for the involvement of the bureaucrats was reduced. So at present in developing countries the de-officialization of the cooperative movement is taking place, which denotes reducing the importance of officials to run the cooperatives.

Catalytic Entrepreneurs

Catalytic entrepreneurs are external agents, or members of outside agencies, whose task it is to get the process of cooperative institutionalization started and to work with and strengthen local cooperatives. These outside cooperative entrepreneurs (or agencies) can be governmental or non-governmental. What makes the "catalyst" different from the bureaucratic entrepreneur is that:

1. he is not working through conventional bureaucratic or technological channels; and
2. the local cooperative institutions he is initiating, promoting and supporting remain autonomous. Self-organsing organisations, i.e., do not become an officialised and regulated part of a governmental or parastatal administration.

Catalytic entrepreneurs are specialists in the initialization, promotion and support of cooperative organisations. The designations for such persons are various. The terms "promoter", "change agent", "facilitator", "motivator" have been used.

To sum up, in cooperative theory and policy, is not aware of any approach which has addressed the connection between entrepreneurial behaviour and the degree of economic success and failure of cooperatives. Policy makers have theoritised, planned and implemented in a virtual vacuum about cooperative entrepreneurship is causally related to the main effects of economic growth (increase in incomes, productivity, employment, living standards), not to include entrepreneurial activity in cooperative policy bias and even policy errors. Preventing the potential of cooperatives for development from being used sufficiently and effectively, when innovative entrepreneurship is a necessary condition for the achievement of economic development in general and an organisation's success in specific, there can be no question that cooperative entrepreneurs will have to be included; without cooperative entrepreneurship, cooperatives cannot succeed, they will not even be established.

Functions of Cooperative Entrepreneurship

The primary function of cooperative entrepreneurship consists of the following.

(a) *Discovering cooperative opportunities:* This denotes the identification of the problems of the members and the capacities of the cooperatives to discharge such problems. In doing so, there are two important tests a cooperative has to undertake, namely, the *market test* and *participation test*. The market test can be undertaken by means of studying the market behavior and to find out ways and means of providing services and supplies effectively and competitively (at a low price) to the members. The second test, namely, participation test denotes the loyalty of the members towards their cooperatives. For the success of the cooperative, the members must express their fuller loyalty by means of actively participating in the management as well as business activities. With regard to business activities, members have to sell their produce only through the cooperatives even during the times of low price and depression period. Likewise, in getting the service of their cooperative, members should show their loyalty by linking their service activities to the cooperative perennially.

(b) *Implement such opportunities effectively and efficiently:* The next stage is the implementation of opportunities explored by the cooperatives to fulfill the needs and desires of the members. Coordination is necessary between members, board, and the executive. They have to keep in mind that they have to face stiff competition from the market economy. To face such economy (private sector) efficiency in service and operations are necessary. Cost of operations must be low and the benefits to be accrued in the form of higher prices and fuller satisfaction must be ensured.

Causes for Cooperative Advantage

The cooperative advantages that will accrue out of cooperative entrepreneurship are as follows:

1. *Monopoly/Market failure:* Monopoly practices followed by private sector led to the exploitation of the producers and consumers. The market forces of demand and supply have been manipulated to the dictates of the monopolist. The cooperative advantage comes out with balancing the market force and benefiting both the producers and consumers.
2. *Transaction cost:* The transaction cost of the cooperatives is always less than other forms of enterprises. Cooperatives operate with efficient personnel and they have learnt the market changes and market forces. The operational efficiency and the interdependence of various cooperatives through vertical and horizontal growth led to the reduction of transaction cost, which are transferred to the members.
3. *Interlinked market:* The cooperative operations are interlinked with each other following the principles of cooperation among cooperatives. Integration between agricultural cooperatives, marketing cooperatives, processing cooperatives, and consumer cooperatives is the best example to express the interlinked market. Such linking of marketing led to the advantage of the producers and consumers and bargaining power of the members has been enhanced.
4. *Uncertainty reduction:* Cooperative entrepreneurship by the cooperative have reduced the uncertainty in all walks of activities. Uncertainty relating to output of production, price trends, market trends, competition, etc have been avoided to the advantage of the members of cooperatives.

5. *Innovations:* Cooperatives have introduced innovations in their operations, which redirected the market trend towards them. Recently in UK the cooperative banks have abolished the service charges for current account and gave a rate of interest to that deposit. This made all other commercial banks to extend this benefit to their depositors.

Stages of Cooperative Entrepreneurship

Robert and Weiss (1988) have explained the process of cooperative entrepreneurship into the following four stages.

1. *Opportunity Search:* This stage consists of identifying the opportunities, no matter what their sources. When cooperatives are doing traditional services for a long time, they have to search for new opportunities for their growth, development, and sustainability.
2. *Opportunity Assessment:* After searching the opportunity, the practicability of the opportunity is to be assessed. Such opportunity assessment may be useful for the future members of the cooperatives.
3. *Opportunity Development:* This is to decide which of the opportunities emerging from assessment should be developed further. The high potential opportunities are critically analyzed and final action required is identified.
4. *Opportunity Pursued (Implementation):* This is to indicate the implementation process and methods of the opportunities selected and developed.

Preconditions for Cooperative Entrepreneurship

While the training of managers will clearly be a critical element in promoting the entrepreneurial spirit in cooperatives, this is only one element in the creation of a favourable climate for cooperative entrepreneurship. Restrictive legislation and regulations which impinge on cooperatives' ability to function as business organisations may have to be removed. Above all, cooperatives must be autonomous and free from outside control. They must become truly democratic and member-governed. Cooperatives must position themselves in such a way as to be able to nurture and develop a culture of entrepreneurship. They must be ready to try out new programmes and not be constrained by bureaucratic formalities. They must be allowed to dispose of their own financial resources and have discretion over their use. They must not be dependent on government, or on donor agencies. They must be prepared to take calculated risks in the interests of providing more effective and efficient services to their members. The following are the pre-conditions for cooperative entrepreneurship:

1. *Training System:* The first precondition for the success of cooperative entrepreneurship is to introduce an effective training system for the managers and the employees of cooperatives. Only through training entrepreneurial skills can be developed to the managers. The training

components should be aimed at harnessing motivation, developing creativity, innovative thinking, imagination and self-assertiveness. They should increase the individuals' ability to plan strategies and tactics, set goals, solve problems, develop negotiating skills, resolve conflicts, and take calculated risks.

2. *Cooperative Legal System:* The cooperative legal system should be flexible and should not unnecessarily tax the cooperatives to go through various procedures and formalities. Less interference should be allowed in the democratic function of the cooperative management. Cooperative being business organisations must be allowed free hand to face competition and challenges.
3. *Autonomy and Freedom:* As per the directions of the principles of cooperation explained by the ICA, cooperatives must be provided autonomy in their operations. There should be less interference from the external agencies like the government and official bodies.
4. *Positioning the Cooperatives to Develop Entrepreneurship:* Every cooperative position its activities to develop entrepreneurship at the three levels, namely membership level, manager level, and bureaucratic level. The membership level entrepreneurship must be given preference to create leadership and continuous growth of the cooperatives.
5. *New Opportunities:* As mentioned earlier, cooperatives must find out new opportunities to do more services for their continued growth and sustainability. By means of extending the area of operation, enlisting new members, and adding new services such new opportunities could be created.
6. *Self-Reliance:* On no account cooperatives should depend on external agencies like government for their financial and other resources. Within the cooperative movement efficient banking and marketing systems should be developed and that system should provide mutual dependence of cooperatives.
7. *Taking Risks:* Cooperatives, in order to promote entrepreneurship must take calculated risks in the interest of providing more effective and efficient service to the members.

Determinants of Cooperative Entrepreneurial Behaviour

1. *Member Awareness:* This is a significant aspect to decide the cooperative entrepreneurial behavior. Awareness of the problems of members, their cooperatives, and vigilance on running their cooperatives are very important to make the cooperative entrepreneurship a success.
2. *Managerial Abilities:* The cooperative must also develop the managerial abilities of its employees to work under competitive circumstance and to discharge the services cost-effectively.

3. *Political Climate:* The political climate of the country also plays a role in determining the cooperative entrepreneurship behavior. In spite of drastic political changes in countries like UK, Japan, etc cooperatives are running successfully. But in developing countries, cooperatives need a favorable political climate to undertake their activities successfully.
4. *Economic Climate:* Free play of economic forces and perfect competition situation must prevail to do services to the members. These are the days where fair trade practices have been promoted by the cooperatives, which are to be followed by other market forces.
5. *Technical Expertise:* Cooperatives, hereafter must add technical expertise to meet challenges and competition. When they enter into new areas of operation they must go for latest technology and they must train their employees by inculcating new skills.
6. *Globalisation:* Globalisation of the economy among countries have opened great opportunities for the cooperatives. Cooperative products can be mutually imported and exported between countries and the cooperative entrepreneurship can go globally.

An ILO View on Cooperative Entrepreneurship

The deliberations at a seminar sponsored by ILO on cooperative entrepreneurship raised the following important points:

- Given the explosion of cooperative in South Africa it is important to distinguish between fake and genuine cooperatives. The ICA statement of identity and principles as well as the 2005 Act provide a basis to assess cooperatives on the ground. This is important because genuine cooperatives should not be overshadowed by 'fly by night' ones merely chasing financial resources. In many ways the Black Economic Empowerment policy thrust from government has politicised cooperatives in a particular way and has encouraged rent seeking as opposed to bottom up member and worker owner driven cooperatives.
- Cooperative entrepreneurship is not a 'silver bullet' but is a key ingredient in cooperative development. For cooperatives operating in a market environment enhancing cooperative entrepreneurial skills is crucial. On the other hand, subsistence and social cooperatives might not need to be driven by cooperative entrepreneurship. In both cases cooperative entrepreneurship should not take away from cooperative principles.
- Cooperative entrepreneurship should not be collapsed into SME frameworks and neither should it reduce cooperatives to another business form. Cooperatives are a distinct institutional form with a values centred institutional model and social character. The hard skills of financial management, marketing, management etc that are required in cooperatives should be encouraged as part of a wider education and

training practice in cooperatives. Most of the successful cooperative movements in the world are grounded in ongoing education and training to build institutional capacity, raise member awareness and ensure skills development. Cooperative entrepreneurship should be part of the culture of cooperative practice and it is an integral part of cooperative ideology.

- Government is busy with various interventions that impact on and close the space for bottom up movement building. In many ways the enabling role of the state, despite the good intentions, easily translates into control. Government is talking about cooperative colleges and various other interventions to build cooperative capacity but all seem to be in a top down framework. Besides government the cooperative movement needs to be challenged to build 'in-house' movement capacity for education and training.
- The economic role and function of cooperatives should not be reduced to poverty reduction. Cooperatives in the global north, in rich countries, play a pivotal role in mainstream economic activity. The multi-class appeal of cooperatives needs to be enhanced to attract different skills and capacities into cooperatives. Professionalising the training for cooperatives becomes important. For example, securing accredited training in diploma's and degrees on cooperative entrepreneurship, management, financial management and so on is crucial in the South African context.

Human Resource Development in Cooperatives: Towards Cooperative EntrepreneurshipThe Changing Environment

In a variety of radically differing political environments cooperatives are being forced to re-examine their basic operating principles in order to survive economically and to continue to serve the needs of their members. In the past, cooperatives in most developing countries were not truly autonomous and member-driven, but instead were dominated, and sometimes controlled, by government. They were, in many cases, instruments of government policies for the achievement of social and economic goals such as rural development, employment promotion, poverty alleviation and so on. Sometimes cooperatives have been utilized for political purposes too.

We are now witness to a rapidly changing economic, social and political environment characterized by the intertwined processes of democratization, decentralization, globalization and adjustment. The effects of these changes on cooperatives are many and vary from country to country and from one type of cooperative to another. In broad terms however, state-controlled cooperatives which are unable to adapt to the new environment face considerable difficulties. The exposure of state-protected "cooperative" monopolies to the competition of the market usually dramatically reduces the market share of these cooperatives and may lead to their disintegration.

On the other hand, strong, viable, autonomous cooperatives which adapt successfully can play an important role in promoting economic and social development through serving the interests of their members and of their communities. Indeed, the global changes of the past few years may, in the long run, create the conditions for the emergence of a strong, dynamic, autonomous, member-controlled, genuine cooperative movement. However, the transition to a market-oriented economy often involves the collapse of the state-controlled cooperative sector and that the autonomous movement is not always able to fill the vacuum.

The International Cooperative Alliance's Identity Statement adopted at the 1995 Centennial Congress in Manchester, England, gives clear expression to the democratic and voluntary nature of cooperative enterprises and to the values which inspire cooperative members, leaders, managers and employees. The Identity Statement is an important milestone in cooperative history in that it firmly locates cooperatives globally as autonomous associations. Without an identifiable character cooperatives will not be able to survive, certainly not as cooperatives, although they may evolve into other types of business organisations.

Whether one regards the global changes of the last decade or so in a favourable or unfavourable light, cooperators would be wise to adopt a pragmatic approach and examine the ways and means by which cooperatives can survive the transition period and develop management strategies which will enable cooperatives to flourish. The increasingly competitive market environment requires additional approaches and aptitudes, which we can loosely categorize under the heading "Cooperative Entrepreneurship".

Of late, the notion of "Cooperative Entrepreneurship" is increasingly being seen as a key to ensuring cooperative survival under the new, competitive market conditions. What is "Entrepreneurship", what does the term mean in a cooperative context and what are the implications for cooperative human resource development (HRD)? The following discussion may give a clear picture on this issue.

Competencies of Cooperative Entrepreneurship

Competencies can be described which has been provided by a recently published ILO Training Package entitled "Know About Business":

A body of knowledge

Knowledge consists of a set or body of information stored, which may be recalled at an appropriate time. The kinds of knowledge necessary in a business involve having information about the market, the customers, the competitors, business management, sources of funding and more.

A set of skills

Skill is the ability to apply knowledge. The skills needed in business may be of a technical nature such as engineering, computing, farming, etc., or of a managerial nature such as marketing, financial management, organisation, planning and leadership.

A cluster of traits

A trait is the aggregate of peculiar qualities or characteristics which constitute personal individuality. A successful entrepreneur takes initiative, is persistent, is concerned for high quality, is oriented to efficiency, solves problems in original ways, takes calculated risks, plans systematically, is assertive and so on.

A balanced combination of these competencies is essential for successful entrepreneurship. What then are the functions performed by the entrepreneur? Peter Kilby suggests the following: Searches for and discovers new information.

Translates new information into new markets, techniques and goods Seeks and discovers economic opportunity Evaluates economic opportunities Marshalls the financial resources necessary for the enterprise Makes time-binding arrangements Takes ultimate responsibility for management Provides for and is responsible for the motivational system within the firm Provides leadership for the work group Is the ultimate uncertainty or risk bearer.

Entrepreneurship in Cooperatives

Cooperatives have a great deal to gain by examining how an injection of entrepreneurial attitudes and approaches can help them achieve their goals and objectives. Indeed, cooperative managers functioning in a competitive market certainly need to shed bureaucratic modes of operation and adopt entrepreneurial approaches if they are to effectively serve the interests of cooperative members. However, in cooperatives special competencies are required by managers, such as:

Knowledge of cooperative principles and practices Knowledge of cooperative law and by-laws Devotion to the cooperative ideal Sensitivity and responsiveness to members' interests and wishes Community orientation.

Moreover, cooperative values, if mobilized effectively, may provide the cooperative with the competitive edge required to ensure the cooperative's success. Peter Davis, Director of the Unit for Membership Based Organisations of Leicester University, UK, has argued strongly that not only are values essential for determining the "cooperative difference" in the market place, but also that "Value Based Management is the future for management". Davis criticizes cooperatives for "not utilizing their human-centred values dynamically in their communications with their customers and employees". Furthermore, he argues that the cooperative enterprise must be managed as an integrated whole, combining business activities and social purpose, avoiding the view that these "sides" are in some way in conflict. He points to the "ethical banking" approach of the UK Cooperative Bank as an example of a cooperative organisation using its values to achieve rapid expansion of the business. Davis writes that the Bank has successfully integrated cooperative values into modern management methods, which he considers to be the key to its prosperity in a very tough competitive environment. He concludes that":

> *....we desperately need managers who have the qualities to take responsibility for leading and building the whole community of members and employees into a social and value based business seeking the fulfilment of the cooperative purpose".*

So far we have considered entrepreneurship in the context of cooperative management capabilities and functions. We can also consider the relevance of entrepreneurship to the individual cooperative member. As the ILO COOPNET/COOPREFORM Coordinator for Asia, K.K. Taimni has written:"

> *....individual members take to entrepreneurship i.e. scan the environment, identify and seize opportunities, assume risks, deploy their own capital and derive benefits. The role of the cooperative is confined here to provide support services, including essential advisory services, so that risk-related losses are minimized and links between a member's enterprise and external agents and markets are effectively established."*

Thus, we are challenged to apply the concept of entrepreneurship to all actors in the cooperative - cooperative members, board members, managers and employees - while maintaining and strengthening the cooperative identity and purpose.

Integrating Entrepreneurial Skills in Cooperative HRD

A critical question to ask, therefore, is to what extent do existing cooperative training institutions and programmes train cooperative members, board members, managers and employees in the competencies required by cooperatives struggling to survive and grow in a competitive market situation? A reorientation of training systems may be necessary if we recognise these competencies as being vital for cooperative sustainability. This reorientation will include the adaptation of curriculum, training materials and methodologies. In addition to more traditional cooperative management training courses on, for example, accounting, business planning, finance, marketing, production, materials, distribution, office administration, data processing, management information systems, personnel management etc., entrepreneurial skills development components should be added. These training components should be aimed at harnessing motivation, developing creativity, innovative thinking, imagination and self-assertiveness. They should increase the individual trainee's ability to plan strategy and tactics, set goals, solve problems, develop negotiating skills, resolve conflicts and take calculated risks. In some cases existing materials from the non-cooperative sector can be utilized but more often new materials will have to be prepared to take account of the special character of cooperative enterprises. Special training will have to be provided for trainers, many of whom are today not able to facilitate the learning of entrepreneurial skills. Cooperative HRD institutions will have to contribute to the strengthening of management consultancy and auditing systems, which, if effective, can provide significant support to the reorientation of cooperatives to the new environment.

Promotion of Cooperative Development

Entrepreneurship is an essential ingredient of cooperative development. Cooperative development always includes the *dual* aspect of cooperatives: development of the cooperative enterprise and promotion (motivating and enabling) of member entrepreneurship.

How to promote cooperatives in order that cooperatives can advance their members more effectively? With what kind of services can cooperatives improve the performance of their member entrepreneurs? How can cooperatives stimulate member innovation of their members and promote those that are working out of the economic core and transform these enterprises into ambitious and glamorous firms?

The primary focus of policy makers, educators, trainers and consultants must be on promoting ambitious and glamorous cooperatives (which probably are rather young) and new cooperatives.

The first thing to do is negative: *not* to do things which handicap or restrain these class of cooperatives. The second thing to do is to *identify* new cooperative entrepreneurs and young cooperatives with highly ambitious/ innovative entrepreneurs. Thus, policy makers and government should make a shift to the promotion of cooperative entrepreneurs and through them member promotion.

External assistance should be actively sought by co-operative leaders and managers with the specific goal of increasing entrepreneurial opportunities and management capacity. This assistance usually takes the form of training courses, project or venture finance, or entrepreneurial advice offered by experienced and well trained "catalytic" entrepreneurs from co-operative movements, NGOs or government institutions.

In that way government policy shifts from direct intervention and promoting state goals to indirect assistance and promotion of member goals. Cooperative entrepreneurship has to be promoted instead of promoting the cooperative sector as a whole. Modern cooperative entrepreneurs will have to learn a minimum of theory in order to understand what they are doing and what needs to be done in order to compete successfully and grow by better promoting their members. Thus, a main emphasis is laid upon cooperative education and training, capacity building or human resources development. A special focus should be given to academic entrepreneurs, thus connecting the worlds of science and business.

16

Conditions and Motives Favour the Organisation of Cooperatives

Conditions that Favour Starting Cooperatives

Certain conditions are needed for starting cooperatives successfully that are to vbe kept in mind by cooperative entrepreneurs. Such conditions are as follows:

(a) The cooperative that is to be started must be *socially viable*. Those who are starting such cooperatives must be willing to provide all needed cooperation. "The persons forming local organisation have to be prepared to cooperate – there has to be a minimum of sociability"

– *Munkner*

(b) The members who are entrusted in starting a cooperative must commit themselves to mobilize *needed resources*. This should be on a voluntary basis and not for a pressure from outside.

(c) There should be the *community of interest* between the proposed members. That means, the proposed members should have a common problem to be solved among themselves. "The persons forming the local organisation have to have at least one economic interest in common, a broader base of interest is favorable"

– *Munkner*

(d) The cooperative must be *economically viable* and provide at short notice tangible advantages for the members individually or as a group, otherwise, the interest in the cooperative will rapidly decline.

(e) There must be the questions to be raised among the members as to why the cooperative must be formed and the uses of *group action*.

(f) The proposed cooperatives must be given the chance to develop on their own. Any stimulation from outside is desirable but should not lead to artificial growth. This is the bane of state-sponsored cooperatives in certain developing countries.

(g) The proposed cooperatives must be given the opportunity of evolving their own rules, regulation and patterns of organisation.

(h) Certain external forces like the governments, taxation policy, land policy, and political developments are to be considered while starting new cooperatives.

Economic and Social Motives to Organise Cooperatives

Economic Motives

The motives for joining the cooperatives are those which have a direct effect on the economic life of members. The members join cooperatives because it promises to be the most effective instrument towards gaining increased income. The joining of cooperative is an attempt to reap relatively higher economic advantage. This can come about by the way of cooperative providing goods and services which are regarded as important or either not available or available but beyond the reach of the member or the members enjoy them but at very high cost.

The cooperation can thus help satisfy this motive of increased income either in the form of:

(a) Reducing the cost of members business

(b) Increased revenue.

Sociological (Emotional) Motives

The urge to join may result from and individual feelings of:

(a) ***Isolation and loneliness***

This is an individual feeling which is regarded as a weak point for change, to be safe they assume that joining the cooperative can thus be an attempt to regain the missing emotional way of life.

(b) ***The search for security*** may also be a motive for joining cooperative. This is normally motivated by a sort of general or individual crisis. The time and magnitude of the occurrence of each crisis can not be known in advance. It can happen with out our knowledge. This magnitude can also be beyond the means of the individual. Individual strength often provides insufficient. This enables the cooperatives that offer relatively more security/insurance through pooled efforts.

(c) ***The search for protection*** can also be motive for joining cooperative because, when the member is integrated into an existing cooperative the group is able to protect itself against physical or spiritual threats from outside. They may feel exploited by other more powerful persons, groups or force against whom they are individually powerless.

In most societies in the developing countries, wisdom, knowledge and status have been considered the function of age. The aged thus tend to dominate and try to maintain the status quo. Without such a protection from modern groups like the cooperatives, the already slow technological development adoption of the new technology would be slower. Thus motive of the individual cooperative member to shift responsibility for modern/ progressive decisions and action which they could otherwise not dare to take because, they may be regarded as running counter to old traditions. So the capacity of the cooperative to jointly accept this responsibility and protect the individual member is very important for introducing and accepting change in the social structure of developing regions.

(d) Some people may also join the cooperative simply because *they want to be seen*. This is often the cause when membership in a cooperative is correctly or incorrectly looked upon and viewed as one outward sign of superiority over another. As a desire to catch up, individuals decide to join the cooperative.

(e) The motive to *avoid being out*. This is often the cause when people discover that virtually every body around them has joined the local cooperative. They have feelings of having been left out and not being normal. Their membership in the cooperative may then result as a response to this.

(f) Some persons also join the cooperative with the motive of not missing out on any unspecified, possible advantage which such an institution may offer. Such people do not join the cooperative because they are sure of the advantages or because they are convinced that they need the cooperative. They do so mainly because if may people join, they believe that so many people can not all be wrong that *one or the other advantage must exist*, and if so, they would not want to miss out.

(g) The urge to join the cooperative may also result from *a desire to adhere to customs or tradition*. This is usually the case in relatively old, often rural cooperative in which a number of families have always lived a face to face life inside the cooperative and one generation seen to bequeath the cooperative as part of the inheritance to the next generation.

(h) Another motive which may give rise to membership in a cooperative is the possibility of using cooperatives *as spiting board to some higher social or political position in the community*.

External Pressure

A motive for some people joining the cooperative may also be that of satisfying some external power under whose pressure they have come. This is the case when revolutionary government which claims to be socialist in nature, regarded cooperative as a socialistic organisation which can serve their aims.

They enact legislation which makes membership mandatory for farmers who seek private use of his plot. Failure to join the cooperative would mean having to give up the only profession and means of livelihood. They have no option but to join the cooperative. A slightly milder variation often comes in the form that access to specific services such as supply of essential consumer goods, subsidising of input credit are made conditional upon membership in the cooperative.

Managerial and Organisational Characteristics of Cooperatives

Managerial and Organisational Characteristics of Cooperatives

The cooperative entrepreneurs should know and consider the following managerial characteristics of cooperatives:

Managerial Characteristics of Cooperatives

1. *Cooperatives are associations of human beings:* Cooperatives are formed by members to solve their economic problems. In that process they have to mobilise capital. It is subordinated to human interests. Capital is not allowed to dominate in cooperatives over human beings.
2. *Democracy in cooperatives:* Cooperative management strictly follows the principles of democracy. All are equal here and 'one man one vote' principle is followed. No single individual is allowed to dominate, by virtue of large number of shares held by him.
3. *Service motive:* Service is the motive and not profit in cooperatives. In doing such service, efficiency is emphasized in cooperative management. P.R. Dubhashi, has viewed that "the principle of efficiency is vital in cooperative management. But in so far as the market mechanism of private enterprise, turns the principle of maximum efficiency into maximum profit, it becomes in compatible with the cooperative management and needs modification".
4. *Equality:* Equality is practiced in cooperative management. All members are given equal opportunity to enjoy the benefits of cooperative and they can exercise equal control without any narrow rise to the level of the president of a National Federation through his leadership.

5. *Application of principles of cooperation*: Cooperatives have to first follow the principles of cooperation laid down by ICA, then they have to go for applying the management process. It has to keep a balance between these two. Weeraman States that "the proper application of cooperative principle is necessary for the success of the movement, for cooperative principles are those which are essential, that is absolutely indispensable to the achievement of cooperatives movements role".
6. *Different aims system:* Cooperatives have to satisfy the aims of different people composed under its management. They are members, office bearers, personnel and government, so it has to harmonize the interest of these complex aims system and to maintain a balance.
7. *The Control Process:* In cooperatives, the members are users and owners. Varied interests of members must be bet with atmost efficiency. In that process cooperatives should not loose their control over factors of production. Prof. Laidlaw, stresses that, "it is a business organisation in which the components of ownership – use – control are integrated by being all vested in one body of people, the members".
8. *Cooperative management is governed by cooperative legislation*: The cooperative societies Act of respective states directly and indirectly control the management of cooperatives. The Registrar of cooperative societies is assigned with enormous powers to interfere in the management of cooperative institutions.
9. *Integrating government policies*: In countries like India cooperative movement had its origin with initiative of government. In the Planning process, specific roles have been assigned to the cooperatives. Here the cooperatives have to sacrifice some of their autonomy and freedom.
10. State (government) interference is quite common in the management of cooperatives in countries like India. Boards are very often dissolved to suit the political convenience of ruling parties.
11. *Cooperatives strive to introduce professional management in their administration:* In that process they have to face so many hurdles and interferences. Without minding that large sized cooperatives and processing cooperatives go a head with professional management.
12. *Tools and techniques of management applied by cooperatives vary from society- to society-* primary cooperative societies, with smaller area of operation and smaller area of transactions offered to use only elementary tools whereas bigger cooperatives use latest and sophisticated techniques of management.
13. *It is an art as well a science:* It is an art as it effects changes or accomplishes goals by deliberate efforts. It is a science as cooperative management strives to acquire body of knowledge through observation, speculation and forecasts, which are capable of verification.

14. *Practice of cooperative management is based on knowledge and responsibility:* Entire gamets of management technique are applied under various situations to get things done, at lesser cost and at the cost of giving enough training and experience to the people concerned.
15. *Cooperative management involves group effect at all levels:* It combines the efforts of all individuals and bodies (Board, general body, etc.) at every stage of activity. At the culmination, the Board and executive sit together to discharge responsibilities.
16. *Economic liberalisation:* Last decade saw the liberalization of the economy world over. The implication was that, private sector has been given a free hand. Till recently, cooperatives have been enjoying lot of privileges from government and they have to loose such privileges in during course. Cooperatives have to adjust themselves to the changing economic climate.
17. *Competition:* Cooperatives are given thorough competition by private and public sector organisations. They have to improve their operational efficiency by means of using modern management techniques. Otherwise they cannot survive in the competition.

Organisational Characteristics of Cooperatives

1. *Business organisation:* Cooperatives are one of the business organisations like the sole enterprise, partnership firms, joint stock companies and public sector organisations. But their motive is service, and not profit like the private organisations.
2. *Homogeneous group:* Cooperatives are organised by homogeneous groups consisting of like minded individuals. People who are having common problems like credit, marketing, housing, etc., joint together and organise cooperatives to solve their problems.
3. *Corporate status:* In developing countries, cooperatives are registered under separate cooperative societies acts/proclamations promulgated by respective governments. A registered cooperative society has legal status and protection from government.
4. *Democracy:* One of the salient organisational features of cooperatives is their democratic character. All members are given equal opportunities and the principle of "one man one vote" is strictly followed.
5. *Cost effective service:* Cooperatives work under competitive situations and they have to provide cost effective service to the members. Almost all types of cooperatives are providing services for a lower cost than the market cost.
6. *Exploitation by middlemen:* Cooperatives, since their beginning have challenged the exploitive forces like money lenders, middlemen, traders and contractors. The combined effort of members have kept these forces at a distance.

7. *Application of modern management tools:* Cooperatives have applied modern management tools and techniques to improve their operational efficiency and customer services. Technology up-gradation takes place in processing and industrial cooperatives.
8. *Team work:* One of the basic organisational characteristics of cooperatives is the effective teamwork at all levels. In majority of the cooperatives cordial employer-employee relationship exists, which favours the effective functioning of the cooperatives.

Governance for Cooperative Entrepreneurship

"Governance is one of the characteristics of any institution that is concerned with governance or management of governance. Governance is the reflection of the quality of management".

The four key components of governance are: accountability, transparency, predictability, and participation. Cooperatives are having good governance. A contributory factor for bad governance is corruption, which is avoided in cooperatives.

(a) ***Accountability:*** Accountability is the capacity to call officials to account for their action. Effective accountability has two components viz., answerability and consequences. Answerability is the requirement to respond periodically to questions concerning one's official action. There is also a need for predictable and meaningful consequences without which accountability is only a formality. Cooperative activities discharged by officials and leaders have accountability.

(b) ***Transparency:*** Transparency denotes low cost access to informations. Reliable and timely economic and financial informations are a must for the cooperatives. Cooperatives never keep secrecy and every member has a right to the information.

(c) ***Predictability:*** Predictability results from rules and regulations, that are clear, known in advance. Lack of predictability makes it difficult for officials to plan for the provision of services. Cooperative laws are clear and things can be predicted.

(d) ***Participation:*** participation is needed to obtain reliable information and to serve as a check and watch dog for the organisation's actions. In a cooperative members and leaders participate in various democratic forums like the board and general assembly meetings.

Some of the possible indicators of good governance that are to be considered by cooperative entrepreneurs as follows:

1. How much of awareness the leaders and members have about the principles of cooperation and the basic value of cooperative philosophy?
2. How clearly they understand the ethical and moral elements which are the essential components of the cooperative philosophy?

3. How different is the cooperative enterprise from a private enterprise or a state enterprise?
4. How conscious are the board members about their rights and responsibilities? To what extent the board members realize that they accountable and answerable to the members who have reposed their confidence in them?
5. How much operational powers are delegated to the chief executive?
6. How smooth are the communication channels between the board and chief executive?
7. How much is the level of transparency in dealing with the employees?
8. How smooth is the channel of communication between the cooperative and its stakeholders and business partners?
9. Whether there is any discipline outlined on the use of assets of the organisation?
10. How often the meetings are held?

To what extent the cooperative institution obeys the directives of the state at the cost of its autonomy and freedom of action?

18

Formalities and Types of Cooperatives to be Organised

Formalities to be followed by Government

In developing countries like Ethiopia, the government has greater responsibility in encouraging and promoting cooperatives. Government has to show a very favourable attitude and set a climate conducive for the growth and development of cooperatives. The tasks, which properly belong to government, can be summarized as follows:

(a) To *create a favourable climate* for the development of cooperatives. By this is meat the removal of obstacles, resistance to unfair competition and to the efforts of private dealers and money-lenders to bind the cooperatives members through permanent indebtedness.

(b) To provide *adequate and clear legislation* on cooperation, regulating the rights and duties of cooperatives and their members, their liability, legal personality and the like. This legislation has where necessary to be supplemented by regulations for its implementation and model bylaws for the cooperatives. These need to cover, among other things, members' contributions to capital, the distribution of surpluses, reserves and similar matters.

(c) To establish an *information and inspection* service for cooperatives, the job of the service being to encourage, to advise and to supervise the cooperatives.

(d) To provide for the *coordination of cooperative* activities with those of the agricultural advisory service, agricultural credit institutions, marketing boards and other relevant government services.

(e) To assist with *education and training* for those on the management committee and the people actually running the business, for the benefit of the cooperatives; and to help in establishing educational schemes for the membership and to promote the spread of cooperative information.

(f) To provide *financial assistance* to cooperatives in the form of grants and loans, as a means of providing working capital or capital for necessary investment in buildings, machinery and so on. Such help should, however, be supplementary only, in order to ensure that cooperatives attempt to provide as far as possible for their own financing needs – from members' share capital, reserves built up from undistributed trading surpluses, voluntary deposits by members and possible loans obtained from or via agricultural credit banks or other credit institutions.

(g) To encourage and assist the *establishment of federations and national cooperative unions*. These, belonging as they do to the cooperative movement of which they form part, need to be put together and managed democratically; and they also need to be able at the appropriate time to take over the advisory and supervisory functions of government from the authorities, together with responsibility for education, inspection and so on.

An international symposium on the dynamic of the relationships between government and cooperatives was held in Tel Aviv in 1964 and came to the following conclusions:

(a) Relations between government bodies and cooperatives should not be a one-way traffic from above, with the cooperatives being used by the authorities as an instrument for the imposition and implementation of government planning. Many countries try too hard to realize political ends through cooperatives. Instead, there has to be "an exchange of capacities and functions of opposed interests and advantages" between government and cooperatives. "These functional relationships need to be realized in a form such that, in the interests of the common good, just balance can be achieved with regard to both functions and powers."

(b) The maintenance of an adequate measure of autonomy by the cooperatives is of great and positive value. An excess of control and interference, or even of support, is harmful to the sound development of cooperation.

(c) In those cases in which cooperatives have come into being autonomously from below, a strengthening of the ties with government may be desirable to ensure greater correspondence between private and public interests..

Types of Cooperatives to be Organised

What Type of Cooperatives can be organised?

The type of cooperative to be organised depends on the social, economic, political, and educational climate of a country. The early cooperatives organised in European countries are more than 150 years old. By that time, the European countries were under the evil effect of Industrial Revolution. Later, when cooperatives were started in Asian and African countries, a century ago, these countries were under the colonial rule of European countries. Cooperatives were started in these countries officially by the colonial governments. The initiative did not come from the users of cooperatives. On the other hand it was trusted from above. This made the cooperatives to have slow growth in many developing countries. In Ethiopia the conditions were different when the cooperative movement was started during 1960s. The foregoing analysis will show what type of cooperatives can be started.

A. According to the economic status of the members of the cooperative
   1. Producers:
      - Farmers, fishermen (compare the Raiffeisen) cooperatives;
      - Dealers and traders;
      - Craftsmen (compare Rochdale)
   2. Consumers
   3. Employees.

B. According to the sector of the economy in which the cooperatives are active
   1. Agriculture
   2. Fishing
   3. Forestry
   4. Industry and manufacture
   5. Retail and wholesale trade
   6. The provision of services (credit and banking, transport, insurance and so on).

C. According to the cooperative's economic functions
   1. Purchasing/supply cooperatives, for the purchase of business essentials and for consumption.
   2. Marketing cooperatives
   3. Processing cooperatives
   4. Cooperatives providing services (credit, insurance, irrigation, transport, tractor services and such like, artificial insemination)
   5. Production cooperatives

D. According to the member-businesses' degree of integration
   1. Complementary activities undertaken by the cooperative in the service of its members – 'auxiliary societies', cooperatives providing services (in general terms, categories *Ci* to *Civ* inclusive).
   2. Partial integration of the member-businesses in cooperative activities: the member-businesses have not only hived off some of

their functions to the cooperatives but have also tied themselves to the cooperative's planning of various activities. These are what is meant by 'integrated cooperatives'.

3. Complete integration, in which the member-businesses are completely subsumed in the cooperative, examples are cooperative farming, joint farming, collective farming and the kolkhoz.
4. Production cooperatives. Here the members are nothing more than workers in the common enterprise.

E. According to the organisational structure (the categorization suggested in Dulfer (11) (pages 56-57).

1. Traditional cooperatives = executive-operated cooperatives. The cooperative in this scheme is but the executive body for the member-firms (compare *Di*). The member-businesses determine the cooperative's activities.
2. Market-linkage cooperatives. These are commonly found in the developed world. The cooperative enterprise is completely autonomous in this case and does no hove close ties with the constituent businesses. The manger of the cooperative implements his own policy, directed towards competition in an open-market economy.
3. Integrated cooperatives. This form is of particular interest in the context of regional development programmes and those connected with irrigation, land reform and settlement projects. The member-businesses, though legally independent, are tied to the cooperative in such a way that its management can take decisions about the activities to be carried out on the individual businesses' premises and the way in which their interests shall be safeguarded. The members do, certainly, keep their autonomy and a certain degree of control over matters relating to production, but they have in doing so to align themselves with a common strategy and a common production plan, drawn up by and under the supervision of the cooperative's top management. Schiller (28) terms this the "cooperative promotion of agricultural production".

F. According to cooperatives' geographical areas of activity

1. Urban cooperatives. This category includes urban consumer cooperatives, house building cooperatives, savings and credit cooperatives for urban salary earners and so on.
2. Rural cooperatives, particularly in agriculture and fishing.
3. Craft and manufacturing cooperatives. These can be either urban or rural.

G. According to the level of organisation (apex systems)

1. Primary cooperatives – mostly at local level.

2. Secondary cooperatives – mostly at a regional level.
3. Tertiary cooperatives or federations of cooperatives – mostly at a national level.

H. According to the cooperatives' legal status
1. Unregistered, therefore not enjoying legal personality.
2. Registered (equaling 'recognised') cooperatives, possessing legal personality:
   - With the liability of the members excluded;
   - With the members having limited liability, their liability being restricted to one or more times the amount of their share;
   - With the members' liability being unlimited. In this case the members are wholly responsible, to the extent of all they possess for the debts of the cooperative.

I. According to the number of tasks assumed by the cooperative
1. Single purpose cooperatives.
2. Single commodity cooperatives.
3. Multipurpose cooperatives.
4. All purpose (= integrated) cooperatives.

19

ILO's Policy on Cooperatives and Potential Surveys

ILO's Policy on Cooperative Organisation

The International Labour Organisation, which is taking good efforts in promoting cooperatives, has given the following guidelines for cooperatives in its Recommendation Number 127 dated 1st June 1966.

Objectives of Policy Concerning Co-Operatives

1. The establishment and growth of co-operatives should be regarded as one of the important instruments for economic, social and cultural development as well as human advancement in developing countries.
2. In particular, co-operatives should be established and developed as a means of:
   (a) improving the economic, social and cultural situations of persons of limited resources and opportunities as well as encouraging their spirit of initiative;
   (b) increasing personal and national capital resources by the encouragement of thrift, by eliminating usury and by the sound use of credit;
   (c) Contributing to the economy an increased measure of democratic control of economic activity and of equitable distribution of surplus;
   (d) Increasing national income, export revenues and employment by a fuller utilisation of resources, for instance in the implementation of system of agrarian reform and of land settlement aimed at bringing fresh areas into productive use and in the development of modern industries, preferably scattered, processing local raw materials;

(e) Improving social conditions, and supplementing social services in such fields as housing and, where appropriate, health, education and communications;

(f) Helping to raise the level of general and technical knowledge of their members.

3. Governments of developing countries should formulate and carry out a policy under which co-operatives receive aid and encouragement, of an economic, financial, technical, legislative or other character, without effect on their independence.

4. (a) in elaborating such a policy, regard should be had to economic and social conditions, to available resources and to the role which co-operatives can play in the development of the country concerned.

   (b) The policy should be integrated in development plans in so far as this is consistent with the essential features of co-operatives.

5. The policy should be kept under review and adapted to changes in social and economic needs and to technological progress.

6. Existing co-operatives should be associated with the formulation and, where possible, application of eh policy.

7. The co-operative movement should be encouraged to seek the collaboration in the formulation and, where appropriate, application of the policy, of organisations with common objectives.

8. (a) The governments concerned should associate co-operatives on the same basis as other undertakings with the formulation of national economic plans and other general economic measures, at least whenever such plans and measures are liable to affect their activities. Co-operatives should also be associated with the application of such plans and measures in so far as this is consistent with their essential characteristics.

   (b) For the purposes provided for in Paragraph 7 and Paragraph 9, subparagraph (1), of this Recommendation, federations of co-operatives should be empowered to represent their member societies at the local, regional and national levels.

Methods of Implementation of Policy Concerning Co-operatives

A. Legislation

9. All appropriate measures, including the consultation and existing co-operatives, should be taken:

   (a) to detect and eliminate provisions contained in laws and regulations which may have the effect of unduly restricting the development of co-operatives through discrimination, for instance in regard to taxation or the allocation of licenses and quotas, or through failure to take account of the special character of co-operatives or of the particular rules of operation of co-operatives;

(b) to avoid the inclusion of such provisions in future laws and regulations;

(c) to adapt fiscal laws and regulations to the special conditions of cooperatives.

10. There should be laws or regulations specifically concerned with the establishment and functioning of co-operatives, and with the protection of their right to operate on not less than equal terms with other forms of enterprise. These laws or regulations should preferably be applicable to all categories of co-operatives.

11. (a) Such laws and regulation should in any case include provisions on the following matters:

(a) a definition or description of a co-operative bringing out its essential characteristics, namely that it is and association of persons who have voluntarily joined together to achieve a common end through the formation of a democratically controlled organisation, making equitable contributions to the capital required and accepting a fair share of the risks and benefits of the undertaking in which the members actively participate;

(b) a description of eh objects of a co-operative, and procedures for its establishment and registration, the amendment of its statutes, and its dissolution;

(c) the conditions of membership, such as the maximum amount of each share and, where appropriate, the proportion of the share due at the moment of subscription and the time allowed for full payment, as well as the rights and duties of members, which would be laid down in greater detail in the by-laws of co-operatives;

(d) methods of administration, management and internal audit, and procedures for the establishment and functioning of competent organs;

(e) the protection of the name "co-operative";

(f) machinery for the external audit and guidance of co-operatives and for the enforcement of the laws and regulations.

(b) The procedures provided for in such laws or regulations, in particular the procedures for registration, should be as simple and particular as possible, so as not to hinder the creation and development of co-operatives.

12. Laws and regulations concerning co-operatives should authorize co-operatives to federate.

Potential Surveys

A potential survey is a systematic appraisal of the economic and possibly social effects, which the realization of a certain project will have, and a survey of the technical problems involved. Co-operatives can be confronted with the need for such an analysis, for example, if a new society or a new branch is to be established, if new activities are to be undertaken, etc. In a wider sense a similar study, though perhaps not so elaborate, should precede any decision which could decisively alter the course of a society.

In smaller matters this analysis can be prepared and assessed by the society's staff or, in the case of societies to be formed, by a pre-co-operative study group of prospective members, but in most cases a qualified economist or engineer, or both, have to be consulted. Within the co-operative sector this type of extension service can usually be contacted through central business organisations, auditing associations or government departments. In some instances surveys are also carried out by international organisations involved in co-operative extension work or by private consulting firms.

Contents of a Potential Survey

1. Background

The background information to be collected is as follows:

(a) General aspects which may affect the project, such as the relevant legislation, the structure of local administration, income statistics, etc., and a general description of the area where the project will be carried out, its geographical factors, climate, communication system, people and customs. In the individual case it may also include specialized information, in rural projects, for example, about soil qualities, rainfall, land tenure and utilization, average farm size, methods of farming, etc.

(b) The scope for development or the need for new facilities, at present as well as in the future, by showing the faults and disadvantages of the present set-up or situation, or by proving, by way of market analysis, the room for expansion.

(c) The suggested target for expansion or the proposed capacity of any new facilities.

(d) The possible approach or method to be used and, if necessary, a comparison of several methods, and the planned location of any facilities.

(e) The time schedule for the realization of the project considering the recruitment and training period for any new staff, the delivery period for any new machinery and the construction time for any new buildings required as well as the most favourable time to start the project with regard to the market.

(f) The size of membership related to the set targets and the possibility of attracting new members.

(g) The expected response from present or prospective members, especially whether they realize the necessity of the project and are willing to co-operate, or what steps can be taken to enlist their collaboration.

2. Market issues

The key questions that should be answered in the Market issues are presented below:

(a) What is the current or projected demand for your proposed products or services? In other words, how many units can you reasonably expect to sell each month?

(b) What are the target markets for this product or service? What demographic characteristics do these potential customers have in common? How may of them are there?

(c) What is the projected supply in your area of the products or services needed for your project?

(d) What competition exists in this market? Can you establish a market niche, which will enable you to compete effectively with other providing this product or service?

(e) Is the location of your proposed business or project likely to affect is success? If so, is the identified site the most appropriate one available?

The market issues should be conducted first because it is critical to the success of the business. If it cannot substantiate through research that adequate demand for the product or service exists, or if it cannot obtain sufficient quality to meet expected demand, then the project is not feasible.

3. Organisational issues

(a) What organisational structure is the right one?

(b) Who will serve on the board of directors?

(c) What qualifications are needed to manage this business?

(d) Who will manage the business (if possible)?

(e) What other staffing needs does the co-op have? How do the staffing needs to change over the next 2-3 years?

4. Technical requirements

(a) The feasibility of using the existing facilities and the present staff for the new task and the possible changes to be made for their adaptation.

(b) Any new facilities and manpower needed and their availability:

1. land and buildings, their size design, outlay and equipment.

2. machinery, type, make, capacity.
3. transport, type, capacity.
4. manpower, required skill and experience, recruitment plan.

Key Questions to answer include:

(a) What are the technology needs for the proposed business?
(b) What other equipment does your proposed business need?
(c) Where will you obtain this technology and equipment?
(d) When can you get the necessary equipment?
(e) How much will the equipment and technology cost?

5. Capital outlay and finance

(a) The total cost of the project assessed according to a detailed list of the costs of any building, machinery or vehicles needed and, if possible, accompanied by tenders of the relevant suppliers.
(b) The required rate of finance calculated on the basis of the expected average lifetime of the invested assets.
(c) The source of finance available for the purpose of the project.

The following financial aspects are to be considered.

(a) *Start-up Costs:* These are the costs incurred in starting up a new business, including "capital goods" such as land, buildings, equipment, etc. The business may have to borrow money from a lending institution to cover these costs.
(b) *Operating Costs:* These are the ongoing costs, such as rent, utilities, and wages that are incurred in the everyday operation of a business. The total should include interest and principle payments on any debt for start-up costs.
(c) *Revenue Projections:* How will you price your goods or services? Asses what the estimated monthly revenue will be.
(d) *Sources of Financing:* If your proposed business will need to borrow money from a bank or other lending institution, you may need to research potential lending sources.
(e) *Profitability Analysis:* This is the "bottom line" for the proposed business. Given the costs and revenue analysis above, will your business bring in enough revenue to cover operating expenses? Will it break even, lose money or make a profit? Is there anything you can do to improve the bottom line?

6. Analysis of operating costs (Includes salary, taxes, interest, etc.)

(a) The breakdown of the expected operating cost including the proportional overhead expenses calculated for various levels of output or development.
   1. based pm estimated costs

2. by comparison with a society which has already carried out a similar project taking into account the cost variations caused by differences in size, location, structure of membership and efficiency in management.

(b) The comparison of differing methods with respect to operating costs.

7. Analysis of expected benefits

The assessment of added revenue gained from the project or of the expected decrease in cost or improvement in service.

8. Final assessment

(a) The comparison of the increased operating cost with the additional revenue expected (break-even graph).

(b) The influence of the new project on the overall profitability of the society.

(c) The reasons which would make the project feasible despite a decrease in profitability, for instance, the long-term effect on the development of the society.

9. Appendix

The appendix should include all those documents, statistics, tenders, drawings to which the text of the survey refers.

20

Organisational Factors

Organisational Factors

While organising a cooperative, certain organisational factors are to be considered. These factors have been drawn from other countries experiences and applied to Ethiopia.

1. Size of a Society

The size of an enterprise is especially important in its economic aspects. One of the problems of every co-operative society is to reach a size, which allows the economic effects of co-operation to gain their full advantage.

1. a monopolistic situation in their area of operation protecting them from competition.
2. A high degree of vertical integration with a central business organisation giving them some of the advantages of large-scale enterprise.
3. A strong co-operative spirit among members manifested in absolute loyalty and volunteer work in the society.

Where these special conditions do not prevail, the expansion of the enterprise must be an essential part of the business policy of a co-operative society. The increase in size may be achieved by:

- attracting new members within the area of operation;
- increasing the area of operation;
- increasing the turnover with the present members in the existing lines or by taking up new activities;
- amalgamation with other societies; and
- buying out competing enterprises.

In practice the lack of capital and of dynamic and imaginative management, the pressure of competition and the parochial attitude of neighbouring societies resisting amalgamation are some of the major obstacles in the way of expansion.

A further problem related to expansion is that in many cases it is only possible to accomplish in fixed stages. The expansion into a higher stage of growth may lead to a temporary decrease in profitability before a further increase in size can fully utilize the new stage.

Problems also exist for those societies that have outgrown their optimum size. Certain cost groups have the tendency to rise disproportionately after a certain stage of development has been reached, for example, the administrative expenses when indirect control replaces direct control or, in the case of supply societies, the distributive costs if the area of operation extends too far. Decentralization through the formation of branches may provide a partial solution to these problems.

Another aspect of size is the sociological effect. Regarding the relationship between the members and the society the optimal size is the small, face-to-face group, where co-operative spirit and loyalty are much more easily instilled than in mass membership. The ideal size in this respect is normally well below the economic optimum. However, in the interests of progress, economic considerations must take priority. The resulting increase in efficiency and of benefits to members makes the question of loyalty less important. In addition, modern methods of public relations can compensate to a certain degree for the loss of direct contact among the members and thus avoid the inner dilution of the society.

2. Location

Location refers to the geographical situation of the society's premises within the area of operation. The selection a suitable location can have considerable influence on the operating costs, the capital requirements, the relationship between members and society, and the contact with market partners.

The factors which have to be considered are:

1. Geographical factors
   - the distance and access to sources of supply, to market outlets and to members;
   - the adequacy of the available transport and communication systems to the market and to members;
   - the availability and comparative costs of power and water;
   - the climate and its effects on working conditions and operating methods.

2. Community factors
    - the availability, skill and cost of local labor,
    - the availability and standard of business services such as banking, insurance, lawyers, accountants, etc.
    - the availability of public facilities such as police, fire brigade, etc.
    - local laws and taxes.

3. Exploratory Meeting

To determine the level of interest in starting and supporting a cooperative, invite potential members to a general meeting. Announce the meeting date, time, and place by letter, or word or mouth. Invite outside advisers.

The leadership group should develop an agenda and select a presiding officer who can conduct a business meeting. Sometimes, and adviser can act as chair or help answer questions. Primary agenda items should include:

- What is the need;
- Possible solutions;
- Cooperative principles and terminology;
- Cooperative operating practices;
- Advantages and disadvantages of a cooperative;
- General risk capital equity and financial requirements; and
- Various forms of member-user commitment needed.

One approach is to have one member of the leadership group discuss the need and another summarise how the proposed cooperative might solve it. In addition, a representative of a successful cooperative might explain its operations, benefits, and limitations.

Allow plenty of time for discussion. Prospective members should be encouraged to express their views and ask questions. All issues raised should be addressed, although answers may be delayed until later meetings when more information becomes available.

Questions to be raised

1. What is cooperative and how is it different from other business?
2. Who controls a cooperative?
3. How much is my initial investment?
4. Will my investment (equity) requirement be determined by volume or by number of members?
5. How much money can I lose if the cooperative fails?
6. Can I get out of the cooperative whenever I want?
7. What are marketing or purchasing agreements and why are they needed?
8. What are net margins and net earnings?
9. What are the patronage dividend?
10. Can we restrict cooperative membership?

4. Steering Committee Formation and Duties

If the group wants a more detailed study after discussion is completed, it should select a steering committee. This group should have a keen interest in the cooperative, be well-respected within the community, and have sound business judgment. Committee members often become the initial organisers and members of the cooperative's first board of directors.

The first function is to select officers of the steering committee, usually at the close of the general informational meeting. Next, establish a deadline for completing a business analysis, including a target date for surveying potential members. Periodic progress meetings retain interest of prospective members.

The steering committee, with the help of one or more advisers, determines if a cooperative is feasible. *First,* it judges whether the proposed cooperative is likely to succeed and benefit its members, *Second,* if the proposal passes this test, the committee prepares a specific, detailed business plan for the new cooperative.

Assistance from specialists in law, accounting, finance, economics, engineering, and cooperative business operations is critical during the business analysis phase.

Economic need is fundamental to the formation and successful operation of any cooperative. The committee should examine what products or services the cooperative could provide, those needed from other source, and whether costs would be reduced or quality improved. Intangible functions also should be considered. Will the cooperative provide a needed service, preserve a market, stabilize prices, or encourage more orderly marketing?

Is the projected initial investment within the financial ability of the potential members involved?

The committee should consider alternatives to starting a new cooperative. Could similar services be provided by another nearby cooperative, either directly or by establishing a branch? I forming a new cooperative is the best alternative, the group should consider linking with regional cooperatives to obtain additional benefits.

A new cooperative should initially limit services to avoid elaborate or costly facilities above those absolutely needed. If successful, services can later be expanded.

5. Member-User Survey

Formal survey techniques are best for estimating potential membership. The adviser usually drafts the survey questionnaire for the steering committee to review.

The following list gives a general idea of the needed information:

1. Member-user experience and capabilities-years in present location, overall success, demand specific to the cooperative venture, and production and marketing success;

2. Variety of products or services to be offered or needed;
3. Period of need services;
4. Current unit value-cost per unit;
5. Member-user-location of use or need;
6. Familiarity with and use of other cooperatives and willingness to join, finance, and use one.

While the questionnaire is being prepared, the steering committee should develop a list of potentially interested member. When the questionnaire is completed and approved, the committee interviews potential members.

The adviser analyzes the survey, prepares a report, and presents it to the steering committee. The results and implications are then discussed at a meeting of all persons surveyed. Survey results should reveal how potential members identify the economic need and the degree of interest in a cooperative to fulfill that need. The survey should indicate the level of support in terms of business volume and if financial commitment is sufficient to organise and successfully operate the cooperative.

Factors determining the initial situations are:

1. *The economic and social relationships within the social groupings* (village, district) where it is sought to bring about the development of co-operative forms of co-operation. An important determinant for these relations is the access to, basic production resources (land, water); e.g. land can be communally owned and/or individually, fairly equitably distributed or otherwise, tilled by its owners, tenants, sharecroppers and/or landless laborers. Where different economic and social groupings co-exist, economic interests also will differ and ask for different forms of co-operative organisation. Co-operative organisation, so promoters should realize, will reduce or worsen inequalities or stabilize them depending on who the beneficiaries are.
2. The *Perception* by the potential members of the co-operative of their economic and social position and of the possibility of bringing about a change in this through joint action. This is decisive for their readiness to organise themselves co-operatively.
3. The potential members' *ability* to solve their problems independently through co-operation. This ability is determined by the locally available knowledge, skills and other means.
4. The functions which are performed by already *existing co-operatives* and similar enterprises, the measure of autonomy granted to them and the extent to which they need assistance and control.
5. The existing *economic order at supra-local level* with its ramifications at local level, in particular the position of private undertakings, state enterprises or official institutions providing services which will not allow, or will oppose, competitive activities by c-operatives in their particular field.

6. The existence or otherwise of co-operative legislation and other statutory provisions.
7. *The physical environment* (precipitation, nature of the soil, etc.) which does not allow of the introduction of new forms of economic enterprises or of the expansion of existing forms.
8. *The available manpower and the requisite funds,* to be supplemented by foreign help if necessary, for manning and equipping the *"promoting machinery"* (= the organisation or complex of organisations which assist the co-operatives).
9. *The available financial resources for provision of credit for co-operative enterprises* insofar as these are not completely self-financing.

Additional Information to be Collected

A. Projected Volume of Business

The best source for these projections comes from the *potential member survey conducted as a part of the feasibility study.* If the business is seasonal, it is important to accurately characterize how production or purchasing and sales occur to determine the appropriate facility and equipment needs.

Market Information

Lenders don't want to finance a proposed business without a market. They want to know who the customers are, if markets have been located, and expected prices and volumes.

Cash Flow

Projected cash flow information may be the most important to the lender. It gives a continuous month-by-month cash income and expense prediction. Key items in eh final analysis are the net cash flow for the month and the ending cash balance. Lenders are particular concerned with the net ending cash balance. Does the cooperative have sufficient funds to operate and pay bills? Is additional borrowed capital needed, particularly for operating during heavy seasonal periods? Can control lable expenses be reduced during periods of low income? Are cash reserves adequate to overcome adverse market swings? And, most importantly, can the cooperative repay its loans? Most lenders want 3 years projections.

Operating Statement

For a new cooperative, the projected operating statement provides and expected picture of operations for one or more years. It contains information on sources of income as well as expenses. The key figure is the "bottom line" that indicates whether net margins (profits) are anticipated. A monthly operating statement provides information to lenders and assists the board in making major policy and management decisions.

Balance Sheet

For the newly formed cooperative seeking financing from outside sources, the projected balance sheet is extremely important. It projects the future value of the cooperative and indicates it solvency and ability to satisfy creditors' claims when due. In summary, it lists the cooperative's assets, liabilities, and net worth.

Loan Package

A summary of scheduled financing needs and sources saves the lender time in assembling the various pieces of data for analysis. It should show major items for which loans and member capital will be spent. These items are extracted from the projected cash flow data. A brief resume of the designated manager should be included in the documents given to the potential lender.

B. Maintain Good Board-Manager Relations

The differing responsibilities of the board of directors and the manager must be clearly understood and carried out.

Directors represent members and are legally responsible for the performance and conduct of the cooperative. All corporate powers of the cooperative, other than those specifically conferred on members, are vested in its directors and outlined in the bylaws an in the State and Federal legal statutes.

Directors' three major responsibilities are to set policies, employ and evaluate the general manager's ability to carry them out, and provide adequate financing for the cooperative.

The board also has some specific management responsibilities such as functioning as trustees for the members in safeguarding their assets in the cooperative; setting goals, objectives, and general policies; adopting long-term strategic plans; employing a competent manger and evaluating performance; preserving the cooperative character of the organisation; establishing an accurate accounting system; adopting an annual operating budget; appointing an outside firm to perform an annual audit; controlling the total operation; and authorizing distribution of cooperative net earnings and redemption of members' equities.

The board, in turn, delegates responsibility for daily operations to a hired general manager or chief executive officer. The general manager hires or discharges employees, including department heads, who with the manager comprise the hired management staff or team.

Responsibilities of hired management include managing or directing daily business activities; carrying out policies set by the board; setting goals and making short-term plans; employing, training, and discharging employees; organising and coordinating internal activities in compliance with cooperative goals and objectives and board policies; keeping complete accounts and records and developing an annual operating budget; and providing the board with periodic reports.

Questions often arise as to the division of responsibilities between the board and hired management. Sometimes they overlap and an exact division cannot be made. Some factors to consider are: the time period-long-term decisions are the responsibility of the board while management makes short-term decisions; idea decisions are usually introduced by the board and actual decisions implemented by management; decisions involving policy are the responsibility of the board, and cooperative functions are handled by management; board primary control activities usually concern the board, while secondary controls pertaining to short-run operations are the responsibility of management. When it comes to staffing, the board hires the manager who, in turn, selects the staff of the cooperative.

Use of policy and procedure manuals and job descriptions along with frank discussions of questions when they arise can help maintain an understanding of the division of responsibility.

Conduct Business like Meetings

A cooperative is a business so its meetings should be conducted in a businesslike manner.

Policy should be established for determining a reasonable quorum for membership and board meetings. A quorum is the specific or minimum percentage of members required to be present to conduct official business. Quorum requirements are sometimes written into State statutes, but should be discussed in the by-laws. As membership expands, the percentage of quorum increases the actual number needed. Setting the quorum too high increases the risk of not getting enough member participants to deal with business matters needing attention.

Parliamentary procedure is a appropriate for orderly group action. It enables the chair to lead a group smoothly and efficiently in determining the wishes of the majority while protecting the rights of minority.

Good meetings just doesn't happen. It results in carrying out several successive steps: planning ahead involves members, following a published agenda, and following through on meeting actions.

Forge Links With Other Cooperatives

An early exercise to determine whether to start a new cooperative was toe investigate the alternative of liking with an existing cooperative that could expand its service territory. Even if starting a new cooperative is the best course of action, the search for beneficial links with other cooperatives should continue.

Alliances with regional cooperatives or other businesses may be valuable sources for supplies, marketing outlets, and related services. Membership in

State and national cooperative associations can keep the new cooperative abreast of what others around the country are doing. These associations can be sources of education and training programmes, legislative and public relations support activities, and help identify sources of special expertise.

C. Things to be avoided by new cooperatives

New organisations are most vulnerable in their early formative years. Here are some tips for new cooperatives to avoid potential pitfalls:

1. *Lack of clearly identified mission:* A new cooperative shouldn't be formed just for the sake of forming one. The potential member-user must identify a clear mission statement with definite goals and objectives.
2. *Inadequate Planning:* Detailed plans for reaching defined goals and the mission are important. In-depth surveys of the potential member-user needs coupled with business feasibility studies are necessary. Stop the organisational process if there isn't sufficient interest in the cooperative by potential member-users or if it isn't a sound business venture. The human cost in time and organisation expense may be better used elsewhere.
3. *Failure to use experienced advisors and consultants:* Most persons interested in becoming member-users of a new cooperative haven't had cooperative business development experience. Using resources persons experienced in cooperative development can save a log of wasted motion and expense.
4. *Lack of member leadership:* Calling on the services of experienced resource persons can't replace leadership from the organising group. Decisions must come from the potential member-user group and its selected leadership. Professional resource persons should never be in decisionmaking positions.
5. *Lack of member commitment:* To be successful, the new cooperative must have the broad-based support of the potential member-users. The support of lenders, attorneys, accountants, cooperative specialists, and a few leaders won't make the cooperative a business success.
6. *Lack of competent management:* Most cooperative members are busy operating and managing their own businesses and lack experience in cooperative management. The directors hire experienced and qualified management to increases the chances for business success.
7. *Failure to identify and minimise risks:* The risk in starting a new business can be reduced if identified early in the organisational process. Careful study of the competition, Federal, State, and local Government regulations, industry trends, environmental issues, and alternative business practices helps to reduce risk.
8. *Poor assumptions:* Often, potential member-users and cooperative leaders overestimate the volume of business and underestimate the costs of

operations. Anticipated business success that ends in failure places the organisers in a "bad light." Quality business assumptions tempered with a does of pessimism often proves to be judicious.

9. *Lack of financing:* Regardless of the amount of time spent in financial projection, most new businesses are underfinanced. Inefficiencies in startup operations, competition, complying with regulations, and delays often are the causes. Often, the first months of business operations and even the first years are not profitable, so adequate financing is important to survive this period.
10. *Inadequate communications:* Keeping the membership, suppliers, and financiers informed is critical during the organisation and early life of the cooperative. Lack of or incorrect information can create apathy or suspicion. The directors and management must decide to whom and how communications are to be directed.

21

Legal Aspects of Organising Cooperatives

Legal Aspects of Organising Cooperatives — A Model of Ethiopia

In Ethiopia, the Co-operative Societies' Manual includes specific guidance on the promotion and organisation of a proposed Co-operative Society and the preparation of an Economic Appreciation of the project, etc. (pages 3-15 of the English version of the Manual). The Manual also includes a copy of Ethiopian Co-operative Legislation (i.e., the Proclamation and Regulations made under it) and Model Rules for five major types of Society.

Sections (a) and (b) of the Economic Appreciation are obviously designed to build up a realistic and relevant "picture" of the area where the proposed Society will be and of the people living and working there. Much of the information may already be available in various government offices (e.g., Administration, Agriculture, Community Development, etc) and it is essential that the co-operative project should relate to the work of other "development agencies" in the area so that all efforts reinforce and support each other. In short, there must be team work in the overall attack on poverty and all the handicaps associated with it. A Co-operative Society will usually be the nucleus providing legal, financial and business organisation for those aspects of an overall programme which need it.

Sections (c) and (d) might be called the "business part" of the Economic Appreciation although it must obviously take into account essential information about the people and the area.

Since Co-operative Societies could be formed in a variety of situations in Ethiopia (e.g., among a group of people not specifically part of some development scheme in Package Area schemes; in Special Scheme area such as WADU, etc.) it is appropriate to list certain things they - would or should – have in common:

1. They should have been formed only because their members wanted to form them: it is wrong for anyone to urge people to form co-operatives. If members have formed a society to "please" anyone but them – selves they will not feel that the problems, which will surely arise, belong to them. Where co-operative have to be formed to carry out special aspects of some development scheme (e.g., a Minimum Package Area scheme) it is all the more necessary to carry out co-operative education amongst members. If all that evolves is a "trading centre" it will not play a full part in the long-term aims of the scheme.
2. They should relate closely to the lives and needs of their communities, and have sound economic aims and business prospects.
3. They should be registered under Co-operative Law and guided, supervised, and audited under arrangements made by the Government official appointed under that Law.
4. They should follow the universally accepted Principles of Co-operation and feel themselves to be part of the wider Co-operative Movement, in order to bring fullest benefits to their members and communities.
5. They should, in due time, help to set up a national co-operative organisation which arranges or co-ordinates the educational, training, trading, advisory and representational services of the Ethiopian Co-operative Movement. The ultimate aim must be a strong, healthy and self-reliant Movement with can play a constructive role in the life of the nation.

Formation and Registration of Co-operative Societies

1. Formation of Co-operative Societies
   - (1) Co-operative societies may, according to their nature, be established at different levels from primary up to the federal level.
   - (2) A primary society shall be established by persons who live or work within a given area.
   - (3) The number of members in a primary society to be established shall not be less than ten.
   - (4) Notwithstanding Sub-Article (2) of this Article the appropriate authority may specify in the directive, the minimum number of members that could make a society economically feasible.
   - (5) A society may sell some of its shares to persons outside its area when the society faces shortage of capital.
2. Types of Societies
   - (1) A society may engage in either production or service rendering activities or in both.
   - (2) The field of activities to be engaged in by any society shall be determined by the by-laws of the society.

3. Name of Society
   (1) Any society shall have its own name.
   (2) Words "Cooperative Society and Limited Liability" shall appear in the name of every society.
   (3) A name or distinguishing mark registered by one society shall not be used by any other society.
   (4) The name of every society shall be written boldly and be put at every place where the society's activities are performed. It should also be written or sealed on every notices letters, other specifications and documents which are signed on behalf of the society.
4. Registration of a Co-operative Society
   (1) Any society shall be registered by the appropriate authority.
   (2) Any society, when established, shall submit an application for registration together with the following particulars to the appropriate authority:
      (a) minutes of the founders meeting;
      (b) the by-laws of the society inn three copies;
      (c) names, address and signature of the members;
      (d) name, address and signature of the members of the management committee of the society;
      (e) a detailed description which proves that the registered members of the society have met the requirements for membership in accordance with the provisions of this Proclamation and the by-laws of the society;
      (f) name, address and signature of members of the societies above primary level;
      (g) plan of the society;
      (h) documents showing that the amount of capital of the society and the capital has been collected and deposited in a bank account, if there is no bank in the area, that it has been deposited in a place where the appropriate authority has designated;
      (i) the description of the land on which the society operates;
      (j) other particular that may be specified in the regulations or directives issued for the implementation of this Proclamation.
   (3) The appropriate authority shall register a society and issue a certificate of registration hen it sis satisfied that the application for registration submitted to it has fulfilled the requirements for registration.
   (4) When the appropriate authority rejects the application for the registration of a society, it shall give a written explanation to the representatives of the society within 15 days. The representatives

may appeal tot eh high court which has jurisdiction on the decision of the appropriate authority.

(5) The certificate of registration issued to a society pursuant to Sub-Article (3) of this Article is in accordance with this Proclamation.

(6) Juridical Personality and Responsibility

(a) Any society registered in pursuance of Article 9 of this Proclamation shall have juridical personality from the date of its registration.

(b) Any society shall not be liable beyond its total asset. It has limited liability.

5. By-laws of Society

(1) Every society shall have its own by-laws.

(2) The contents of the by-laws shall include the following particulars:

(a) name and address of the society;

(b) objectives and activities of the society;

(c) working place (area) of the society;

(d) requirements necessary for membership of the society;

(e) the rights and duties of members of the society;

(f) the powers, responsibilities, and duties of management bodies;

(g) conditions for withdrawal and dismissal from membership;

(h) conditions for reflection appointment, term of office and suspension or dismissal of the members of the management committee or other management bodies;

(i) conditions for calling of meeting and voting of the society;

(j) allocation and distribution of profit;

(k) auditing;

(l) employment of workings;

(m) other particulars not contrary to this Proclamation.

(3) By-laws of society may be amended by the special resolution of the general assembly. However, the amendment of the by-laws of the society shall be effective on the date of its submission to and registration by the appropriate authority.

(4) Where the Society decides on the amendment of its by-laws three copies of the amendment and the special resolution of the society made in accordance with this Proclamation shall be submitted to the appropriate authority within 30 days from the date of the decisions.

(5) The appropriate authority shall register the amendment and give evidence or its registration to the society where it is satisfied that the amendment of the by-laws was made in accordance with this Proclamation of this Proclamation.

22

Stages in Organising Cooperatives

Because each situation is unique, there is no specific recipe for forming a cooperative. The steps for starting a cooperative recommended here may be considered as guidelines by cooperative entrepreneurs.

A. Steps to Starting a Cooperative

Like other businesses, every co-op starts with the recognition of a need or an opportunity. One or two people willing to put in some time and energy can spark a group interested in starting a co-op.

Members of such a group have a mutual need that can be addressed through joint action. They could, for example, lack a market for their products or lack necessary supplies or services. Acting together to address that need, they can achieve something which none of them could achieve alone.

Basic Steps in Starting a Cooperative

1. Hold an organising meeting; establish steering committee.
2. Conduct a feasibility study.
3. Hold a meeting of potential members to report on the results of the feasibility study.
4. Incorporate the co-op by filing articles of incorporation and bylaws.
5. Prepare a business plan.
6. Secure financing for the co-op.
7. Recruit/Admission of members for the co-op.
8. Hire co-op management and staff.
9. Hold the co-op's first membership and board meetings.
10. Start Cooperatives.

1. Hold an organising meeting and establish a steering committee

(a) A core group of interested individuals should hold an informational meeting of potential co-op members and others in the community. The primary purpose of the meeting is to explain the identified need and how a co-op would address it.

It is important that the group come to general agreement on the nature and importance of the problem and the potential for a cooperative to address it. Such an agreement will become the group's shared vision, so it is worth spending as much time as necessary to achieve it.

(b) Provide informational handouts that explain what a co-op is and how it would work. Also provide information about the steps involved in starting a co-op so people have a sense of what they may be getting into. Determine the level of interest in exploring a co-op among meeting participants.

Many organising groups have found it helpful to invite speakers from other cooperatives in order to highlight their success stories. This often gives meeting participants a more down to earth vision of what a co-op is and how it can work for them.

(c) A steering committee should be formed of participants at the meeting which will coordinate activities on behalf of the group. Committee members must be able to provide leadership to the larger group and be willing to put some time and energy into researching the feasibility of the proposed cooperative.

(d) Allow plenty of time for questions and discussion. A meeting like this often works best if it is led by an experienced facilitator. In many cases, it is necessary to hold more than one meeting to give all interested parties in the community a chance to participate.

Typical Steering Committee Members

1. President

   Often the "project champion." Facilitation skills a big plus.

2. Vicr President

   May chair key subcommittee.

3. Treasurer

   Manages funds. May lead business plan phase. Accounting skills a big plus.

4. Secretary

   Coordinates all communications. Computer skills a big plus.

5. Non-officers

Group Dynamics (Adapted from Henehan)

Various issues must be resolved to proceed:

- Potential members must see that the benefits in adopting a cooperative approach are attainable.
- Individuals must emerge who are willing to assume a leadership role and take the agreed-upon vision to the next steps.
- A level of trust and confidence must evolve within the group.
- The creative tension between visionaries and doers must be harnessed effectively. It cannot be allowed to prevent the group from moving forward.
- Participants must be convinced that the initial risks and costs in adopting the proposed approach are outweighted by the potential benefits to be obtained.
- Roles of members, management and board members should be clear to all.
- Everyone involved should have confidence that the proposed organisation is the best alternative available.

Typical Sub-committee Areas:

- Business plan committee;
- By-laws & policies committee;
- Purchasing & construction committee; and
- Personnel committee.

2. Conduct a Feasibility Study

(a) The steering committee can either conduct a feasibility study (using the guidelines provided), or hire a consultant to carry out the study. The purpose of a feasibility study is to examine critical opportunities and obstacles that might make or break the proposed cooperative business. The feasibility study should give the group a good idea of whether the co-op is likely to be successful as a business.

The critical issues that a feasibility study analyzes include the number and interest level of potential members; market issues (can the co-op get better prices, better quality or better services than potential members currently get through other means?); operating costs; start-up costs; and availability of financing.

If insurmountable obstacles are discovered in the feasibility study, the development of the cooperative should be abandoned or shelved before too much time and money has been expended.

(b) In some cases, local or state governments or foundations may provide financial or technical assistance with the feasibility study. *The quality of the feasibility study is critical because it will influence all future decisions on the development of the co-op.* Don't hesitate to bring in outside expertise when you need it.

Contributions by potential co-op members are often used to help cover the cost of a feasibility study. These members will be the primary beneficiaries of the cooperative, so naturally they should assume some responsibility for the financial costs of assessing its feasibility.

3. Report on the Results of the Feasibility Study

(a) The steering committee should hold a follow up meeting with potential co-op members to report on the results of the feasibility study. A summary of the feasibility report should be distributed to participants, and the full report made available to anyone who wishes to see it. Allow plenty of time to discuss the report and ensure that potential members understand the results.

(b) Be sure to spend time reviewing the financial section of the report. The preliminary financial projections should tell the group how much equity will be required from each member of the co-op, and whether or not the co-op is projected to return any patronage refunds (shares of the profits) to members during the first few years of operation. These are key pieces of information that will influence each person's decision about whether to join the co-op.

This should be a major decision point. If the feasibility study indicates that the co-op is not a viable business, or if sufficient commitment does not exist among the group, the steering committee should not proceed with forming the co-op.

4. Incorporate the Cooperative and file Articles of Incorporation and Bylaws

(a) In most states, a cooperative has to be incorporated under the appropriate state statute in order to conduct business. Most states have statutes specifically governing cooperatives. The articles of incorporation describe the kind and scope of the cooperative's business. Incorporation takes place when a co-op files its articles with the secretary of state. If the steering committee wishes to, it may draft the articles of incorporation and bylaws. Make sure to have a lawyer who is familiar with cooperatives review these documents before they are presented to the membership.

(b) The bylaws state how the cooperative will conduct business, and must be approved by the membership. Note that a co-op can start out with very basic bylaws and refine them after the business plan has been developed.

(c) As soon as the cooperative is incorporated and thus exists as a legal entity, two members of the steering committee should open a bank account in the co-op's name. This account will be used to deposit equity contributions from new members.

(d) *A note about stock:* Articles of Incorporation allow the steering committee to decide whether the co-op will issue stock or not. We recommend that the co-op do so. In recruiting new members, it can be an important symbolic act to hand over a stock certificate to each individual who joins the co-op. Many new members feel more comfortable having something in hand to show for their contribution. Some potential members also find a stock cooperative easier to understand than a non-stock structure. Blank stock certificates are available at most office supply stores. Just fill in the blanks to indicate the number of shares each member buys and the cost per share.

5. Prepare a Business Plan

(a) If the feasibility study results are favorable, the steering committee carries out or hires a consultant firm to develop a detailed business plan. The business plan serves two primary purposes: to provide a blueprint for the development and initial operation of the co-op and to provide supporting documentation for potential members, financial institutions and other investors.

(b) A typical outline of a business plan includes a description of the company, a market analysis, research and development related to the co-op's product or service, a marketing and sales plan, a description of the organisational structure and key personnel, and financial data.

(c) In most cases, a new co-op will need to borrow capital from a bank or other lending institution in order to get started. The business plan serves a vital function in describing to the bank the co-op's goals and how it plans to accomplish those goals. Most lending institutions will not consider a loan request that is not accompanied by a detailed business plan. In addition, it is a very useful document when recruiting new members to the cooperative.

(d) Few steering committees have sufficient skills to develop a thorough business plan. Obtaining technical assistance can make the difference between a business plan that gets a loan and one that does not. Note that many state governments offer grants and loans to assist start-ups with technical assistance and business planning.

A cooperative's business plan should include many of the components of a business plan for any type of firm. However, there are additional considerations for cooperatives which should be addressed in a well thought out plan. For example, cooperative finance involves a number of unique aspects such as the variety of ways to raise or revolve member equity. Governance structure should be spelled out in the plan to insure that an effective decision making capacity is designed. Will voting be by member, proportional to patronage, or proportional to investment? Member rights and responsibilities in relation to the cooperative should also be presented.

Financial projections should be built on several scenarios reflecting the impact of various member actions, such as a given percentage of members not meeting their patronage or investment obligations. What level of losses or prices might members be willing to tolerate? What happens if a share of members over produce or find more attractive alternatives?

6. Secure Financing

(a) Cooperative businesses vary greatly in the amount of capital they need to get up and running. The business plan should include the amount and type of financing needed by the co-op and a strategy for obtaining it. The steering committee and its advisors are responsible for implementing this strategy.

(b) Virtually all co-ops require some level of member financing, usually in the form of stock purchases or membership fees. Member financing not only provides equity for the co-op, it also provides a financial base that helps other investors, particularly banks, feel more secure in investing in the co-op. The steering committee should prepare a membership application for new members to fill out and sign. It should identify the member's name, address, and phone number; the number of shares of stock being purchased (or the amount of the membership fee if it is a non-stock co-op); and a stated agreement that the new member agrees to belong to and abide by the bylaws and contracts of the co-op. Each member's initial financial contribution should be collected at the time the membership application is submitted.

(c) In addition to member equity, most co-ops need to borrow money to get started and to maintain their operations. Loans can come from banks and other financial institutions (including several national banks for cooperatives).

7. Recruit/Admission of Members

(a) Laying the groundwork for the co-op's membership base needs to begin when the steering committee first meets. During their organisational phase, many co-ops hold meetings for potential members, conduct surveys and mail organising updates to them, and collect initial down payments on membership fees.

All of these activities provide a good indication of the level of interest in, and commitment to, the co-op. Thus, when the time comes to actually "ante-up" and join, potential members are more primed to act. Even so, the steering committee may need to recruit new members in addition to those who have attended one or more of the organisational meetings. *This should be a major decision point. If the co-op is unable to obtain the necessary debt financing, or if sufficient commitment does not exist among potential members to provide sufficient equity capital, the steering committee should not proceed with developing the co-op at this time.*

8. Hire Cooperative Management

(a) Some new co-ops identify management personnel early in their organising process, especially if one or more key individuals are already known to members of the steering committee. However, recruiting staff personnel is listed as a later step in the co-op formation process because the co-op is not a definite "go" until the necessary financing has been secured.

One or more of the key individuals can be hired as consultants at an early stage with the mutual intent that they will work for the co-op once it is formally established. This approach also has the effect of making investors feel more comfortable about financing the co-op because proposed management staff have been identified. For some lenders, competent management is the most important thing they look for in making a loan decision.

9. Hold Co-op's First Membership & Board Meetings

(a) After financing has been secured and sufficient members have signed up, the first general membership meeting is convened. There are two major pieces of business that must be conducted at this meeting:

- the members adopt the co-op's bylaws; and
- the members elect a board of directors for the co-op.

This meeting marks the transition from a steering committee and interim leadership group to a formally elected board and legally approved bylaws.

Allow enough time for members to look over the bylaws and ensure that they are thoroughly understood before the vote takes place. There may be a few amendments suggested; these and the bylaws are approved by majority vote.

In their capacity as owners, members elect the board of directors to function as their representatives in overseeing the administration of the co-op. *It is this mechanism through which a cooperative is member-controlled.* As the members' representatives, the board's primary responsibilities are to develop policies, conduct long-range planning, hire and supervise the co-op manager, and guide the co-op in pursuing its mission and goals.

(b) The new board of directors should hold their first board meeting shortly after the first membership meeting. Among other duties, the board should elect officers, develop job descriptions for management personnel, and initiate the hiring process, if necessary.

10. Start Operations

(a) During the initial phase of the co-op's operations, management should concentrate on implementing the business plan. It is vital that frequent communication between staff, board and members be maintained during this period. Some co-ops have lost touch with their members after start-up, and have found that to be a recipe for disaster. Management and board need to make sure the co-op is meeting the needs of the members over time. Do this through regular newsletters and member surveys.

(b) Another way to maintain good communication between staff, members and board is to conduct educational seminars for them. Remember that continuous education is one of the cooperative principles. It enables members to participate in the co-op's affairs and make fully informed decisions regarding them.

A strong co-op is built on a foundation of involved members. Without an active base of members who are willing to work towards the success of the co-op, the co-op is bound to fail.

Starting a cooperative can be a lengthy and somewhat arduous process. It can also be very rewarding to see the fruits of your labour turn into economic and social benefits for you and your community.

The steering committee takes responsibility for seeing the organising process through to the end. Be patient and give yourselves the time to conduct each development stage carefully.

Don't get discouraged if the process appears to get bogged down. Bring in outside technical assistance as needed, and solicit advice from others who have been down the same road

Additional Information Related to Starting A Cooperative

Bylaws, Membership Application, Member Meetings

Bylaws

Bylaws are the rules and regulations that govern the day-to-day working and regular functioning of a cooperative society. They are equal to the Articles of Association followed by a private company. A bylaw can be amended to suit the needs of the cooperative. Bylaws state how the cooperative will conduct business and must be consistent with both State laws and the articles.

Bylaws usually have membership requirements and lists rights and responsibilities of members; Grounds and procedures for member expulsion; how to call and conduct membership meetings, methods of voting, how directors and officers are elected or removed, and their number, duties, terms of office; time and place of directors meetings; requirement to conduct business; handling of losses; treating nonmember business; dissolution of the cooperative; and the process for amending the bylaws.

Also covered is how the board is structured to represent the membership, given geographical distribution and size of the membership and the scope of business and function of the cooperative. Directors may be selected to represent areas based on membership density, to reflect commodities or services to be handled, or some other basis that provides equitable representation. The organising committee's recommended management structure should include the basis for director representation, voting methods, and board officers, and their terms.

An outline of the major topic areas that the bylaws should cover appears below.

Membership

Identifies the qualifications for eligibility and procedures for joining the cooperative, including requirements for purchase of stock, if any. Describes the procedure by which membership may be ended, either voluntarily or involuntarily.

Meetings of Cooperative Members

Identifies the date for the annual meeting; how and when any special meetings may be held; requirements for notice of upcoming meetings; procedures for voting and requirements for a quorum; order of business at the annual meeting.

Directors and Officers

Specifies the number and qualifications of directors; procedures for electing directors and length of terms; election of officers by the board; frequency of board meetings and requirements for notice of board meetings; any special meetings; compensation of board members and requirements for a quorum.

Duties of Directors

States the director's specific powers and responsibilities, including: guiding the cooperative and articulating its mission, goals, and policies and periodically reviewing those goals. Authorizes directors to employ a manager, define the manager's duties, determine his or her compensation and evaluate his or her job performance. Specifies the director's responsibility to maintain an.appropriate accounting system and have the co-op's books audited or reviewed annually. This section also specifies the board's responsibility to indemnify directors, officers and management against liability.

Duties of Officers

Specifies the duties of the president, vice president, secretary, and treasurer. Also describes the terms of officers and excused absences from board meetings.

Membership Capital Contributions

Specifies the required equity contribution by members and the method by which the co-op will collect the contribution; what type of stock the cooperative has the authority to issue; and any requirements regarding the co-op's stock certificates.

Profits and Losses

Specifies how the co-op's profits, if any, will be distributed based on each member's patronage with the co-op. In addition, any losses experienced by the co-op must be allocated across the membership.

Nonmember Business

Specifies how the cooperative will distribute the benefits, if any, resulting from business with non-members.

Dissolution

Identifies a procedure for dissolving the cooperative, and specifies the distribution of any remaining assets.

Amending the Bylaws

Specifies a straightforward method by which the bylaws may be amended.

Contents of bye-laws

The bye-laws must contain:

1. The name and the trade name of the cooperative, which may be freely chosen, as long as there is no confusion possible with the name of another cooperative already registered and as long as the public is left in doubt about the limited financial liability of the members.
2. The locality of the head office, its postal address and possibly the conditions for a transfer.
3. The definition of the objective (including the indication of whether the cooperative is a single or a multi-purpose cooperative).
4. The conditions and procedures for admission, resignation, exclusion and suspension of members as well as eligibility criteria. These must reflect the particular character of the cooperative in question, as also reflected by its being a primary, a secondary or a tertiary cooperative.
5. The value and minimum number of the shares to be subscribed by each member. The GA ensures that the economic means of the least affluent members form the basis for the decision.
6. The procedure and conditions for the subscription and payment of the shares and, possibly, of additional shares. Shares may be paid in cash, kind, labour, service or by leaving the share of the surplus, to which a member is entitled, with the cooperative.
7. The type of financial liability of the members for the debts of the cooperative the administration of the registers.
8. The conditions and procedures for convening GAs (form of notice, fixing and notifying the agenda, election of the president of the session, preferably not a member of the board of directors, quorum and voting, number of delegates by section or by region if any, etc.).

9. The size of the board of directors and, possibly, of the supervisory committee; the conditions of eligibility to the various offices, the duration of the mandates and their possible remuneration; rights and obligations of officers, mode of decision taking.
10. The conditions and procedures for convening the board of directors and, if any, the supervisory committee (quorum, voting, etc.).
11. Financing: capital formation, constitution of the legal and of the statutory reserve funds.
12. Surplus distribution and contribution to cover losses.
13. The distribution of the capital in case of resignation, exclusion or liquidation.
14. Definition of the financial year.
15. Auditing.
16. Conditions and procedures for voluntary dissolution.
17. Arbitration procedure;
18. Decision making;
19. Specification of any other legal matter; and finally
20. The procedure for modifying the bye-laws.

Membership Application

The application, signed by the member and approved by the board of directors, is the legal proof that a patron is a member. A cooperative should have a completed membership application on file from every member. Membership and the amount of business done with members and nonmembers are important factors for certain activities.

A membership certificate may be issued to each member as evidence of entitlement to all of the rights, benefits, and privileges of the association.

Member Meeting

Further action is usually needed to accept those members who have subscribed for shares or agreed to become members.

If members of the first board of directors have not been named in the bylaws, they should be elected at this meeting or the steering committee can be converted as Board of Directors.

Here are some suggestions for selecting the first board of directors:

- Use a nominating committee to develop a panel of candidates for the board;
- Select only members as candidates;
- Nominate two candidates for each position; and
- Vote by secret ballot.

Implementing the Business Plan

Officers of the cooperative are elected and directors assigned to individual or committee responsibilities to implement the business plan.

Members may be assigned to committees, but at least one board member should be on each committee to enhance communications. Target dates are established for important events such as groundbreaking, construction completion, dedication or open house, and full-capacity operations.

The board needs to act immediately on some specific items:

- Conduct a membership drive;
- Adopt a form of membership application or subscription;
- Acquire capital;
- Initiate steps to hire a manager;
- Authorize officers or employees to handle cooperative funds and issue checks;
- Design and install an accounting system.
- Provide for bookkeeping and auditing services;
- Print bylaws, and other member documents for distribution to all members;
- Bind officers and employees in accordance with bylaws.

Membership Drive

Cooperative normally have open membership. Initially they may have a selective membership policy. Members should feel a responsibility to recommend other believed to be qualified users. That's why it's important for members to understand what their cooperative is, how it operates, its benefits, and its limitations.

People join cooperative primarily for economic benefits-services and increased income. Most people want to be shown the advantages of cooperative membership. If those benefits are not evident, few prospects will join and even if they do, they probably won't regularly patronize the cooperative.

New members may be asked to join by purchasing shares or paying a membership fee and signing and application. The applicant should get a receipt for funds collected. The cooperative must follow up with membership and related material.

Accurate accounting of money is an extremely sensitive issue. The cooperative should retain an independent accounting firm to assist in recording funds prior to the collection of substantial amounts of money. Now, we can look into the rights and responsibilities of members, board of directors, chairman, vice chairman, manager and chief account in the Ethiopian context.

Elections

Elections are conducted routinely as per the bylaws of the cooperative. Every year one-third of the directors will be relieved and elections will be conducted for the post of the directors. Elections can be conducted during the ordinary general assembly meeting as well as during the special general assembly meeting. The members must be given prior intimation by the presiding officer (usually the chairman of the cooperative) relating to the date of election and the nomination by the members. Elections to the posts of president, vice-president, secretary and other office bearers will be conducted among the members of the board of directors.

Members, General Assembly and Board

Members

Cooperative management starts with membership, members formulate the broad general policies of the cooperative and elect the Board of Directors to supervise the execution of these policies. The manager and his staff put into practice the policies prescribed by the members under the guidance of the Board of Directors. This division of activities places important responsibilities on members, which should not be taken lightly.

The Obligations and Rights of Members

Obligations

Principle

Membership is linked to rights, these being conditioned by the discharge of obligations. The law and subsidiary legislation must ensure that this rule is respected, even in cases where social rules tend to override these rights and obligations.

In no case, must the social mechanisms based on family ties, race, age, religion or any other affiliation to a group affect the independence and the equality of the members.

Personal Obligations

By belonging to a cooperative, members commit themselves to:

- Respect the bye-laws as well as all the decisions taken in the general assembly, whether they voted for their adoption or not.
- Abstain from any activity detrimental to the objective of their cooperative.
- Membership in several cooperatives having the same objective and territory must not automatically be considered as harming the cooperative(s).
- Participate actively in the life of the cooperative. This obligation may not, however, be enforced.

Financial Obligations

Membership in a cooperative implies the following financial obligations:

- Each member must subscribe to and pay for the minimum number of shares fixed by the bye-laws;

- Each member is financially liable for the debts of his or her cooperative. This liability is at least equal to the amount of shares subscribed.

In order to compensate, at least in part, for the financial weakness inherent to most cooperatives, the law or the bye-laws may impose an obligation on the members to make supplementary payments in case the cooperative is unable to pay its debts. This may result in an unlimited financial liability of the members.

The amount of these supplementary payments may be the same for each member, it may be determined as prorata of the transactions made by each of the members, according to the method used to distribute the surplus, or according to the number of shares held by each member. If not specified in the law, the type of financial liability of the members must be explicitly dealt with in the byelaws in order to protect the interests of third parties.

Because of the status of legal personality of cooperatives, this financial liability commits the members towards their cooperative only, and not towards the creditors of the cooperative. It extends beyond the termination of membership, during a period to be specified in the law. As a rule, a member must contribute to the discharge of only those debts which show in the balance sheet at the time of the end of his or her membership.

Other Obligations

One might envisage obliging the members to use, to a certain extent at least, the services of their cooperative. Although favouring in the short run the development of the cooperative, such a rule would in time have a negative influence on the competitiveness of the cooperative and it might violate competition law.

Rather than reasoning in terms of legal obligations, one might consider that cooperators have the moral duty to work with their enterprise. Furthermore, it is up to the cooperative itself to offer sufficiently attractive services to its members. In order to guarantee a certain stability in specific cases, the cooperative might have to conclude individual contracts with each of its members.

Furthermore, exceptions are possible particularly in the case where the members decide to make an important investment, the success of which depends on the members using that facility. Members could then temporarily be forbidden to look elsewhere for the rendered services.

Rights

Personal rights

Each member has the right to:

- use the installations and services of the cooperative;
- participate in the general assembly, propose a motion therein, and vote;
- elect or be elected for an office in the cooperative;

- obtain at all times, from the elected bodies of the cooperative information on the economic situation of the cooperative;
- have the books and registers inspected by the supervisory committee.

Jointly as a group (minimum number to be determined), the members can also:

- convene a general assembly and/or have a question inscribed on the agenda of that GA;
- ask for an additional audit.

Financial Rights

The members have the following financial rights:

They receive a share of the surplus in the form of a bonus, calculated as prorata of their transactions with their cooperative (patronage bonus), and/or a limited interest on the paid-up shares.

When terminating their membership, they can ask that the paid-up shares be reimbursed. Losses or devaluations may be deducted from the nominal value of these shares.

In the case of liquidation, members receive a share of the remaining sum, if any, unless the bye-laws stipulate that this must be credited to another cooperative or to a charitable organisation.

Members participate in management in a number of ways. The most important are when they:

(a) Adopt and amend by-laws,
(b) Elect and remove Board of Directors,
(c) Approve changes in capitalization and major additions to plants and services,
(d) Decide on the appropriation of net surplus,
(e) Approve annual activity plan and budget,
(f) Make a decision on audit reports.
(g) Consider the annual report of the Board of directors controlling committee and making a decision,
(h) Become active in the cooperative affairs by attending meetings, serving on committees, accepting special assignments, and genuinely backing the cooperative,
(i) Abide by the decision of the majority,
(j) Keen informed about the cooperative by studying annual reports, talking with board of directors & employees,
(k) Defend the cooperative and its management when it is unjustly criticized or attacked.

In order for cooperative members to exercise control, they must take action by legally called meetings. They by-laws should specify the procedure to be followed in calling meetings. The highest body in the cooperative is the general meeting. All members of the cooperative should attend meetings.

23

Feasibility and Viability Studies for Cooperative Enterprises

Feasibility Studies

Feasibility studies – also termed project evaluation, pre-construction survey, etc. – are systematic appraisal of the economic and possibly social effects which the realization of a certain project will have, and a survey of the technical problems involved. Co-operatives can be confronted with the need for such an analysis, for example, if a new society or a new branch is to be established, if new activities are to be undertaken, etc. In a wider sense a similar study, though perhaps not so elaborate, should precede any decision which could decisively alter the course of a society.

In smaller matters this analysis can be prepared and assessed by the society's staff or, in the case of societies to be formed, by a pre-co-operative study group of prospective members, but in most cases a qualified economist or engineer, or both, have to be consulted. Within the co-operative sector this type of extension service can usually be contacted through central business organisations, auditing associations or government departments. In some instances feasibility studies are also carried out by international organisations involved in co-operative extension work or by private consulting firms.

In most cases the study is carried out according to a schedule similar to the following:

1. Terms of Reference

In this preface it should be established on whose authority the study is being made, and the exact objectives it is to pursue. For the further course of the study it is important that this purpose is clearly stated. It should also include the course the study will follow and the source of information on which it will rely.

2. Introduction

The introduction must present the background information to the project:

(a) General aspects which may affect the project, such as the relevant legislation, the structure of local administration, income statistics, etc., and a general description of the area where the project will be carried out, its geographical factors, climate, communication system, people and customs. In the individual case it may also include specialized information, in rural projects, for example, about soil qualities, rainfall, land tenure and utilization, average farm size, methods of farming, etc.

(b) The scope for development or the need for new facilities, at present as well as in the future, by showing the faults and disadvantages of the present set-up or situation, or by proving, by way of market analysis, the room for expansion.

(c) The suggested target for expansion or the proposed capacity of any new facilities.

(d) The possible approach or method to be used and, if necessary, a comparison of several methods, and the planned location of any facilities.

(e) The time schedule for the realization of the project considering the recruitment and training period for any new staff, the delivery period for any new machinery and the construction time for any new buildings required as well as the most favorable time to start the project with regard to the market.

(f) The size of membership related to the set targets and the possibility of attracting new members.

(g) The expected response from present or prospective members, especially whether they realise the necessity of the project and are willing to co-operate, or what steps can be taken to enlist their collaboration.

3. Market Analysis Research

The key questions that should be answered in the Market Analysis section of the feasibility study are presented below:

(a) What is the current or projected demand for your proposed products or services? In other words, how many units can you reasonably expect to sell each month?

(b) What are the target markets for this product or service? What demographic characteristics do these potential customers have in common? How may of them are there?

(c) What is the projected supply in your area of the products or services needed for your project?

(d) What competition exists in this market? Can you establish a market niche, which will enable you to compete effectively with other providing this product or service?

(e) Is the location of your proposed business or project likely to affect is success? If so, is the identified site the most appropriate one available?

The market analysis should be conducted first because it is critical to the success of the business. If you cannot substantiate through research that adequate demand for your product or service exists, or if you cannot obtain sufficient quality to meet expected demand, they you project is not feasible. You should not continue to the next step in the feasibility study.

4. Organisational Issues

(a) What organisational structure is the right one for you?
(b) Who will serve on the board of directors?
(c) What qualifications are needed to manage this business?
(d) Who will manage the business (if possible)?
(e) What other staffing needs does the co-op have? How do you expect staffing needs to change over the next 2-3 years?

5. Technical Requirements

(a) The feasibility of using the existing facilities and the present staff for the new task and the possible changes to be made for their adaptation.
(b) Any new facilities and manpower needed and their availability
  (i) land and buildings, their size design, outlay and equipment.
  (ii) machinery, type, make, capacity.
  (iii) transport, type, capacity.
  (iv) manpower, required skill and experience, recruitment plan.

Key Questions to answer include:

(a) What are the technology needs for the proposed business?
(b) What other equipment does your proposed business need?
(c) Where will you obtain this technology and equipment?
(d) When can you get the necessary equipment?
(e) How much will the equipment and technology cost?

6. Capital Outlay and Finance

(a) the total cost of the project assessed according to a detailed list of the costs of any building, machinery or vehicles needed and, if possible, accompanied by tenders of the relevant suppliers.
(b) The required rate of finance calculated on the basis of the expected average lifetime of the invested assets.
(c) The source of finance available for the purpose of the project.

The following financial aspects are to be considered.

(a) *Start-up Costs:* These are the costs incurred in starting up a new business, including "capital goods" such as land, buildings, equipment, etc. The business may have to borrow money from a lending institution to cover these costs

(b) *Operating Costs:* These are the ongoing costs, such as rent, utilities, and wages that are incurred in the everyday operation of a business. The total should include interest and principle payments on any debt for start-up costs.

(c) *Revenue Projections:* How will you price your goods or services? Asses what the estimated monthly revenue will be.

(d) *Sources of Financing:* If your proposed business will need to borrow money from a bank or other lending institution, you may need to research potential lending sources.

(e) *Profitability Analysis:* This is the "bottom line" for the proposed business. Given the costs and revenue analysis above, will your business bring in enough revenue to cover operating expenses? Will it break even, lose money or make a profit? Is there anything you can do to improve the bottom line?

7. **Analysis of Operating Costs** (Includes salary, taxes, interest, etc.)

(a) The breakdown of the expected operating cost including the proportional overhead expenses calculated for various levels of output or development.

 (i) based pm estimated costs;

 (ii) by comparison with a society which has already carried out a similar project taking into account the cost variations caused by differences in size, location, structure of membership and efficiency in management.

(b) The comparison of differing methods with respect to operating costs.

8. **Analysis of Expected Benefits**

The assessment of added revenue gained from the project or of the expected decrease in cost or improvement in service.

9. **Final Assessment**

(a) The comparison of the increased operating cost with the additional revenue expected (break-even graph).

(b) The influence of the new project on the overall profitability of the society.

(c) The reasons which would make the project feasible despite a decrease in profitability, for instance, the long-term effect on the development of the society.

10. **Appendix**

The appendix should include all those documents, statistics, tenders, drawings to which the text of the feasibility study refers.

Example: Study of the possibilities of expanding a co-operative marketing society

(a) what is the present economic situation of the society?

(i) area of operation, membership.
(ii) Activities, turnover.
(iii) Management and staff.
(iv) Balance sheet and other records.

(b) Is there scope for an expansion of the established activities?

(i) by increasing the membership:

- Are there farmers in the area of operation who are eligible for membership but who are not yet members?

  What is the degree of competition from other marketing institutions in the area?

  What can the society do to attract these farmers despite competition? Can it improve services or give better prices?

(ii) by increasing the area of operation:

- Are there co-operative marketing societies already working in adjoining areas? If so, is an amalgamation feasible of possible?
- What other marketing institutions have established themselves in the adjoining areas, and could the society competed with them?
- What effect would the increased average distance between member and society have on he marketing costs?

(iii) by increasing the turnover per member:

- Are the present members completely loyal to the society? If not, what can be done to improve this situation? Does the possibility of introducing delivery contracts exist?
- Can the society initiate a scheme by which he members increase their production, e.g. new farming methods?

(c) Is an expansion along the current lines desirable? Can the market absorb more produce without a significant fall in price?

(d) Is there scope for expansion by taking up new activities?

(i) by marketing other farming products not yet covered?

- What other crop or animal product is produced in the area in sufficient quantity to give a basis for organized marketing?
- For which of these products is there a suitable market?
- What competition would the society have to face in this field?

(iii) by taking up other activities such as credit, supply, or other services:

- For which of these activities is there a sufficient demand among members or prospective members?
- What competition would the society have to face in any of these fields?

(e) Would the society be able to cope with an expansion in connection with:

(i) top management?

- Is the present management capable of taking on additional functions? If not, are there suitable facilities for further training? And would the present management be able and willing to undergo such training?
- Is the present management willing to shoulder new responsibilities? If not, would and increase in salary act as an incentive?
- Would it be possible and feasible to replace the present management with more experienced persons?

(ii) staff?

- Is the present staff adequate in quantity and quality to cope with an increase in work and duties?
- Are there staff training facilities?
- Can the society recruit additional experienced staff?

(iii) facilities?

- Are the present facilities of the society adequate for additional functions with regard to space, equipment and transport?
- What new investments would be necessary? And what would be the cost?
- What are the possibilities of securing the necessary finance?

What sources are available?

(f) How would the increased costs compare with the additional revenue? Is the overall profitability of the society maintained, increased, decreased or endangered?

Merits of Feasibility Studies to Cooperatives

1. Whenever a new cooperative is to be organized, the scope for the viability and survival of such cooperative can be predicted.
2. Whenever cooperatives open new branches or offices, the success of such new units could be predicted accurately by cooperatives.
3. In raising deposits and mobilising resources, feasibility studies can help the cooperatives by suggesting new methods and measures.
4. Sick units and dormant cooperatives can be revived by using feasibility studies.
5. Cooperatives work under competition. What type of competition they face could be ascertained by feasibility studies.
6. The relations of the consumers and the members of cooperatives could be examined by this method. Their problems could also be solved.
7. Reactions and attitudes of Government towards their co-operatives could be predicted by this method of research.
8. Whenever cooperatives introduce new products the success of such new products can be predicted by this method.

9. The market share of bigger cooperatives can be surveyor and steps can be suggested to increase the market share in future, by this research.

Viability Studies

A viability study is an economic analysis of the past and present performance of an enterprise, a department or a special project, of the soundness of its financial structure and economic basis, of its competitiveness, and of the capabilities and efficiency of its management. It is based on the figures obtainable from the accounts of the enterprise and from any supplementary statistics available.

Viability norms and applications may vary from cooperatives to cooperatives. Such variations may be as follows:

(a) *Cooperative Banks:* For cooperative banks, agricultural credit cooperatives and cooperatives which are undertaking banking business the viability norms will be based mainly on the banking services undertaken and customer attraction aspects.

(b) *Producers' Cooperatives:* For producers' cooperatives like agricultural producers' cooperatives, manufacturing cooperatives, weavers' cooperatives, etc the viability norms can be based on production efficiency, operational efficiency, input-output relations, and cost considerations.

(c) *Service Cooperatives:* For service cooperatives like consumer cooperatives, cooperative supermarkets, etc the viability indicators are customer satisfaction, efficient customer service and price considerations.

(d) *Marketing Cooperatives:* Marketing cooperatives are one of the prominent cooperative organisations. Their viability can be decided on the basis of their operational efficiency, marketing services undertaken; price provided to producers and input services provided.

(e) *Cooperative Training Centers:* For such institutes the viability is decided by factors like number of training programmes conducted, quality of training programmes, efficiency of training instructors and the managerial abilities inculcated by such institutions.

In general, viability norms for all types of cooperatives can be fixed on the following criteria:

1. *Organisational Aspects:* The general structure of the society, its organisation, activities, volume of business and membership. The society should have adequate membership and it should have enough number of activities to satisfy the needs of the members. Later stage the society can increase its number of activities. Likewise, the volume of transaction is an important aspect. The society should have adequate volume of business to manage the recurring costs of the society. Any society must attain a break-even analysis within three years of its starting.

2. *The financial structure:* Any cooperative to be viable should be strong in its financial basis. The ultimate objective goal of a cooperative should be to stand on its own leg and to be self-reliant in its resources. The other financial aspects are as follows:
   (a) *The solvency and stability of the society:* This denotes that a cooperative should be able to raise its own resources and it should keep its credibility in the eyes of the members, depositors, creditors, government and the public.
   (b) *The self-sufficiency in finance:* This is considered to be one of the most important criteria for the viability of a cooperative. As far as possible, a cooperative should mobilize resources by way of owned funds (consisting of share capital and reserves). When this source is not successful, the cooperative can resort to raising of resources by way of accepting deposits from the members and non-members. Borrowings will lead to dependency on other agencies and a cooperative may have to sacrifice its own financial freedom thereby inviting the interference of such creditors.
   (c) *The capital intensity,* i.e. the relationship of fixed assets to total assets – This factor denotes that a cooperative, in the long run must be able to build strong assets in order to face any financial and business challenges. This will also facilitate the cooperative to face competition in the open market.
3. *The Financial Viability:* A cooperative can attain financial viability by mobilizing its own funds. In addition to such self-reliance in resources a cooperative can attain the financial viability through the following measures:
   (a) *Administrative Cost:* As far as possible a cooperative must try to check the administrative cost to the total cost of operations. Another way of keeping the administrative cost under control is by way of increasing the operational efficiency, volume of business and services by having the same staff structure.
   (b) *Recovery of Loans:* This is one of the significant viability norm for cooperative banking institutions or cooperatives engaged in lending operations. The loans must be recovered in time. Any overdue loan will increase the financial commitment of the cooperative. It will lead to unnecessary locking of capital and the cost will increase by means of paying additional interest for overdue loans. So, an efficient loan recovery measure is a strong indicator for a viable society.
   (c) *Length of Operations:* This denotes the loaning and other service operations of a cooperative is short term or long term in nature. Depending on the length of operations, a cooperative must raise its resources properly. Short term resources should not be employed for long term ventures. Prior planning is necessary in raising resources and deploying the funds.

(d) *Investment of Funds:* As cooperatives are coming under the purview of the central bank of a country (National Bank of Ethiopia), in investing their funds the cooperative has to follow the guidelines given by the central bank of the country. Within the purview of such regulations, a cooperative must invest its funds productively and remuneratively in the form of loans, investments and related aspects.

(e) *Growth and Diversification of Activities:* A cooperative, in order to attain viability must grow year after year as well as it must diversify its operations, having the main objective of fulfilling the basic needs of members. Diversification of functions will ensure a cooperative to distribute the financial and business risks equitably.

(f) *Sources and Costs of Funds:* As discussed earlier, a cooperative must be self-reliant in its resources. While raising the resources it must see that the cost should be cheaper and the overhead charges should be minimum. For example, while raising deposits, a cooperative can concentrate on current deposits and savings deposits, which are cheaper than on completely relying on fixed deposits.

4. *The performance of the society:* Finally, the performance of a cooperative in terms of its profitability, productivity and earning power will decide its viability.

(a) *The profitability:* An enterprise is basically profitable if the income of the period under consideration meets the current expenditure. For the purpose of comparison this relationship can be expressed as:

Income/Expenditure

Absolute profitability is assured if the result is more than 1.0. Relative profitability is indicated by the figures after the decimal point. In the case of co-operative enterprise the relative profitability will normally remain well below 2.0.

The maximum profitability of enterprise is reached if it can achieve the highest revenue with the lowest costs. As co-operatives are restricted in their revenue by the principle of 'service at cost', a society can reach its maximum profitability by putting the main emphasis on reaching an optimal cost structure.

(b) *The productivity:* Productivity is measured by an input-output analysis. As the correlating of the output or results of the society to the individual factors of production, i.e. labour, capital and organisation, is extremely difficult, if not impossible, productivity is usually measured as one-factor-productivity (I-III below) or as overall-productivity (IV). The measurement can be based on quantity or value, though it is only feasible to measure the out put in quantity if it has a degree of uniformity. Possible relationships are:

Turnover or output/
W.H. (working hours) or labour costs

Turnover or output/
Interest on the average capital*
Invested in the business.

$$\frac{\text{Turnover or output}}{\text{Average capital invested in the business}}$$

$$\frac{\text{Turnover or output}}{\text{Cost of management (salaries + expenses)}}$$

$$\frac{\text{Turnover or output}}{\text{Total operation cost.}}$$

A co-operative society has reached its maximum productivity if it can realize a maximum of service to the members at minimum cost.

(c) *The earning power:* This is an indicator of success comparing profit with invested capital. The earning power of a co-operative society can be established in two ways:

The earning power of the capital owned:

$$\frac{\text{(patronage refunds and similar payments + interest paid on share-capital + allocations to the reserve fund + estimated additional benefits to members in the form of price advantages compared to the market)} \times 100}{\text{average capital owned i.e. equity capital, during the period considered}}$$

II the overall earning power:

$$\frac{\text{(as under I + interest paid on capital borrowed)} \times 100}{\text{average total capital invested in the society during the period considered.}}$$

The desirable rate of earning power depends, in the case of the individual society, on the degree of risk involved in its activities, though the invested capital should at least earn the current commercial rate of interest on capital borrowed.

24

Preparation of Business Plan in Cooperative Enterprises

Business Plan

A business plan is a written document that contains information, an organisation that has collected converted into comprehensible and workable plans that can be understood by all parties involved with the business. All aspects concerning the business are addressed by the business plans, including what, why, how, when and where of the business opportunities, as well as all the activities, goals and strategies thereof.

This is a well written statement which outlines the major activities of the business and any future plans for the business. This will act as a guideline when various annual operational budgets are formulated. Business plan manly is presented to financial institutions when sourcing finance. Before releasing their funds, the financiers would want an assurance from the business that it is a going concern and what ever project they want to venture in will be viable.

Business plan is supposed to involve all line managers and employees of an organisation. The use of expert help may be important but the entrepreneur's own input is of vital importance as the plan should contain achievable targets of which the owners and employees are capable of setting.

Business plan should be based on achievable assumptions. As the plan relates to the future there is a need to make a careful assessment of the current and future economic and political conditions which may have a direct impact on the operations of the business. Targets set should be achievable and supported with previous achievements made by the business.

There is no universal way of producing a business plan but here are some of the important sections which are supposed to be found in an ideal business plan.

The uses of and reasons for a business plan:

- It gives direction to the business management and activities
- It helps to identify objectives, problems and also opportunities
- Performance standards are set
- Performance is evaluated and monitored
- It provides a written business tool that can serve as a decision-making tool
- A backing for obtaining capital or finance
- Both the entrepreneur and employees use the business plan for guidance
- It is used for obtaining new business

BUSINESS PLAN TEMPLATE FOR AGRICULTURAL COOPERATIVE UNIONS

Cover Sheet

This contains the basic information about the cooperative business, such as name of the cooperative business. There is a need to have an attractive cover which will captivate the read to read more from the business plan.

An Executive Summary

This contains a summary of the information which is contained in the overall business plan. As reader may not be able to scrutinize every detail of the plan, the executive summary should present an overview of what information the business plan is going to relate. The executive summary need to be brief as it is just an abbreviated version of the business plan.

Table of Contents

The table of contents is an important section which is always undermined. The table of contents assists the readers of the plan to quickly trace where to find a particular section or a specific issue.

Business Background

It Contains information about the cooperative enterprise or members of the venture team, together with an indication of the contribution of each person to starting or acquiring business. Would be investors, financiers and the future managers of the business are interested in the details in respect of how the idea for the product or service was developed, why it was decide to start or acquire the a business and what process of the business acquisition or start up entailed. The background gives the appraisal or the financier an understanding of the original mission envisaged by the cooperative enterprise and whether there has been any positive or negative deviation from those original objectives of the business. The business background section contains basic information about the proposed business the projects which the business require to venture in. The contents are:

- the name of the current owner of the business;

- location of the business;
- objectives of the business;
- the reasons for sale of the business;
- the description of any proposed project;
- registered address of the business;
- owner's personal details; and
- business form.

A well written background helps to give the appraiser of the business plan the impression that the bidder knows the operations of the business.

I. Description of the Cooperative

1. Profile of the Union
   - 1.1. Name of the Union:
   - 1.2. Location: Region Zone Woreda
   - 1.3. Date of establishment:
   - 1.4. No. of households in the area of operation:
   - 1.5. No. of Member primaries:
   - 1.6. Individual members: Male Female Total
2. The competitors
   - 2.1. Who are your competitors?
     - (a) Private traders
     - (b) Wholesalers
     - (c) Others (specify)
   - 2.2. What are the strategies used to face competition.
     - (a) Purchasing efficiency (inputs)
     - (b) Selling efficiency (output)
     - (c) Marketing services
     - (d) Price mechanism
3. Competencies
   - 3.1. Who are your customers?
     - (a) Individuals
     - (b) Private institutions
     - (c) Government institutions
     - (d) Cooperatives
     - (e) Others (specify)
   - 3.2. What is the mechanism used by you to verify customers satisfaction?
     - (a) Daily complaint by the customers
     - (b) Suggestion box
     - (c) Grievance day (weekly/fortnightly/monthly)
     - (d) Complaint by phone, letter correspondence, etc.

3.3. How many institutional customers you have at present? ________

3.4. What type of institutional customers are they?
   (a) Wholesalers
   (b) Private companies
   (c) Government organisations
   (d) Cooperatives
   (e) Others (specify)

3.5. What are the steps taken by you to enlist more institutional customers?

3.6. What are the future businesses you would like to add? (mention business like consumer activities, transport services, etc).

II. Organisational Analysis

1. Committee members

1.1. Name the types of committees of your union.
   (a)
   (b)
   (c)

1.2. How many members are there in each committee?
   (a) ____________ committee: ______________ members
   (b) ____________ committee: ______________ members
   (c) ____________ committee: ______________ members

1.3. Give the educational qualification and experience of committee members.

Sl. No.	Committee Member/Name	Level of Education	Experience as Committee Member	Women Participation		Remarks
				Number	%	

1.4. What are the steps taken by you to organise new primaries and to enlist more primaries as members?

1.5. During last three years how many general assembly meetings were held?

Year	Number of Meetings	Date of Meetings	Number Attended	Remarks

1.6. During last three years how many committee meetings were held?

Year	Number of Meetings	Date of Meetings	Number Attended	Remarks

1.7. Give the details of training programme undergone by the committee members.

Sl. No.	Type of Training	Conducted by Whom	No. of Participants	Duration

1.8. Give the details of your future training programmes for the coming three years.

Year I

1.

2.

Year II

1.

2.

Year III

1.

2.

1.9. Give details on number of exposure visits arranged.

Sl. No.	Visit (Place)	Conducted by Whom	No. of Participants	Duration

1.10. Give the details of your future Exposure visits for the coming three years.

Year I

1.

2.

Year II

1.

2.

Year III

1.

2.

2. Manager and Staff

2.1. Give the details of the staff (manager & other employees)

Sl. No.	Name and Designation	Age	Qualification (Education)	Experience (Years)

2.2. Give the details of future recruitment of staff.

Year/ Sl.No.	Nature of job	Number of Staff Required	Age	Required Qualification (Education)	Experience (Years)
Year I					
Year II					
Year III					

2.3. What is the timeframe fixed to recruit new staff? (How many staff to be recruited in each forthcoming year?)

2.4. Training programmes undergone by the staff

Sl. No.	Type of Training	Conducted by Whom	No. of Participants	Duration

2.5. Give the details of your future training programmes (for employees) for the coming three years.

Year I

1.

2.

Year II

1.

2.

Year III

1.
2.

2.6. Give details of exposure visits

Sl. No.	Visit (Place)	Conducted by Whom	No. of Participant	Duration

2.7. Give the details of your future exposure visits (for employees) for the coming three years.

Year I

1.
2.

Year II

1.
2.

Year III

1.
2.

III. Marketing and Sales Analysis

1. Growth strategy (monthwar and yearwar)

1.1. What was the growth strategy followed by you for the last three years in terms of input and out marketing?

Year	Input Marketing		Output Marketing	
	Target	Achievement	Target	Achievement
Year I				
Year II				
Year III				

1.2. What is the future growth potential proposed by you for the future three years.

Year	Input Marketing		Output Marketing	
	Quantity	Value	Quantity	Value
Year I				
Year II				
Year III				

2. Procurement Strategy
   2.1. Procurement timings every day
   2.2. Fixation of procurement responsibility to each staff
   2.3. Purchasing/procurement target

Year	Procurement	
	Target	Achievement
Year I		
Year II		
Year III		

2.4. Purchasing/procurement plan for future three years.

Year	Procurement	
	Quantity	Value
Year I		
Year II		
Year III		

2.5. Storage facility (existing)

Sl. No.	Storage		Capacity (in sq.mts)	Type (Modern/Traditional)
	Owned	Hired		

2.6. Future plan to construct/hiring/increase the storage capacity (for three years – 2007, 2008, 2009)

Sl. No.	Type of Store	Timeframe to Complete the Process (Year)
1.	Owned	
2.	Hired	
3.	Capacity increase	

2.6. Steps to avoid wastage, pilferage during procurement stage and storage stage. (state the steps taken by you in this regard)

3. Pricing Strategy

3.1. Mention the price strategy followed by you for the last three years.

Year	Commodity	Open Market Price	Cooperative Price	Diffrence
Year I	1			
	2			
	3			
	4			
	5			
Year II	1			
	2			
	3			
	4			
	5			
Year III	1			
	2			
	3			
	4			
	5			

3.2. Mention the price strategy for the future three years.

Year	Commodity	Cooperative Price
Year I	1	
	2	
	3	
	4	
	5	
Year II	1	
	2	
	3	
	4	
	5	
Year III	1	
	2	
	3	
	4	
	5	

3.3. Who decides the pricing policy for input purchasing and output sales?
 (a) Committee members
 (b) Manager
 (c) Both committee member and managers
 (d) Any other, specify.

3.4. What are the future pricing strategies you propose to follow to face competition from private traders?

3.5. Do you have any future plan to create price Fluctuation Fund or similar arrangements to face price loss during input marketing and output marketing?

4. Sales Strategy

4.1. What are the market arrivals of various commodities? (for current year)

Sl. No.	Commodity	Harvest Month	Market Arrival Month	Remarks
1.				
2.				
3.				
4.				
5.				
6.				

4.2. Market arrivals of various commodities proposed for future three years?

Sl.No.	Commodity	Harvest Month	Market Arrival Month	Remarks
Year I				
1.				
2.				
3.				
4.				
5.				
6.				
Year II				
1.				
2.				
3.				
4.				
5.				
6.				

(Contd...)

Sl.No.	Commodity	Harvest Month	Market Arrival Month	Remarks
Year III				
1.				
2.				
3.				
4.				
5.				
6.				

4.3. What is the purchase/procurement made by you for the current year?

Year/ Sl.No.	Commodity	Quantity (in qtnls.)	Value	Remarks (in Birr)
1.				
2.				
3.				
4.				
5.				
6.				

4.4. What is the proposed purchase/procurement for the future three years?

Year/ Sl.No.	Commodity	Quantity (in qtnls.)	Value (in Birr)	Remarks
Year I				
1.				
2.				
3.				
4.				
5.				
6.				
Year II				
1.				
2.				
3.				
4.				
5.				
6.				

(Contd...)

Year/ Sl.No.	Commodity	Quantity (in qtnls.)	Value (in Birr)	Remarks
Year III				
1.				
2.				
3.				
4.				
5.				
6.				

4.5. What is the incentive (commission) given to the sales force (manager, committee members, salesmen)?

4.6. What is the future plan to give incentive to sales force?

5. Transport and Communication Services

5.1. What is the transport arrangement made by you for input marketing and output marketing?

Year	Type of Transport		Transport Charges Paid (if hired)	Remarks
	Owned	Hired		
Year I				
Year II				
Year III				

5.2. Do you have any future plan to purchase your own vehicle? Yes/No

If yes, give details.

5.3. What is the current communication facilities you have?

(a) Phone facility
(b) Mobile Phone
(c) No phone/mobile facility

5.3. What is the future (Yearwar) communication facilities youwould like to add?

1. Phone facility
2. Mobile Phone

IV. Financial Analysis

1. Members Stake

1.1. What is the value of a share in the cooperative union?

1.2. What is the minimum shares fixed to become the member of the union?

1.3. Do you have any future plan to increase the share contribution by primary SACCOs to the union? Yes/No.

If yes, explain the scheme yearwar.
Year I -
Year II-
Year III -

1.4. What is the amount of compulsory savings prescribed for primary SACCOs?

1.5. Is there any future plan to increase the compulsory savings? Yes/No.
If yes, explain the scheme yearwar.
Year I -
Year II-
Year III -

1.6. Capital base

Year	Share Capital	Reserve/Retained Earnings	Compulsory Deposits	Borrowings from NGO	Borrowings from Govt.	Borrowings from Commercial Banks
Year I						
Year II						
Year III						

1.6.1. Give your future plan of increasing capital base.

Year	Share Capital	Reserve/ Retained Earnings	Compulsory Deposits	Borrowings from NGO	Borrowings from Govt	Borrowings from Commercial Banks
Year I						
Year II						
Year III						

V. Cost and Profitability Analysis

1. Break-even Analysis

1.1. In which year the union started functioning?

1.2. In which year the union started earning profit?

1.3. Mention the profit/loss for the union since its establishment.

Sl. No.	Year	Profit	Loss	Remarks
1.	First Year			
2.	Second Year			
3.	Third Year			
4.	Fourth Year			
5.	Fifth Year			
6.	Sixth Year			

1.4. Proposed profit for future three years.

Sl.No.	Year	Profit
1.	2007	
2.	2008	
3.	2009	

1.5. Mention the income areas of the union.

Year	Income Sources				Total
	Input Distribution	Grain Marketing	Marketing Charges	Others	
Year I					
Year II					
Year III					

1.6. Proposed income areas of the union.

Year	Income Sources				Total
	Input Distribution	Grain Marketing	Marketing Charges	Others	
Year I					
Year II					
Year III					

2. Cost Analysis

2.1. Give the details of the following cost/expenditure areas.

Year	Expenditure Areas							Total
	Rent	Salary	Hiring (Vehicle)	Office Exp. (Electricity, Tax, etc.)	Travel (Perdiem)	Marketing Cost	Other	
Year I								
Year II								
Year III								

2.2. Give the details of the following cost/expenditure areas for future 3 years

Year	Expenditure Areas							Total
	Rent	Salary	Hiring (Vehicle)	Office Exp. (Electricity, Tax, etc.)	Travel (perdiem)	Marketing Cost	Others	
Year I								
Year II								
Year III								

3. Profit Analysis

3.1. Pattern of the distribution of profit

Year	Profit	Dividend	Reserves	Retained Earnings	Others
Year I					
Year II					
Year III					

3.2. Pattern of the distribution of profit for future 3 years.

Year	Profit	Dividend	Reserves	Retained Earnings	Others
Year I					
Year II					
Year III					

4. Ratio Analysis

1. Give the following statements for calculating ratios
1. Budget and actual statement for the years 2004, 2005 and 2006.
2. Profit and loss account (Income & expenditure statement) for the years 2004, 2005 and 2006.
3. Balance sheet for the years 2004, 2005 and 2006.

25

Project Management for Cooperative Entrepreneurs

Cooperatives undertaking special projects such as a move or major expansion should distinguish between "operations" and "project." I will make such a distinction, present a view of project management, and suggest how it can function within our cooperative businesses.

The challenge of managing a retail natural foods cooperative is one that is steeped in many dimensions, ranging from the daily detail to the large long-term vision, from employee relations to member relations, from customer service to serving a board of directors, from community relations and market presentation to systems development. Often, to those aware of these needs, the list of priorities can be overwhelming.

While some of these challenges can be viewed as unique to cooperatives, they are not unlike the general challenges of management. In any context, it is important to keep the management process simple in order to be effective. Partly for this reason, it is useful to distinguish between operations management and project management.

"Operations" vs. "Project"

Operations represents ongoing activities or flow, defined through systems and formula. The daily operations of a grocery store are a series of related systems that have an ongoing and sustaining synthesizing energy: buying, receiving, stocking, merchandising, front end, accounting, etc. It is a struggle to build successful systems (and they always need refinement and modifications) that will yield a perpetual or near-perpetual process of ongoing desired results. Once those results are forthcoming and somewhat stable, a basic formula is in place: For every dollar of sales, x per cent goes to cost of goods, x per cent to labour, x per cent to other expenses, and x per cent to net profit.

Of course there is constant change within these operational systems and formulas, but the basic structure maybe sustained. "Operations" has a life of its own. Complacency is dangerous, and analysis, review, training, change, and innovation should be built into the formula. The formula will require fixing from time to time. Generally, the more the operational formula encompasses — such as market and financial awareness, opportunities for innovation, focus on the big picture, mission, and vision — the stronger the business will be.

A project, on the other hand, represents change or innovation and is temporary or short term. Projects are usually untested and risky. Unlike ongoing operations, a project has a specific beginning and end. A project has a clear goal to achieve, and the achievement of that goal represents the end of a successful project. Of course, many projects can also end in failure. Projects can range from short and small to long and large. Development of a new system for cutting cheese, creation of a new newsletter format, introduction of a new product line, development of an annual promotion calendar, and moving to or opening a new store can be viewed as projects.

Healthy "operations" should generate, support, and integrate "projects." Unlike manufacturing production, where research and development have a clearer and more recognized role, wholesale and retail distribution often overlook innovation because daily operations dominate. Project development can thus be a valuable means for operations/distribution to develop and keep innovation as priority. A healthy "operations" should have lots of productive and successful projects continually beginning and ending. As these projects become part of the ongoing formula, there is less need to label them as projects.

All projects have a number of things in common: A clear goal or objective, a timeline, a "sources and uses' budget, and their own energy, excitement and support. Most importantly, they all have a need for effective project management.

Four important aspects of good project management are:

1. the effective handling of people;
2. always maintaining a focus on exactly what needs to be done next;
3. honestly assessing yourseif and your situation at all times; and
4. remembering that you need all the help you can get from within and outside of your co-op.

Why project management?

Cooperatives of all sizes must be able to respond rapidly to today's changing economic conditions in order to survive and prosper. Private business has successfully used project management to adapt to different conditions. There are clearly many opportunities and needs for project management within cooperative businesses. We can illustrate the primary features and concerns of project management by focusing on relocation/ expansion of retail natural food cooperatives.

Project management is a term that originated in the engineering and construction fields. It was originally technical, rigid, specialized, and confining in its usage. In recent years, project management has broadened in acknowledging and emphasizing the process and human factors involved in projects. Cooperatives might find value and special relevance in this broader concept at a developmental level. Cooperatives often are slow to respond or make decisions, and tend to be overly bureaucratic. The basic tools ofproject management, properly used, can help cooperatives overcome these tendencies and be more responsive.

By clearly defining the process involved in relocation and expansions and by developing high quality project management, cooperatives will be better able to compete and survive in the marketplace. New stores will be opened in a shorter timeline, without reinventing the wheel each time.

The Basics

Project management can be defined as the planning, organizing, directing and controlling of resources, aimed at achieving a relatively short-term goal or objective. The standards for successful project management center around time, cost and performance.

The performance standards are clearly and briefly specified in the project goal and should be reviewed throughout the project at or before key decision points.

Development Timeline

Stage I	Feasibility	Commitment, planning, strengthening, positioning, initial contacts with lenders, site search and securing	(3 months - 3 years)
Stage II	Preparing for Leasehold Improvements or Construction Design, bids Financing		(2-6 months)
Stage Ill	Leasehold Improvements or Construction		(2 - 6 months)
Stage IV	Prepare for Opening		(1 - 2 months)

Note: End of Stage I — Sign lease or purchase agreement with contingencies
End of Stage II— Close on financing, remove contingencies, final decision point. No turning back!

The primary tools of project management are a timeline and a budget.

A realistic project timeline is a very helpful planning tool. The timeline will be modified a number of times, but it should be developed and used from the beginning of the project. Relocation/expansion projects typically have four stages, with each stage having a number of components — many of them occurring simultaneously. (See sidebar.)

"Sources and Uses" Budget

The "sources and uses" development budget is the simplest and most powerful of tools, yet it is so often forgotten, neglected, or misunderstood. (See my article and sidebar on "Sources & Uses Development Budget," CG#33, March-April 1991.) It is simply a listing of all the sources and uses of funds, with total funds equaling total uses. Generally, any of the sources can be applied to cover any of the uses.

In the case of a co-op retail relocation project, sources include: the co-op's cash reserve (or a large portion of that reserve), new equity from members, member loans, donations, sale of equipment, landlord's contribution, vendor loans, vendor credit (extended terms), community or city funds (loans or grants), regional loan funds, the National Cooperative Bank, and local banks. The owner's share (i.e., the co-op's) should be 25-40 per cent of the total, and the owner's share plus subordinated funds should be 40-60 per cent of the total.

The uses include acquisition, construction or leasehold improvements, equipment, additional inventory, fees (consulting, architect, legal, financing) and project management costs, start-up promotional, staffing, and training costs, business disruption, occupancy costs prior to opening, moving costs, working capital allowance to cover first year operating losses, and a 10 per cent overrun alllowance. There are standard guidelines for ratios and costs per square foot that are used to create a sources and uses budget.

The key is to be creative. List as many sources (and uses) as you can. Costs (and hidden costs) are almost always higher than you originally plan for. Play with the numbers. After an initial draft of sources and uses has been created, develop a financial pro forma and model for at least years 1, 2 and 3 of the new operation. The pro forma should include income statements, cash flow, capital budgets, balance sheets, and a special section that shows the co-op's ability to service debt.

It is important to acknowledcge and again emphasize the role of creativity among the qualities of successful project management in cooperatives. Relocation/expansion projects are extremely challenging for cooperatives, requiring creativity, innovation, and commitment to change in order to overcome all the hurdles that will be encountered along the way. The project timeline and "sources and uses" budget are planning tools and management tools that allow you to manipulate and massage the plan. They enable you to see the whole project on one or two sheets of paper. I view them as stretching tools, enabling you and your group of supporters or potential supporters to expand to the possibilities and realities of the project.

The Job

What does it take to be a successful project manager for a cooperative relocation/expansion project? Foremost, it requires a person with enormous dedication and perseverance to see a project through from start to a successful finish. These projects are very challenging and consuming of energy and resources. Skilled management is required to develop and effectively utilise those resources in a responsible and timely manner, while building and sustaining positive energy throughout the project.

The obvious candidate for a relocation/expansion project manager is the co-op's general manager. A general manager should be able to provide the required leadership and focus the project requires. However, the general manager is also responsible for ensuring continued strong performance from the current store as well as planning for the operation of the new store. If the general manager is to be the project manager, then a capable assistant manager or management team will need to assume a large share of the general manager's duties, as the project requires 25 per cent, then 50 per cent, then over 75 per cent of the general manager's time.

If the general manager is not the project manager, then the general manager (or management) should hire or contract with a project manager who will report directly to the general manager. Potential candidates include employees (preferably mid-management), professional project managers or consultants, or a candidate found or recruited through an open hiring.

Key Qualities

A project manager for a retail cooperative relocation project should have skills and qualities in the following areas:

- *Organisation and decision making:* Be well organised and able to achieve timely and successful results. Demonstrate an ability to manage multiple tasks and focus, both within the project and in addition to the project. Be able to work independently and be selfmotivated, without becoming lost, isolated, or unaccountable. Be a creative and effective problem solver and a timely decision maker, knowing when and how to seek appropriate support, both within and outside the co-op. Seek and coordinate professional advice and services.
- *Leader and champion:* Serve as a strong and credible leader and champion for the project. Be an effective team builder throughout the project, promoting excitement and good energy among a diverse group of stakeholders and supporters. Respect, praise, and cultivate all participants. Motivate, and push the project as needed, again, with respect, honesty, positive energy, and a desire to learn more every day.
- *People skills:* Demonstrate effective people skills and clear communication to all involved in the project. Be flexible and responsive. Delegate responsibility and authority with successful results. Be an effective negotiator and fund raiser at all opportunities.

- *Analysis and financial management:* Bring appropriate analysis into the project as a means to test and support your good intuitivejudgment. Have a full overview of the project's financial goals and status in your head, and provide effective and timely financial management of the project.
- Commitment and humor: Offer strong commitment to your task, combined with common sense. Have or acquire an abundant sense of humor. Enjoy yourself as well as others.

Formidable Challenges

After working as a project manager, and also providing consultation and support to other project managers, we can conclude this review by commenting on some of the major challenges a project manager will encounter:

- Combining project management with one's regular job. Or more aptly, adding a project manager role to a job that is already full time or more. Some general managers are able to do this and effectively delegate. Respect your abilities. don't take on the imossible.
- Becoming isolated from the organisation. A project manager needs access to and support from operational resources, and should seek to involve all elements of the organisation at different stages of the project. The organisation needs to take ownership of its project.
- Managing stress and sustaining positive energy. Project managers can't sacrifice themselves as martyrs to the project without inviting failure. Take care of yourself during a project that seems to lengthen each day. The project manager sets the tone and by serving as an example should encourage other participants to take care of themselves. When the project is finally over and the new store opens, the real demanding work begins. Be ready.
- Developing clear channels of accountability and support within the co-op. The project manager needs to be fully empowered to do their job. There should be clarity as to the roles within the organisation, the key decision point in the project timeline, and who makes those decisions.
- Developing an effective base of outside support and assistance for a project manager. An informal "development team" composed of a few key people within the co-op and a handful of outside supporters who have particular areas of strength and expertise can be loosely brought together on an as needed basis by the project manager to provide support and honest critique. The makeup of this development team can fluctuate and depends in part on the current stage of the project. The group itself has no formal authority, but serves as a valuable resource to the project a project manager who is confident and secure with their own abilities and limitations can gain immeasurably by openly seeking assistance and support from a variety of sources. A project manager needs to organise, facilitate and build their own support team.

26

Synchronising Cooperative Entrepreneurship and Social Innovation

The Operating Hybrid Synergies Behind

Economic development originates and fosters in relation to the strength and health of the local entrepreneurship and depends on the rate of its generation and equally to the intensity of its sense of social responsibility, its innovation quotient and its index of management capabilities. Entrepreneurial density, innovative propensity and management capability in the society in a particular period determine the character and future of economic development. Entrepreneurs are rarely mentioned in connection with cooperative development, which reflects the state of entrepreneurship in conventional economic thinking, where entrepreneurs are more often than not a missing category.

Cooperative Entrepreneurship – Framework

Cooperative entrepreneurship denotes the application of entrepreneurship talents and outcome to the cooperative institutions. Unlike the independent, individual entrepreneurs, cooperative entrepreneurs vary in nature and component. Cooperative entrepreneurship refers to a role or a set of roles whose influences are conditioned by characteristics of group members. The personalities of the entrepreneurs are influenced by the situation. But the true entrepreneurship though individual oriented has got a collective group foundation in cooperatives. Cooperative entrepreneurs collectively engage in the enterprise activity for the economic interest of themselves. Cooperative entrepreneurship should function collectively and should have courage to stand up when something wrong is done and should be capable of owning a mistake openly. Such cooperative entrepreneurs will not only succeed but will also make the cooperatives a succeed story in the world.

Cooperative Advantage Through Entrepreneurship

The cooperative advantages that will accrue out of cooperative entrepreneurship are: Monopoly/Market failure; Transaction cost; Interlinked market; Uncertainty reduction; and Innovations.

Stages of Cooperative Entrepreneurship

Robert and Weiss (1988) have explained the process of cooperative entrepreneurship into the following four stages.

1. *Opportunity Search:* This stage consists of identifying the opportunities, no matter what their sources. When cooperatives are doing traditional services for a long time, they have to search for new opportunities for their growth, development, and sustainability.
2. *Opportunity Assessment:* After searching the opportunity, the practicability of the opportunity is to be assessed. Such opportunity assessment may be useful for the future members of the cooperatives.
3. *Opportunity Development:* This is to decide which of the opportunities emerging from assessment should be developed further. The high potential opportunities are critically analyzed and final action required is identified.
4. *Opportunity Pursued (Implementation):* This is to indicate the implementation process and methods of the opportunities selected and developed.

The Six Stages of Social Innovation

There are identified six stages that take ideas from inception to impact. These stages are not always sequential (some innovations jump straight into practice or even scale), and there are feedback loops between them. They can also be thought of as overlapping spaces, with distinct cultures and skills. They provide a useful framework for thinking about the different kinds of support that innovators and innovations need in order to grow.

1. Prompts

All innovations start with a central idea. But the idea itself is often prompted by an experience or event or new evidence which brings to light a social need or injustice. Some organisations initiate the prompts themselves - using feedback systems to identify possible problems. Creative leaders can use symbols and demonstrations to prompt social imagination. In many cases, research, mapping and data collection are used to uncover problems, as a first step to identifying solutions. The prompts are triggers for action. They may take the form of imperatives; that some action is needed without specifying what that action is. Those running ideas competitions for the crowd sourcing of innovations say that it is the stage of framing a good question which is the key to the competition's success. All of the methods that follow are not only prompts, but also steps towards refining the question and generating a solution.

2. Proposals and Ideas

Asking the right question is the first step to finding the right answer. But once the right question has been framed, there are then a series of methods for searching out and suggesting solutions. Some of these methods are specifically designed to encourage creativity and new ideas – such as competitions and prizes, online platforms and idea banks. Others are adapted from neighbouring fields, such as the arts and product design. Open innovation describes the process of harnessing the distributed and collective intelligence of crowds. It is based on a number of principles including: collaboration, sharing, self-organisation, decentralisation, transparency of process and plurality of participants.

3. Proto typing and pilots

Once a promising idea has been proposed, it then needs to be tested in practice. Ideas develop through trial and error, and constant refinement. It's very rare for an idea to emerge fully formed. There are many methods in use for testing ideas out and refining them, ranging from the formal methods of randomised control trials to pilots and experiments. Social entrepreneurs often dive into practice and hope to learn quickly without using formal evaluations or tests, and one of the common themes of contemporary social innovation is that it often works best by moving quickly into practice, rather than spending too long developing detailed plans and strategies.

4. Sustaining

Only a minority of ideas will survive tests and pilots. Even promising ones may simply not be sufficiently effective, or sufficiently cost effective. When an idea or cluster of ideas is new, there are likely to be many competing alternatives. Usually just a few of these survive. Public feedback may be key, but evaluation methods also have a vital role to play since there is always an element of judgement in determining what counts as success or failure. But the ability to judge innovations, and screen out a high proportion, is critical to the success of an innovation system. Trying to keep too many ideas alive may starve the best ideas of the resources they need to be sustained.

5. Scaling and diffusion

There are many methods for growing social innovations – from organisational growth and franchising to collaboration and looser diffusion. Some of these involve scaling – a metaphor taken from manufacturing. Others are better understood as more organic – 'cut and graft', with ideas adapting as they spread, rather than growing in a single form. Indeed, most social ideas have spread not through the growth of an organisation but through emulation. The supply of ideas and demand for them tend to co-evolve: there are relatively few fields where there are straightforward solutions which can simply be spread. There are currently pressures to promote mergers and takeovers within the grant economy. However, in a distributed economy a different conception of scale is needed, one that focuses on economies of information and communication and structures that can deliver that. Organisations within the social economy have less compulsion to organisational growth and more towards collaborative networking as a means of sharing innovation.

6. Systematic change

The most transformative innovations have been the ones that combine many elements in a new way. The welfare state combines legal rights, service delivery systems, assessment tools and tax collection models. Systemic innovation is very different from innovation in products or services, and usually very different from innovation in business. It involves changes to concepts and mindsets as well as to economic flows: systems only change when people think and see in new ways. It involves changes to power, replacing old power holders with new ones. And it usually involves all four sectors – business, government, civil society and the household. Systemic innovations can be suddenly pushed forward by a crisis, or a disruptive technology. More often they are the result of slow but cumulative processes entailing changing infrastructures, behaviours and cultures.

The Hybrid Synergy Process of Cooperative Entrepreneurship

The following figure clearly presents the hybrid synergy process of cooperative entrepreneurship.

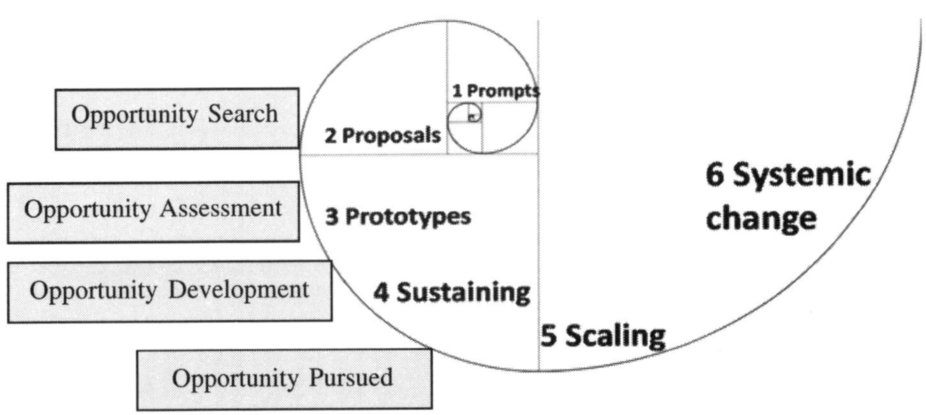

Fig 26.1: **Hybrid Synergy Process of Cooperative Entrepreneurship**

The different stages of cooperative entrepreneurship and various stages of social innovation process are merged together and the hybrid process can be the hybrid synergy process of cooperative entrepreneurship.

27

ICA in Promoting Cooperative Entrepreneurship

Role of ICA in Promoting Cooperative Entrepreneurship

International Cooperative Alliance (ICA) was started in 1895. It has its regional offices at Geneva (for Europe), New Delhi (for Asia), Nairobi (for East Africa), Burkina Faso (for West Africa) and Costa Rica (for Americas). An additional office is opened at Singapore. The headquarters was shifted from London to Geneva during 1995. The Each Africa's office was shifted from Tanzania to Kenya in the year 1998. At present ICA's membership exceed 230 member organisations. ICA admits only member countries National Federations as its member.

The objectives of the ICA are as follows:

1. To provide a forum for the world cooperatives.
2. To expand the cooperative movement in all countries.
3. To concentrate on cooperative education and training of member countries.
4. Empowerment of women.
5. Special attention to youth.
6. Organising regional and global level seminars and conferences on cooperative areas.
7. Publication of cooperative literature and periodicals.

What Does ICA Do?

ICA's priorities and activities center on promoting and defending cooperative identity, ensuring that cooperative enterprise is recognised form of enterprise that is able to compete in the market place.

1. ICA raises awareness about cooperatives. It disseminates information materials including the ICA Digest and other communication means and jointly celebrates with the United Nations the International Day of Cooperatives every year.
2. ICA is the voice of the cooperative movement – ICA has special status with a number of multinational institutions including the UN agencies, Council of Europe, the regional development banks, and others.
3. ICA ensures that the right policy environment exists to enable cooperatives to grow and prosper. It helps its members in their lobbying for new legislations and more appropriate administrative procedures that respect the cooperative model, its principles and values.
4. ICA provides its members with key contacts and information on best practice. It facilitates contacts between cooperatives for trading purpose and intelligence sharing in a wide range of areas. It organises meeting, workshops to address key issues affecting cooperatives and allows discussion among cooperators from around the world.
5. ICA provides technical assistance to cooperatives. Through its development programmes at global and regional levels, it promotes capacity building, advice, and financial support to the cooperative movement.
6. It ensures that right policy environment exists to enable cooperatives to grow and prosper.

Fields of Action

Following are the important field activities emphasized by the ICA for the cooperatives:

1. *Food and nutrition:* The activities of ICA are focused to the increase of food production and offering of nutritious food to the population, especially in developing countries. It has been pointed out that 600 million people in rural areas of the developing countries lack access to land. Re-distribution of land through the cooperatives is suggested to increase food production.
2. *Urbanization and cooperative movement:* It is estimated that by the year 2000, half of the population in the Third World would leave in urban communities. This presupposes the migration of rural population to urban population. Slum improvement is one of the urgent policy areas in developing countries. Here, there is large scope for the cooperatives in the fields of housing cooperatives and consumer credit.
3. *Employment and industry:* Cooperative organisations must offer viable alternatives to other forms of industrial organisations and must undertake labour-intensive production techniques through industrial cooperatives. Industrial cooperatives in urban areas can offer income-generating opportunities for both men and women. Such cooperatives can restrict the rural migration to the urban areas.

4. *Savings, credit and insurance:* The cooperatives must raise considerable part of their resources from the members themselves. Cooperative banks can make contributions to the establishment and expansion of cooperative organisations in a financially sound way. The same is true for cooperative insurance societies.

Priorities for Cooperatives

The following priorities for cooperatives have been laid by the ICA:

1. *Development towards self-reliance:* The governments in developing countries must provide time-bound plans to provide help to the cooperatives. Ultimately, the cooperatives must be self-reliant in financial and other resources.
2. *Democracy:* In an effort to democratize the cooperatives organisations, enlightened membership must be built through cooperative education. In the cooperative educational activities, stress should be laid on the involvement of women.
3. *Involvement of women:* The ICA shall assist in the attainment of true cooperative democracy and to allow the participation of men and women on equal terms. Supporting the programmes for women like literacy campaigns, nutrition education, income generating projects, and developing thrift and loan cooperatives.
4. *Professional management:* Cooperative organisations must improve their services only through professional management. Therefore, an effective system of cooperative staff training is necessary.
5. *Education and training:* The education and training for members as well as committee members are vital for the cooperative performance. Without these, the desired level of quality of popular participation in the control of cooperatives cannot be expected.
6. *Effective personnel policy:* In order to retain the skilled staff, cooperatives must establish comprehensive personnel policies including adequate recruitment and training, competitive salary system, job security and career possibilities.
7. *Promote national and apex organisations:* The promotion of national and apex cooperative organisations is an important part of the development of autonomous cooperatives.
8. *Research:* It is necessary that due attention must be given to the examination of the needs of technical assistance, project identification, feasibility studies, monitoring and evaluation of cooperative programmes.

These elements should be includes in all ICA supported projects, including seminars and conferences.

Part – III

Cases in Cooperative Entrepreneurship

Cases for Cooperative Entrepreneurship

CASE-1

Collective Entrepreneurship as a means for Sustainable Community Development

A Cooperative Case Study in South Africa

Land reform and the support of emerging entrepreneurs is a key, is a key element of South Africa's overall development strategy. Its success will determine the extent to which rural incomes, currently only 20 per cent on average of urban incomes, will increase, and the extent to which food security and political stability will be ensured.

So far, after ten years of democratic government, the results from rural development in South Africa are mixed. The GEM indicated that South Africa has a low entrepreneurial activity rate compared to other low income developing countries (GEM 58). Many communities in rural areas are living in poor conditions. By stimulating economic activities, this problem can be alleviated. Efforts should therefore be to stimulate economic activities by involving members or local entrepreneurs and at the same time keep the generated wealth in the community.

Much emphasis is often placed on the agricultural and the small business sector to create jobs and alleviate poverty in rural areas. These two sectors can undoubtedly make a contribution to economic development as long as obstacles in its way are bridged and the many difficulties faced by entrepreneurs are eliminated or addressed effectively. One way to do this, is for entrepreneurs to form cooperative alliances. Many entrepreneurs in the same industry have been forced by these difficulties to organise and to form cooperatives. Not only does this strengthen the position of small businesses to compete with big businesses and survive, but it also contributes to community development. Earnings produced by cooperatives are returned to the member/owner and the end result is that this wealth is kept within the community. Thereby the goal of job creation and uplifting of communities are reached. Looking at the definition of the cooperative, namely an autonomous association of individuals united voluntarily to meet their common economic, social and cultural needs through jointly owned and democratically controlled enterprises, it is obvious why this is the ideal type of business to support and develop community entrepreneurship. The ability to take advantage of the economies of scale, while retaining individual identity, is appealing to entrepreneurs.

The cooperative will only be successful if it promotes the wealth of its members and provide competitive products and services. This will only be possible if the cooperative can survive, innovate and adjust to changes in the economy. The aforementioned can be achieved if there is an effective combination of the entrepreneurial skills and the cooperative type of business with the advantages it can offer. A prerequisite however is that entrepreneurs should have a knowledge of basic business skills and know how to apply it to their cooperative. The presence of collective entrepreneurship can offer the cooperative the opportunity to capitalize on individual talents together with wisdom and collective energy. All this will contribute to a competitive advantage and a successful cooperative.

In this paper, I focus on the constraint of institutional structures and entrepreneurial skills of farmers and non-farmers in rural areas. I also report results from a survey of socio-economic conditions, farming practices and entrepreneurial orientation conducted in 2005 amongst a cluster of seven communities in South Africa's North-West province. These communities were resettled on its land in 1994 after having been stripped thereof under the previous political regime. In addition to the survey results I also report, as case study, the establishment of a cooperative as an appropriate mechanisms for promoting collective entrepreneurship in the community.

Source with thanks:

Dr Louw van der Walt

Professor in Entrepreneurship
Potchefstroom Business School
North West University
South Africa
Tel: +27 18 299 1365
Fax: +27 18 299 1416
E-mail: pbsjlvdw@puk.ac.za
The Eight West Lake International Confere

CASE-2

Green Cooperatives

A Strategic Approach Developing Women's Entrepreneurship in the Asian and Pacific Region

The Asian and Pacific region is home for over 60 per cent of the world's population and more than 70 per cent of the region's population lives in rural areas and primarily involved in agriculture. Integrating and empowering rural women by promoting women's entrepreneurship in green cooperatives has been recognized as an important approach to alleviate rural poverty and enhancing sustainable rural development. The promotion of women's entrepreneurship in the area of green cooperatives is a vital approach where women can play pioneering role for income generating activities, employment opportunities and improve quality of life for sustainable development. Furthermore, many reside in rural areas and agricultural employment comprises primary source of income for women. Women's development in the region depends on improving the situation of rural communities. The results from this paper show that, the sales volume of womenlink in South Korea has increased 24 times, from 267, 329,000 Korean won in 1990 to 6, 652, 929, 000 Korean won in 2005. However, women lack access to land credit, or production inputs, inadequate knowledge and business experience of cooperatives is limited. In conclusion, women's entrepreneurship through green cooperatives, capacity building and information can enable them to produce and market their green products.

Source with thanks:

Saikou E. Sanyang and **Wen-Chi Huang**

National Pingtung University of Science and Technology,

1, Shuehfu Rd, Neipu, Pingtung 91201, Taiwan Graduate Institute of Agribusiness Management, National Pingtung University of Science and Technology, Taiwan

World Journal of Agricultural Sciences 4 (6): 674-683, 2008

ISSN 1817-3047 © IDOSI Publications, 2008

CASE-3

Workers Cooperatives and Collective Entrepreneurship

History reveals that cooperatives were established by working people to respond to the industrialisation and capitalism. Workers came together and formed cooperatives to meet their daily needs and to create a better society to live in. The vision of cooperatives is not profiteering but to share and improve the socio-economic conditions of the members and the community to which they belong to. Collective entrepreneurship and concern for community are the basic pillars of the very foundations of the co-operatives worldwide. There are many success stories right from the Rochdale cooperative enterprise to SEWA today. However, cooperative movement has come a long way from being used by the governments as one of the tools of development to independent, competitive collective enterprise which is confronting the challenges of WTO, open market and globalization. Cooperatives are the only business enterprises, which operate on certain common values and principles, which keep their community at the top of their agenda. Co-operative values safeguard and promote the basic culture of the particular society in which they live and operate from. Importance of community and collective entrepreneurship is even being recognised by the private sectors and Panos Mourdoukoutas suggests that to enhance revenues, the firms must achieve organisational mutations and permutations, turning themselves from hierarchical managerial units into entrepreneurial network. These entrepreneurial networks are communities that share a common fate. Against this backdrop, an attempt has been made to analyze the strengths of workers cooperatives and its role in sustaining community culture through success stories basically from two states of India Gujarat and Delhi. However, few examples have also been collected from other countries such as US.

Collection and analysis of secondary data from primary information such as visit to co- op, discussions with co-operators and members and from website. The two success stories have been collected from primary sources. However, to depict the overall situation of workers collective in India and see the bigger picture – variables like number of worker cooperatives, financial position, membership, business, community welfare programs etc and leadership, management, income employment and related aspects were collected from secondary sources.

Collective entrepreneurship is popular mode of business and profit earning among worker cooperatives. In terms of employment generation and empowerment of community, case studies suggest satisfactory trend.

However, cooperatives are yet to be independent from the government control and need to be strengthened to face the competition from open market. This case also attempted to examine the impact of the cooperatives on the community in keeping cultural values intact. Inspite of success, these enterprises are facing serious constraints in operating in the open market and it's relevance in socio- cultural and economic empowerment of the community needs to be examined in the light of strengths, opportunity and challenges of the time.

Source with thanks:

Savitri Singh

Advisor Gender Programme International Co-operative Alliance
Regional Office for Asia & the Pacific 9, Aradhana Enclave
Sector-13, Ring Road, R.K Puram, New Delhi (India)
E-mail: savitrisingh@icaroap.coop

CASE-4

The Challenge of Entrepreneurship in Agricultural Cooperatives

Collective action seems a logical strategy to achieve the integration of smallholders into dynamic markets. Organising small farmers into producer organisations has long been a common development intervention to increase their bargaining power vis-à-vis other actors in the value chain. Cooperatives offer such a possibility by means of organizing and empowering individual small producers through a commonly owned enterprise.[1] This form of organisation is not all at new, but the context in which farmer cooperatives in developing countries have to operate today is quickly changing.

New challenges associated with emerging consumer demands, global standardization processes, market concentration, stricter market requirements and price instability require different roles and capacities from cooperatives operating in agri-food value chains worldwide. Their purpose – the empowerment of small producers – has not changed, but nowadays they need different means to achieve that goal. Instead of holding on to the defensive role they used to play in the past (such as trying to set more favourable prices for producers by reducing the market share of intermediaries, for instance), cooperatives are now challenged to take on a more pro-active role in marketing, updating their organisational structure and engaging in value chain integration. A successful transition to this new role requires the acquisition of particular managerial capacities, especially in the domain of 'collective entrepreneurship', as Michael Cook and Brad Plunkett have called it.[2]

Apart from the more conventional features of entrepreneurs, such as being alert to new opportunities, capacity to change organisational structures, good judgement in uncertain conditions and risk-taking attitudes, in order to deal successfully with current challenges, cooperatives also require the capacity to build new partnerships and to make strategic use of networks and relations with other stakeholders. It is worth mentioning that such a transition towards a more entrepreneurial mindset is also conditioned by the socio-political context. For example, cooperatives that were created according to restrictive models, were under government control or operated in a protective environment may find a move towards more entrepreneurial performance much harder.

Entrepreneurship and cooperatives: what does the theory tell us?

How difficult is it for cooperatives in developing countries to develop entrepreneurial skills? From the point of view of economic organisation theory, cooperatives are likely to be confronted with several obstacles in this process. First, due to its multiple owners and purposes, the entrepreneurial function within a cooperative tends to be less clearly allocated than in an investor-owned firm. Moreover, members have a greater incentive to devote time to private entrepreneurial tasks on their own farms, since the returns to entrepreneurial efforts at the cooperative level will always be distributed among the group. Second, capital accumulation tends to be a problem in cooperatives, due to the fact that dividends have to be paid to a large number of members. Capital constraints could mean that wages offered to managers are not high enough to attract the most entrepreneurial ones.[3]

Entrepreneurship and the Development Sector

As argued above, current trends in the agri-food sector call for interventions to strengthen the entrepreneurial capacity of farmer organisations. Furthermore, the theory suggests that there may be some big obstacles to surmount. But is the development sector prepared to undertake such task? Has the entrepreneurial approach already been internalized by development cooperation agencies?

The development sector has traditionally stressed the importance of farmer organisations primarily as tools of political empowerment, advocacy and representation. This was a logical stand at a time when the state played a more important role in steering rural development, setting prices of agricultural products, allocating resources and regulating commercialization. It may yet be misleading nowadays in countries with liberalized agricultural markets and in a context of the growing importance of global agri-food chains. As for their market function, development practitioners have – in part due to their suspicion of (especially large) private commercial agents – promoted cooperatives as countervailing power to existing market forces, which in many developing countries reflect historically very unequal class relations. Above all, cooperatives are conceived by the development sector as agents of social change. They are expected to raise the voice of their constituency against prevalent unjust social and economic relations, and to be an engine of local development. The development sector therefore tends to stress the notion of social entrepreneurship in cooperative development.[4]

Development interventions at the cooperative level have been devoted to different dimensions of organisational strengthening, but often overlooking the economic one.[5] Yet, treating cooperatives not as business partners but as 'recipients' of international cooperation can increase the risk of creating dependency on foreign aid, and may hamper the development of the necessary skills to compete successfully in the market.

Private Sector Entrepreneurship

For private firms, the main benefit of working with cooperatives rather than with multiple individual small producers is lower transaction costs, which include the costs of coordination, establishing and monitoring contracts, quality control of products and collection, sorting and grading practices, etc. Hence, due to these lower costs and economies of scale, cooperatives can have considerable competitive advantages, particularly in sectors that are dominated by small producers.[6]

Compared with the development sector, the private sector holds a rather different vision of the entrepreneurship of cooperatives. Private firms want to source products that meet their demands and standards. They look for reliable business partners who can deliver products in specific volumes, at a good price, on schedule, and that meet quality and other specific requirements. Compared with the 'project mindset' of development practitioners, the private sector has a more instrumental view of entrepreneurship (based upon business performance). Firms will clearly define their expectations and the performance indicators before they start any collaboration (which is not always the case with NGOs). And although firms are often prepared to offer support to the development of producers' organisations (suppliers)– for instance, through training, provision of computers, pre-financing, etc. – they only work with cooperatives that already have a certain level of 'doing good business'.[7]

Strategic Partnerships

How then to combine the collective, social and instrumental views of cooperatives' entrepreneurship? Are partnerships between these three sectors and visions feasible and can they be fruitful? Indeed, such alliances – unthinkable few decades ago – are starting to evolve, framed by a value chain perspective. One example of such a partnership is the recently created tradehouse Yiriwa, located in Mali, which aims at trading organic products. Yiriwa cooperates with farmers as shareholders in a public–private partnership. The initiative is supported by KIT Sustainable Development Fund, ICCO, AKO and local producers. An export-oriented private enterprise was launched, with the unusual features that the interests of farmers' organisations are represented, it is partially funded by resources from international cooperation, and development agencies also participate as co-owners of the business.

Such alliances may be appealing not only to small-scale and purposefully created enterprises, but also to large and 'mainstream' firms. The 'inclusive business' approach adopted by SNV in Latin America, for instance, is based on this idea. It targets conventional private lead firms interested in strengthening the capacity of their small-scale (and often vulnerable) rural providers. The development sector is aware that their interventions often fail due to lack of markets or uncertain sales. Private companies are in a much better position to facilitate (and profit from) the creation of stable markets, so in principle the door should be open for collaboration. Nonetheless, plenty of challenges await those actors willing to engage in such innovative coalitions.

Challenges Ahead

There are crucial challenges for each of the three sectors. For agricultural cooperatives in developing countries, one of the main issues is how to deal with the inevitable tension between engaging in new entrepreneurial relations while also remaining an organisation that is truly controlled by, and works for the benefit of, its members. The experience of cooperatives in the Netherlands suggests that when managers become more autonomous they gain some entrepreneurial freedom (essential to adapt to new market situations), but at the expense of loss of direct influence of the members on the business. Professionalization and internationalization of cooperatives may result, unintentionally, in the exclusion of their more vulnerable (and less competitive) members. The risk that cooperatives undertaking governance changes towards more entrepreneurial settings drift away from the interests of their members is also present in developing countries. On the other hand, is a board of directors that consists of small farmers (normally with limited education and access to information) capable to deal with the rising challenges of dynamic agri-business? The ability to solve this apparent contradiction between efficiency and equity,[9] and to find the right trade-off between a business orientation and the promise of social inclusion, are among the key features that make the cooperative's entrepreneur unique.

One of the key challenges for the development sector is how to adopt also a more business- oriented vision without becoming part of the mainstream business (keeping its identity). For instance, what difference does it make when a development agency becomes an investor? Is it only that it is more willing to bear higher risks if the business is expected to be more inclusive?

For the private sector, probably the main question at stake is to convince managers that social concerns are not just a matter of building a good corporate image, but of adopting an ethical approach towards society. The private sector has to become aware that it has the power to change the living conditions of millions, and has a very important role to play in ameliorating global inequalities. The current crisis should encourage the emergence of new business models, able to deal with social and environmental concerns.

Overall, the critical matter is how to mainstream the partnerships between these three sectors without jeopardizing inclusiveness, which at the end of the day is the key element that will hold all the parties together.

This article is based on the ideas developed during the workshop 'Entrepreneurial capacity and value chain innovation in agricultural cooperatives', which took place during the CERES summer school at CIDIN,

Radboud University Nijmegen, in July 2009. We are grateful to Hedwig Bruggeman (AgriProFocus), Suzanne Nederlof (KIT), Cees van Rij (Agriterra) and Frank Kraaijkamp (van Weely Koffie) for their valuable contributions to the organisation and execution of this workshop. We are also indebted to all the participants for the rich exchange of experiences, as well as to Bertus Wennink (KIT) and Bert Helmsing (ISS) for their helpful comments on an earlier draft of this article.

Source with thanks:

Roldan Muradian and **Ellen Magnus**

October 07, 2009 Roldan Muradian and Ellen Mangnus

http://www.thebrokeronline.eu/en/Special-Reports/Special-report-The-power-of-value-chains/The-challenge-of-entrepreneurship-in-agricultural-cooperatives

CASE-5

Young Dairy Farmers Opt for Their Own Cooperative

's-Hertogenbosch, the Netherlands - They may be young and critical, but that doesn't mean that young dairy farmers don't appreciate the value of the dairy cooperative Campina for their own dairy farms. Cooperative entrepreneurship is not passé, at least not according to most of the five hundred young Campina dairy farmers from the Netherlands, Germany and Belgium who attended the international Campina Young Farmers Day in's-Hertogenbosch (the Netherlands). The majority are the business successors of present Campina members.

Throughout the day the young farmers discussed and debated in Lower House style on the theme 'Dairy basics – Why a dairy cooperative in a growing dairy market?' On viewing incisive statements on the market, cooperation, Campina and entrepreneurship, the young farmers had to physically choose between 'agree' or 'disagree'. They were of course expected to argue their choices. The object of the debate was to obtain transparency and answers to the questions.

At the end of the day Campina chairman Kees Wantenaar concluded: "I've just seen a large group of very ambitious entrepreneurs. You can see that people are facing the future with an open mind. That's the strength of this cooperative."

Cooperative Entrepreneurship is not passé

The theory 'Cooperative entrepreneurship is passé' induced the shuffle of hundreds of feet. The young farmers moved en masse to the 'disagree' square.

From the 'agree' square someone explained: "If as a dairy farmer you are large enough and there are more of you, then you can drive a milk truck together." From the 'disagree' square came the unwavering rejoinder: "Did you hear what he said? Farmers undertaking to do something together. That's cooperation." "The cooperative is one of the strongest forms of entrepreneurship. It's the most sincere involvement in an organisation you can imagine", said Timo Huges, general director of FloraHolland. He is one of the experts with whom the young farmers can consult on this day. He further defines the cooperative: a cooperative must always demonstrate it has added value to its members (the owners).

A Wonderful Challenge

In times where dairy farmers are having a field day, that's a wonderful challenge. Worldwide it appears that the demand for dairy is growing structurally faster than supply. The rosy prospects can be attributed to the growth in population and prosperity outside Europe. When young dairy farmers are asked how they can capitalise on this growth, they often reply: "As an individual member you cannot capitalise on the world market: Campina has to do that." Folkert Beekman, secretary of the Dutch Dairy Commodity Board confirms this: "Because dairy organisations are entering these growth markets, dairy farmers should soon discover that they can still sell the extra milk they supply at a good price." International growth is therefore another of the arguments for the exploratory merger talks between Campina and Friesland Foods.

Investing in Brands and Innovations

Where more mature markets are concerned, such as those in Western Europe where Campina has a strong position, the motto is: invest in brands and innovations. These wise words were addressed to the young farmers by Wouter de Bruijn, managing director at Campina. Brands and innovations are essential to stay in favour with consumers. And that in its turn is necessary to pay the member farmers a structural and competitive milk price.

Golden Generation of Dairy Farmers

Whatever the case may be, the prospects for dairy farmers are better than they have been in years. This point was brought home to the young farmers by Campina dairy farmer Hay Zeegers from Wellerlooi (near Venlo, the Netherlands). "I'm jealous of you people. I've been a dairy farmer for 40 years. In the nineteen seventies we produced so much milk that we created butter mountains that even the Russians weren't able to get through. And now there is a shortage of milk! You are the golden generation; if you are good entrepreneurs, you can earn a good living."

Source with thanks:

http://www.frieslandcampina.com/english/news-and-press/news/jonge-veehouders-kiezen-voor-hun-cooperatie.aspx

CASE-6

Entrepreneurs in the Cooperative Business

You know who an entrepreneur is. He or she is someone who creates a business after identifying an opportunity, assembling the required resources and taking risks to go after it. You probably heard of corporate entrepreneurship. These are individuals in a corporation who behave as an entrepreneur but are not risking their "own" capital. They are called intrapreneurs.

Co-operative entrepreneurship is a new branch of entrepreneurship as it applies to the co-operative movement. If individuals and corporations can do it, why can't the co-operative movement? Can they be creative, innovative and take moderate risks?

Recently the Cooperative Development Division of the Ministry of Labour and Small and Micro enterprise Development hosted an event titled "Co-operative Entrepreneurship Workshop" at Cipriani Labour College.

The Commissioner of Co-operatives, Karyl Adams opened the event. Its objective was to show the importance of entrepreneurship and how it can be applied to the movement. This workshop also explored the "why" and "how" in adopting entrepreneurship.

The cooperative movement is a key player in not only improving its membership economically and socially but plays a major role in economic development. Collectively, cooperatives (financial and non- financial) hold about $10 billion in assets.

Some are like small banks offering similar services while others engage in marketing, consumer, fishing and agricultural activities. A cooperative is different from a corporation which seeks to maximise profits. A cooperative is founded not on selfishness but on volunteerism and democratic principles.

One of the feature speakers was Dr. IC Imoisili, an international consultant and a cooperative expert with the Co-operative Division. He sited data from the International Labour Organisation (ILO) which showed that cooperatives generated 100 million jobs globally, 20 per cent more than multinationals. Cooperatives were a dominant form in some countries with high market shares; Dairies (Norway) 99 per cent, Coffee (Kenya) 70 per cent, Credit (Cyprus) 30 per cent and Banking (Finland) 34 per cent.

Dr. Imoisili's research showed that the leading sectors were Consumer cooperatives (35%), Service cooperatives (31%) and agriculture/animal husbandry (25%). He pointed to some areas that had some potential for cooperatives and be of importance for national development. These include agriculture (for food security), hospitality (for tourism development), exporting (for foreign exchange) and junior cooperatives (for youth leadership development).

Other consultants presented their views on the new world that cooperatives operated in and gave some examples of successful adaptation of entrepreneurship principles. Ms Ermine Christopher-Salino said that cooperatives were not immune to changes in their environment.

Their world was a borderless one, with greater need for differentiated products, increased competition, more research and development, divergent needs of its membership and increased awareness of social and environmental issues. She said cooperatives must respond to these changes but more importantly they must embrace entrepreneurship to move their organisations to the next level.

I presented some examples of successful cooperative entrepreneurship. One such was the Vigia Chico fishing cooperative in Mexico that was involved in the lobster business. They faced the challenges of over fishing and middlemen making all the profits. They came up with the idea of dividing up the ocean floor into lots for each member.

This innovation plus creating cages as artcifical habitats, was instrumental in protecting the lobster population. Vigia Chico also allied with other cooperatives to market their product under a brand name and so removing the commoditisation pressure. This meant they now could sell more lobsters at a higher price and make more money.

Three other cooepratives presented their success stories in applying entrepreneurship locally. Mega credit union, Eastern, boasted about some innovations. They introduced the debit card to its members. Its growth was astronomical with over twenty thousand (20,048) transactions conducted in August 2010.

Eastern Credit Union also gives financial support to its members who want to start or grow their enterprises.

These include maxi-taxi operators, fashion designers and artisans who benefit from both business and technical support and assistance. So in effect, Eastern creates and supports entrepreneurs through entrepreneurship programmes. Of course, Eastern is famous for its La Joya multi-purpose facility. This "jewel" houses the administrative HQ, a gym, auditorium, pre-school, courtyard and a money spinner for them.

Another organisation, Tobago Nutrition Cooperative (TNCSL) is a worker co-op that has a number of entrepreneurial initiatives of its own. It operates as a caterer and supplies the school nutrition programme. It has diverisfied into suppling the private sector including the growing tourist business. This means the co-op has reduced its exposure in these recessionary times. The third co-op to showcase its entrepreneurial ability was Caribbean

Agrarian located in Tabaquite. This company is one of the pioneers of convenience packs. They process vegetables into ready to cook packages and sell them to supermarkets like Hi lo and JTA. This innovation started back in 1987 when they saw a need driven by a customer who was time poor.

They have since expanded from the original callaloo packs to chucky veg, patchoi, chow mein and seasoning packs. They grow their own produce and source the balance from other farmers. This supply chain gives them a competitive advantage in these times of fluctuating supply and prices.

Ladi Franklyn, another management consultant gave her take on what cooperatives need to do to get entrepreneurship infused into the organisation. She pointed out that a strong visionary board with robust leadership can make a big difference. The paradigm shift must start from above with a strong commitment as entrepreneurial activities require risk taking and creative thinking. Resistance to change has to be dealt with and be forgiving of mistakes.

Franklyn further advised the 100 or so cooperative members that the cooperative spirit must change to being more aggressive and proactive.

Cooperatives should become risk takers but more so calculated ones. Being able to conduct feasibility studies and be aware of their members needs in the pursuit of opportunities. In addition to being innovative, they must be close to the customer so to they can churn out new market shifting products. But changing the mind set to an entrepreneurial one requires training. Entrepreneurship as a skill can be acquired and so the need for management development.

The workshop ended with participants presenting their views on this new concept called cooperative entrepreneurship. Will they go back and become more entrepreneurial? If Eastern and Caribbean Agrarian with humble beginnings did it, maybe as true leaders they will inspire others in the movement to do so.

Source with thanks:

http://www.newsday.co.tt/businessday/0,128745.html (the paper is given as such to understand entrepreneurship in cooperative business)

CASE-7

Social Entrepreneurship Case Study

Kallari Cooperative of Ecuador

Indigenous communities around the world face seemingly insurmountable odds against national governments and corporations that seek to explore, and often exploit, the peoples and their land. Indigenous communities around the world face seemingly insurmountable odds against national governments and corporations that seek to explore, and often exploit, the peoples and their land. The Quichua of the Ecuadorian Amazon too face such problems; oil exploration in their territory often means that they are removed from their lands and become dependent on the government for basic needs which they were once able to meet. Although many indigenous groups in the Ecuadorian Amazon have appealed to the government to forbid or limit oil exploration in their territory, the government does not have an incentive to stop oil exploration irrespective of the permanent damage it has on the fragile ecosystem. There are also many instances when the Quichua are persuaded to give up their territory through manipulative means.

When I studied abroad in Ecuador, I came to know of the *Kallari* Cooperative's cafe in the capital city of Quito. The cooperative is made up of hundreds of Amazonian Quichua families who create arts and crafts and manufacture their own chocolate, giving the families a sustainable way of generating income without having to exploit their land through logging and oil exploration. As a self-sustaining community, the cooperative has been able to preserve their way of life without growing dependent on the government while sharing their culture and stories of resilience with the world.

Kallari chocolates are manufactured entirely by the collective and are scrumptious; social entrepreneurship never tasted this good.

Lessons to be Drawn

The Kallari cooperative works because it engages the community it is working for/with; every member of the community is a stakeholder with an important role to play, from the administrative aspects, to manufacturing chocolate or creating crafts. The community themselves see the value in their work. When a community feels it has the talents and manpower to succeed, the community feels it is in control of its destiny and mobilization becomes easier. As a social entrepreneur it is important to work with a community by first asking the community what its needs are, then inviting the community to be a part of the solution.

Source with thanks:

http://vijana.fm/2010/02/04/social-entrepreneurship-case-study-kallari-cooperative-of-ecuador

CASE-8

Entrepreneurship in the Development of Worker Cooperatives in the United States

Nonprofit development organisations play an important role in providing technical expertise in the startup of new firms and in the conversion of existing businesses in the USA. This study explores the characteristics and practice of entrepreneurship in the development of worker cooperatives. This is the first phase of a larger study that will look at cooperative development organisations and cooperative entrepreneurs. In the first phase, the unit of analysis has been the development organisations. This research is based on interviews conducted between June 2004 and March 2005. Interviews will have been conducted with 11 cooperative developers in 8 organisations that have created worker cooperatives or democratic employee stock ownership companies (ESOP's).

Historically, cooperatives have been created to provide economic advantages for those not effectively served by the mainstream economy. In the 1800's, family farmers organized agricultural cooperatives to secure better prices for their products. Credit cooperatives were started for people not served by commercial banking institutions in the early 1900's. Housing cooperatives have provided safe affordable housing for low-income renters. Today, worker cooperatives are viewed as a way to develop community businesses to provide better quality jobs for workers.

While cooperative entrepreneurs share many of the characteristics of the civic entrepreneur, the difference is that accountability to the community is subordinated to the priorities set by their membership and the strategic requirements of their businesses. In cooperatives with strong ties to their community, the cooperative entrepreneur may also be a civic entrepreneur. The study has found that cooperative entrepreneurs are often the staff or development team during the startup phase.

In-depth interviews were conducted with staff that have been involved with the startup or conversion of at least one worker cooperative or democratic ESOP. Respondents were asked to describe the experiences of conversion or startup of new democratic ESOP's or worker cooperatives. Through the interviews, models of intervention have been identified. The study has sought to answer the following research questions:

1. Is an individual focus on cooperative entrepreneurs an appropriate unit of analysis or is cooperative entrepreneurship more typically embodied in a group of entrepreneurs?

2. Do cooperative development organisations play an entrepreneurial role in the startup of the firms?
3. What do they believe motivates a person to become an entrepreneur to develop a business for a group of cooperative members rather than going it alone to develop their own venture?
4. How are cooperative entrepreneurs recruited by development organisations?
5. What professional skills and training are considered important for successful cooperative entrepreneurs?
6. What has been their experience in developing cooperatives?
7. How does the cooperative entrepreneurial experience differ from that of other social and conventional entrepreneurs as described in the literature?
8. Are there specific issues or problems that are identified by the cooperative development firms that have social policy implications for future development of worker cooperatives?

Source with thanks:

Christina Clamp, School of Community Economic Development, Southern New Hamps

http://www.eteo.mondragon.edu/ocs/viewpaper.php?id=28&print=1&cf=1

References

Abalkin, Leonid. 1988. Reviving the Cooperative Movement. *World Marxist Review 31* (June): 53-59.

Abbott, J.C. 1987. Agricultural Marketing Enterprises for the Developing World with Case Studies of Indigenous Private, Transnational, co-operative and Parastatal Enterprises. Cambridge: Cambridge University Press.

ALRO 1991. A Study Report on Agricultural Land Reform Cooperative Development. Bangkok: Kasetsart University.

Andre Hirschfeld. 1977. "Some Thoughts on Cooperative Socialism, "Anthology of Cooperative Thought", Vol. III.

Anschel, Kurt R., Russell H. Brannon and Eldon D. Smith. 1969. Agricultural Cooperatives and Markets in Developing Countries. New York: Praeger Press.

Attwood, Donald. 1989. Does Competition Help Co-operation? *The Journal of Development Studies,* 26 (October): 5-27.

Babcock, John. 1999. *Farmboy: Hard Work and Good Times on a Farm that Helped Change Northeast Agriculture*. Ithaca, NY: DeWitt Historical Society of Tompkins County.

Banerjee, Abhijit, Timothy Besley, and Timothy Guinnane. 1994. Thy Neighbour's Keeper: The Design of a Credit Cooperative with Theory and a Test. *The Quarterly Journal of Economics 109* (May): 491-515.

Barnes, Donald, and Christopher Ondeck. 1997. *The Capper-Volstead Act: Opportunity Today and Tomorrow in Commemoration of the 75th Anniversary of the Capper-Volstead Act*. Report Presented at the National Council of Farmer Cooperatives' National Institute on Cooperative Education, Annual Conference, Pittsburgh, PA. Published online by the University of Wisconsin Center for Cooperatives. Retrieved June 15, 2007, from www.uwcc.wisc.edu/info/capper.htm.

Bartlett, Will, John Cable, and Saul Estrin. 1992. Labour-managed Cooperatives and Private Firms in North Central Italy: An Empirical Comparison. *Industrial & Labour Relations Review,* 46: 103-118.

Baumgardner, James. 1988. The Division of Labor, Local Markets and Worker Organisation. *Journal of Political Economy* 96 (June): 509-527.

Ben-Ner, Avner. 1984. On the Stability of the Cooperative Type of Organisation. *Journal of Comparative Economics 8*(3): 247-260.

Berman, Katrina, and Matthew Berman. 1989. An Empirical Test of the Theory of the Labour-managed Firm. *Journal of Comparative Economics 13*(June): 281-300.

Bernard, T. And Speilman, V. 2009. Reaching the Rural Poor Through Rural Producer Organisations? A Study of Agricultural Marketing Cooperatives in Ethiopia. Food Policy 34: 60-69.

Berry, Brian J.L. 1992. *America's Utopian Experiments: Communal Havens from Long-wave Crises*. Hanover, NH: Dartmouth College—University Press of New England.

Bhuyan, Sanjib. 1992. *Agricultural Cooperatives and Vertical Integration: A Theoretical Analysis*. Unpublished Master's Thesis (M.S.), University of Nebraska, Lincoln.

Bijman, J. And van Dijk. G. 2009. Corporate Governance in Agricultural Cooperatives: A Perspective from The Netherlands. Paper Presented at the Workshop "Rural Cooperation in the 21st Centry: Lessons from the Past, Pathways to the Future, Rehovot, Israel, June 2009.

Birchall, Johnston. 1994. *Co-op: The people's business*. New York: St. Martin's Press.

Blanc, Francois, and Richard Matthewman. 1995. Cooperatives et gestion communale en elevage: Un apercu comparatif entre pays en voie de developpement anglophones et francophones. [French] *Annals of Public and Cooperative Economics/Annales de l'Economie Publique Sociale et Cooperative 66*(September): 253-274.

Boehlje, M. 1996. Industrialisation of Agriculture: What are the Implications? *Choices* (4): 30-33.

Bogetic, Zeljko, and Dennis Heffley. 1992. Market Syndicalism and Market Imbalances. *Journal of Comparative Economics 16* (December): 670-687.

Bonin, John, and Louis Putterman. 1993. Incentives and Monitoring in Cooperatives with Labour-proportionate Sharing Schemes. *Journal of Comparative Economics 17* (September): 663-686.

Bonin, John, Derek Jones, and Louis Putterman. 1993. Theoretical and Empirical Studies of Producer Cooperatives: Will ever the Twain Meet? *Journal of Economic Literature 31* (September): 1290-1320.

Bonn, John. 1984. Membership and Employment in an Egalitarian Cooperative. *Economica 51* (August): 295-305.

Bowen, E.R, The Cooperative Road to Abundance. New York: Henry Schuman, 1953, p. 144.

Bowles, Samuel, Herbert Gintis, and Bo Gustafsson. (Eds.). 1993. *Markets and Democracy: Participation, Accountability, and Efficiency*. Cambridge, UK: Cambridge University Press.

Bradley, Forrest. 1995. Tapestry of Success: A History of Tennessee Farmers Cooperative and its First 50 Years of Cooperation. LaVergne: Tennessee Farmers Cooperative.

Brake, J. et al. 1972. "The NAtional Agricultural Cooperatives Federation: An Appraisal", Korean Agricultural Sector Study (KASS), Special Report 1, Mechigan State University, East Lansing.

Breimyer, Harold [Reviewer]. 1992. Farmers, Cooperatives, and USDA: A History of Agricultural Cooperative Service [Book Review]. U.S. Department of Agriculture, 1991. *American Journal of Agricultural Economics 74* (August): 843-845.

Brown, Leslie [Reviewer]. 1989. Worker cooperatives in America [Book Review]. University of California Press, 1984. *Canadian Review of Sociology & Anthropology 26* (August): 689-691.

Buccola, Steven, and Abdelbagi Subaei. 1985. Optimal Market Pools for Agricultural Cooperatives. *American Journal of Agricultural Economics 67* (February): 70-79.

Burger, Paul. 1997. *Market Area Modeling and Network Analysis of an Agricultural Cooperative System Using a Geographic Information System*. Unpublished Doctoral Thesis (Ed.D.), Oklahoma State University, Stillwater.

CAD.1991. Annual Report on Financial Statistics: Agricultural Land Reform Cooperatives. Bangkok: Ministry of Agriculture and Cooperatives.

Carter, Neil [Reviewer]. 1989. Worker Cooperatives in Theory and Practice [Book Review]. Open University Press, 1988. *Political Quarterly 60* (April/ June): 247-250.

Centre de Gestion des Cooperatives. 1996. Profile of World Agricultural Cooperation. Montreal: Ecole des Hautes Etudes Commerciales.

Certainly not in the same league (cooperatives seek diversity). 1995. *Economist 335*(April 29): 76.

Chinchanker and Namjoshi. 1977. "Cooperation and Welfare," Cooperation and Dynamics of Change, Bombay: Somaiya Publishing House.

Chowdhury, PK.; Huq, MA.; Rahman, SA. 1987. Cooperatives as Institutions for Development of the Rural Poor. Kotbari: Academy for Rural Development.

Clark, Thomas R. 1999. The Limits of State Autonomy: The Medical Cooperatives of the Farm Security Administration, 1935-1946. *Journal of Policy History 11*(3): 257-282.

Clayre, Alasdair. 1980. *The Political Economy of Co-operation and Participation: A Third Sector*. New York: Oxford University Press.

CLT (1993). The Second Conference Proceedings: Chuan 1 with Cooperative Development 24- 25 Feb. 1993. Bangkok: Cooperative League of Thailand.

Clyde Filley A.M, Cooperation in Agriculture, John Willey & Sons Inc, New York, 1929.

Cobia, David. (Ed.). 1989. *Cooperatives in Agriculture*. Englewood Cliffs, NJ: Prentice Hall.

Cook, M. And Plunkett, B. 2006. Collective Entrepreneurship: An Emerging Phenomenon in Producer Owned Organisations. Journal of Agricultural and Applied Economics 38 (2): 421-428.

Cook, Michael L. 1995. The Future of U.S. Agricultural Cooperatives: A Neo-institutional Approach. *American Journal of Agricultural Economics 77* (December): 1153-1159.

Cook, Michael L. 1997. *Cooperatives—Their importance in the Future Food and Agricultural System: Proceedings of a January 1990 Symposium*. Washington, DC: National Council of Farmers Cooperatives and the Food and Agricultural Marketing Consortium.

Cook, Michael L., and Constantine Iliopoulos. 1999. Beginning to Inform the Theory of the Cooperative Firm: Emergence of the New Generation Cooperative. *The Finnish Journal of Business Economics* 4: 525-535.

Co-operate and Prosper (Mondragon). 1991. *Economist 311* (April 1): 61.

Cooperative Marketing Act: 60 years. 1986. *Farmer Cooperatives 53* (October): 4-19.

COOPERATIVES IN EUROPE 2000", Bologan, Italy/30.11.98.

CPD (1989). A Study on the Growth of Agricultural Cooperatives in Thailand 1978-1987. Bangkok: the Cooperative Promotion Department.

Craig, Ben, and John Pencavel. 1992. The Behaviour of Worker Cooperatives: The Plywood Companies of the Pacific Northwest. *American Economic Review 82*: 1083-1105.

Craig, Ben, and John Pencavel. 1993. The Objectives of Worker Cooperatives (Pacific Northwest). *Journal of Comparative Economics 17* (June): 288-308.

Craig, Ben, and John Pencavel. 1995. *Participation and Productivity: A Comparison of Worker Cooperatives and Conventional Firms in the Plywood Industry* (Brookings Papers on Economic Activity). (Microeconomics, 121-160, 173-174; Related Material: Discussion, 161-172).

Credit Union History. 1999. *Credit Union Management 22*(2): 21.

D'Aspremont, Claude, Alexis Jacquemin, and Jean Jaskold Gabszewicz. 1985. Cooperative Agreements and Conflicts of Interest. *European Economic Review 27*(February): 1-2.

Dasgupta, Siddhartha. 1997. *Cooperative Land Tenure Contracts Under Asymmetric Information*. Unpublished Doctoral Thesis (Ph.D.), Department of Agricultural Economics, Texas A&M University, College Station.

Datta, AK. 1984. Landlessness in Bangladesh: The Processes and Mechanisms; a Survey of Research. 1984, 1 Bangladesh; Community Development Library.

David W. Cobia, Cooperatives in Agriculture, Prentice Hall, New Jersy.

Davis, P. 1996. "Towards a Value-Based Management for Membership-Based Organisations", in the Journal of Cooperative Studies, Vol. 29, No. 1, May 1996.

Digby, Margarat. 1960. The World Cooperative Movement, London: Hutchinson University Library, 1960.

DiMarcello, Carol. "ICA: Building Community Jobs by Replicating Model Worker Co-ops." Online. World Wide Web. Available at http://www.wisc.edu/uwcc/info/ica.htm.

Article gives a Brief Description of how ICA helps out the Worker Cooperatives. It includes a Five Phase Plan that it follows.

Don, Yehuda, Nava Kahana, and Avi Weiss. 1992. Theoretical and Applied Aspects of Labour-managed Firms: Editors' Introduction. *Journal of Comparative Economics 16*(December): 567-572.

Dorrien, Gary. 1986. *The Democratic Socialist Vision*. Totowa, NJ: Rowman & Littlefield. Drabenstott, Mark. 1994. Industrialisation: Steady Current or Tidal Wave? *Choices* (4): 4-8. Dunn, John. 1988. Cooperatives Best hope for Farmers' Economic Survival: Senate Study. *Farmer Cooperatives 54* (January): 10-14.

Duelfer, Eberhard. and Jahani Laurinkari [Eds]. 1994. The International Handbook of Cooperative Organisations. Goettingen: Vandenhoeck und Ruprecht, 961 pages.

Durant, Will. 1939. Story of Civilisation - the Life of Greece, New York: Simon and Schuster.

Earle, John. 1985. Draining the Ostia Marshes: A Co-operative Achievement. *History Today 35*(July): 27-32.

Earnest Poisson, the Cooperative Republic, Manchester. The Cooperative Union Ltd., 1925.

Egerstrom, Lee, Pieter Bos, and Gert Van Dijk. (Eds.). 1996. *Seizing Control: The International Market Power of Cooperatives*. Rochester, MN: Lone Oak Press.

Egerstrom, Lee. 1994. *Make no Small Plans: A Cooperative Revival for Rural America*. Rochester, MN: Lone Oak Press.

Ellerman, David. 1984. Theory of Legal Structure: Worker Cooperatives. *Journal of Economic Issues 18* (September): 861-891.

Erba, Eric. 1996. *Comparisons of Costs and Efficiencies Between Cooperative, Proprietary, and Captive Fluid Milk Processors: A Neural Network Approach*. Ithaca, NY: Cornell University, Department of Agricultural, Resource and Managerial Economics.

Ergstrom, Lee (1994). Make No Small Plans: A Cooperative Revival for Rural America. Rochester, Minnesota: Lone Oak Press Ltd., 294 pages.

Estrin, Saul [Reviewer]. 1984. The Economic Analysis of Producers' Cooperatives [Book Review]. St. Martin's Press, 1984. *Journal of Comparative Economics 9* (December): 462-464.

Estrin, Saul, and Jan Svejnar. 1993. Wage Determination in Labor-managed Firms Under Market-oriented Reforms: Estimates of Static and Dynamic Models. *Journal of Comparative Economics 17* (September): 687-700.

Fairbairn, Brett. 1989. *Building a Dream: The Co-operative Retailing System in Western Canada, 1928-1988*. Saskatoon, SK: Western Producer Prairie Books.

FAO. 1986. Profile of Agricultural Cooperatives in Selected Asian Countries. Bangkok: FAO Regional Office for Asia and Pacific.

Filimonova, N., and I. Ermakova. 2005. Farmers' Dairy Cooperatives in the USA: Structure and Tendencies of Development. *Mezhdunarodnyi Sel'skokhozyaistvennyi Zhurnal* (3): 24-26.

Franz C Helm. 1968. The Economics of Cooperative Enterprises, The Cooperative College, Tanzxania & University of London Press.

Gartrell, David and Bernard Paille. 1997. Wage Cuts and the Fairness of Pay in a Worker-owned Plywood Cooperative. *Social Psychology Quarterly 60* (June): 103-117.

Gauthier, David. 1986. *Morals by Agreement*. Oxford, UK: Clarendon Press.

Gehres, Donald J. 1968. Report on Cooperatives in Guatemala. A Report Prepared for US-AID, Guatemala, May.

Gephart, Robert P. 2002. A Cooperative Approach to Local Economic Development. *Administrative Science Quarterly 47*(4): 736-739.

Gerber, Allen. (Ed.). 1996. *The Practical Approach to New Generation Cooperatives: An Exchange of Cooperative Experience from Renville, Minnesota*. St. Paul: Minnesota Association of Cooperatives.

Goddard, Ellen. 2002. Factors Underlying the Evolution of Farm-related Cooperatives in Alberta. *Canadian Journal of Agricultural Economics/Revue Canadienne D'Agroeconomie 50*(4): 473.

Goodman, David, and Michael Watts. (Eds.). 1997. *Globalising food: Agrarian Questions and Global Restructuring*. New York: Routledge.

Gray, Thomas, and Charles Kraenzle. 1998. *Member Participation in Agricultural Cooperatives: A Regression and Scale Analysis*. Washington, DC: U.S. Department of Agriculture, Rural Development, Rural Business-Cooperative Service.

Guinnane, Timothy W. 2001. Cooperatives as Information Machines: German Rural Credit Cooperatives, 1883-1914. *The Journal of Economic History 61*: 366-389.

Gumpert, David E. "How to Really Create a Successful Business Plan." Boston: Inc. Magazine Publishing, 1994. McLaughlin, Harold J., "Building Your Business Plan." New York: John Wiley & Sons, 1985. Osgood, William R. "Basic of Successful Business Planning." American Management Association, 1980.

Guttman, Joel, and Adi Schnytzer. 1989. Strategic Work Interactions and the kibbutz-kolkhoz Paradox. *Economic Journal 99* (September): 686-699.

Hakelius, Karin. 1996. *Cooperative values: Farmers' Cooperatives in the Minds of the Farmers*. Doctoral Thesis, Swedish University of Agricultural Sciences, Department of Economics, Uppsala, Sweden.

Hamilton, Neil. 1994. Agriculture without Farmers. *Successful Farming 92* (April): 28-29.

Hans Hedlund (Edr). 1988. Cooperation Revisited, Scandinavian Institute of African Studies, Uppasala.

Harris, Andrea, Brenda Stefanson, and Murray Fulton. 1996. New Generation Cooperatives and Cooperative Theory. *Journal of Cooperatives 11*: 13-28.

Harris, Andrea. 1998. *Agricultural Co-operatives: An Introduction and Start-up Guide*. Vernon, BC: Ministry of Agriculture and Food.

Harter, Lynn M., and Kathleen J. Krone. 2001. The Boundary-spanning Role of a Cooperative Support Organisation: Managing the Paradox of Stability and Change in Non-traditional Organisations. *Journal of Applied Communication Research 29* (3): 248-277.

Haruna, Shoji. 1987. Random Input Price and the Theory of the Competitive Cooperative Firm. *Journal of Comparative Economics 11* (March): 81-95.

Haynes, Curtis, and Jessica Gordon Nembhard. 1999. Cooperative Economics: A Community Revitalisation Strategy. *The Review of Black Political Economy 27*: 47-71.

Hazell, Peter B.R. and Sidney Hoos. 1962. "Cooperative Enterprise and Organisation Theory", Journal of Farm Econoics, 44, pp. 275-290.

Henehan, Brian, Bruce Anderson, Timothy Pezzolesi, and Robert Campbell. 1997. *Putting Co-operation to Work* (A Guidebook Developed for Cooperating for Sustainability: Achieving a Sustainable Agriculture through Cooperation Teleconference). Ithaca, NY: Cornell University, Cooperative Enterprise Programme.

Henehan, Brian, Bruce L. Anderson, Timothy P. Pezzolesi, and Robert L. Campbell. "Putting Cooperation to Work: A Guidebook for Educators, Advisors, Consultants and Rural Economic Developers." Pages 65-76. *Gives Potential Pitfalls, New Cooperative Tendencies, and Various Guidelines Concerning Management.*

Henry, Stuart. 1985. Community Justice, Capitalist Society, and Human Agency: The Dialectics of Collective Law in the Cooperative. *Law & Society Review 19* (2): 303-327.

Herndon, Cary. 1984. *Vertical Integration by Regional Milk Cooperatives in the Southwest: Potentials and Problems*. Unpublished Doctoral Thesis (Ph.D.), Oklahoma State University, Stillwater.

Hindmoor, Andrew. 1999. Free Riding off Capitalism: Entrepreneurship and the Mondragon Experiment. *British Journal of Political Science 29*(1): 217-224.

Holmen,H.(1987). "The Impact of Egypt's Agricultural Cooperatives on Rural Development". Social-Change. 17: 2, pp. 26-34.

Horowitz, Ira. 1991. On the Effects of Cournot Rivalry Between Entrepreneurial and Cooperative Firms. *Journal of Comparative Economics 15* (March): 115-121.

How to Start a Cooperative. Pages 13-14. Author Unknown. *Gives Twelve Detailed Steps of how to Start a Cooperative.*

Ichiishi, Tatsuro. 1990. A Contribution to the Macro Theory of Comparative Economic Systems. *Journal of Comparative Economics 14* (March): 15-32.

ILO. 1964. Housing Cooperatives. Geneva: International Labour Office, 154 pp.

ILO, Cooperative Management and Administartion (Second revised edn), Oxford & IBH Publishing Co.Pvt Ltd, New Delhi.

International Cooperative Alliance. 1979. Recent Changes, Trends and Developments of the Cooperative Movement in South-East Asia. New Delhi : The Model Press Private Ltd.

Ireland, Norman, and Peter Law. 1983. A Cournot-Nash Model of the Consumer Cooperative. *Southern Economic Journal 49* (January): 706-716.

Jake Carlyle. 2005. A Cooperative Economy, What Might It Look Like? Exploring Tasmania's Economy and the Environment, Paper given at the Hobart Conference: Community. Future, 15 October 2005.

Jentoft, Svein, and Anthony Davis. 1993. Self and Sacrifice: An Investigation of Small Boat Fisher Individualism and its Implication for Producer Cooperatives. *Human Organisation 52* (Winter): 356-367.

John Jacques (Edr), Manual on Cooperative Management, Cooperative Union, Holyoake House.

John Winfred and V.Kulandaiswamy. (nd) History of Cooperative Thought, Rainbow Publications, Coimbatore, India.

Jones, Derek, and Jan Svejnar. 1985. Participation, Profit Sharing, Worker Ownership and Efficiency in Italian Producer Cooperatives. *Economica 52* (November): 449-465.

Jones, Derek. 1985. The Economic Performance of Producer Co-operatives within Command Economies: Evidence for the Case of Poland. *Cambridge Journal of Economics 9*(June): 111-126.

Jones, Derek. 1987. The Productivity Effects of Worker Directors and Financial Participation by Employees in the Firm: The Case of British Retail Cooperatives. *Industrial & Labour Relations Review 41* (October): 79-92.

Kamat G.S. (nd). New Dimensions of Cooperative Management, Himalaya Publishing House, New Delhi.

Kang, Suk. 1988. Fair Distribution Rule in a Cooperative Enterprise. *Journal of Comparative Economics 12* (March): 89-92.

Kaswan, Jaques. 1992. *Projecting the Long-term Consequences of ESOP vs Co-op Conversion of a Firm on Employee Benefits and Company Cash* (Research Report 5). Davis: University of California at Davis, Center for Cooperatives.

Kausar, MMB.1987. What Eludes Rural Prosperity. Pakistan Agriculture. 9: 10, pp. 38-42.

Keillor, Steven J. 2000. *Cooperative Commonwealth: Co-ops in Rural Minnesota, 1859-1939*. St. Paul: Minnesota Historical Society Press. ISBN 0-87351-377-0.

Kempe.R.Hope, "Cooperative Socialism and the Cooperative Movement in Guyana" Review of International Cooperation, London: ICA, 1975.

Kiesling, Lynne. 1996. Institutional Choice Matters: The Poor Law and Implicit Labour Contracts in Victorian Lancashire. *Explorations in Economic History 33*: 65-85. (Related Material: Discussion in 34: 56-76, January 1997).

Kilby, P. (Ed.): Entrepreneurship and Economic Development, Collier-Macmillan Canada, (Toronto, 1971).

Kimball, Miles. 1988. Farmers' Cooperatives as Behaviour Toward Risk. *American Economic Review 78*(March): 224-232.

King, R. 1973. Land Reform: The Italian Experience. London: Butterworth & Co (Publishers) Ltd.

Klatt,W. 1976. 'Land and Labour in Asian', in J.R.Brown and S.Lin (ed.) Land Reform in Developing Countries, pp. 56-98. Hartford: The University of Hartford.

Koller Fred E. 1957. "Cooperatives in a Capitalistic Economy." Agricultural Cooperation (Ed). Minnapolis: University of Minnesota Press.

Korovkin,T. 1988. The Politics of Agricultural Cooperativism: Peru, Dissertation Abstracts International, A Humanities and Social Sciences. 48: 12, p. 3188; Diss., York University, Canada.

Kreitner, Philip Colman. 1981. *The Theory of Economic Cooperation: U.S. New Generation Food Co-ops and the Cooperative Dilemma*. Doctoral Thesis (Ph.D.), University of Michigan, Ann Arbor, 1978. Ann Arbor, MI: University Microfilms International.

Krishnaswami O.R and V.Kulandaiswamy. 2000. Cooperation – Concept and Theory, Arudra Academy, Coimbatore, India.

Kulandaiswamy.V. 2002. Text Book of Cooperative Management, Arudra Academy, Coimbatore, India.

Kulkarni, R. and Krishna Rao. 1956. Agricultural Marketing in India, with Special Reference to Coopertive Marketings of Agricultural Produce in India. Bombay: Cooperators Book.

Kulkarni. K.R. in Theory and Practice of Cooperation in India and Abroad Vol. I, Bombay: Cooperators' Book Depot, 1962.

Kurz, Mordecai. 1985. Cooperative Oligopoly Equilibrium. *European Economic Review 27* (February): 3-24.

Lacy, William, and Lawrence Busch. 1988. Biotechnology: Challenge and Opportunity for Agricultural Cooperatives. *Policy Studies Journal 17* (Fall): 203-214.

Larson, Adlowe. 1969. "Universalities of Cooperation" in Anschel et al. [eds], Agricultural Cooperatives and Markets in Developing Countries. New York: Praeger.

Lawless, Greg. University of Wisconsin Center for Cooperatives. "Four Phases of Cooperative Development". *The Four Phases include Pre-development, Feasibility Study, Business Plan, and Business Start-up.*

Laycock, David. 1989. Representative Economic Democracy and the Problem of Policy Influence: The Case of Canadian Co-operatives. *Canadian Journal of Political Science 22* (December): 765-792.

Lerman, Zvi, and Claudia Parliament. 1990. Comparative Performance of Cooperatives and Investor-owned Firms in U.S. Food Industries. *Agribusiness 6* (November): 527-540.

Lerman, Zvi, and Claudia Parliament. 1991. Size and Industry Effects in the Performance of Agricultural Cooperatives. *Agricultural Economics 6* (October): 15-29.

Lichtenstein, Jack. 1990. *Field to Fabric: The Story of American Cotton Growers.* Lubbock: Texas Tech University Press.

Lin, Justin Yifu. 1993. Exit Rights, Exit Costs, and Shirking in Agricultural Cooperatives: A Reply. *Journal of Comparative Economics 17* (June): 504-520.

Louis Smith, P.F., Evolution of Agricultural Cooperation.

Macpherson, IAN. 1996. Cooperative Principles for the 21st Century. International Co-operative Alliance, Available also on the internet, http://www.coop.org/ica/info/enprinciples.html

Malcolm Sargent. 1982. Agricultural Cooperation, Gower Publishing Co. Ltd, England.

Mansbridge, Jane. (Ed.). 1990. *Beyond Self-interest.* Chicago: University of Chicago Press.

Manu, G.Nelson, R.E. Thiongo, J.: Know About Business, international Training Centre of the ILO – Turin, (Italy, 1996).

Maslennikov V. 1983. The Cooperative Movement in Asia and Africa, Progress Publishers, Mascow.

Mathur,K. 1979. 'Administrative Institutions, Political Capacity and India's Strategy for Rural Development', in Inayatullah (Approaches to Rural Development in Asia: Some Asian Experiences, p. 5. Kuala Lumpur: APDAC.

Mellor, John W. 1971. Performance of Private Trade and Cooperatives. Cornell University Occasional Paper No. 87.

Mellor, Mary, John Stirling, and Janet Hannah. 1988. *Worker Cooperatives in Theory and Practice*. Philadelphia: Open University Press.

Merrett, Christopher D., and Norman Walzer. 2003. *Cooperatives and Local Development: Theory and Applications for the 21st Century*. Armonk, NY: M.E. Sharpe. ISBN 0-7656-1123.

Michigan Alliance of Cooperatives, Cooperative Action, Summer 1997 page 6-7. *Gives Strategy that the Michigan Alliance and Various Others Practice for Cooperative Development.*

Mickiewicz, Tomasz. 1996. The Spatial Dimension of Transformation: Time Pattern and Ownership Factors on the Micro Level. *Europe-Asia Studies 48* (November): 1187-1202.

Milanovic, Branko. 1982. The Austrian Theory of the Cooperative Firm. *Journal of Comparative Economics 6* (December): 379-395.

Miller, David. 1981. Market Neutrality and the Failure of Co-operatives. *British Journal of Political Science 11*: 309-329. (Related Material: Discussion in *13*: 125-128, January 1983).

Minnesota Association of Cooperatives. 1997. *Cooperatives talk Minnesotan: Examining Cooperative Business*. St. Paul: Minnesota Association of Cooperatives.

Mitchell, Janet. 1990. Perfect Equilibrium and Intergenerational Conflict in a Model of Cooperative Enterprise Growth. *Journal of Economic Theory 51* (June): 48-76.

Molinas, Jose. 1998. The Impact of Inequality, Gender, External Assistance and Social Capital on Local-level Cooperation. *World Development 26* (3): 413-431.

Morgan, Zoe. 2006. Case Study—The Co-operative: Mutual Benefits of Staff Engagement. *Brand Strategy* (June): 50.

Munkner H.H and A. Shah, Creating a Favourable Climate and Conditions for Cooperative Development in Africa, ILO, Geneva, 1993.

Murray. 1999. Cooperatives and Member Commitment. The Finnish Journal of Business Economics, pp. 437-418.

Nakkiran.S. 2000. A Treatise on Cooperative Management, Rainbow Publications, Coimbatore, India.

National Cooperative Bank. "How to Organise a Cooperative." *A Brief Pamphlet Explaining what a Cooperative is, Types of Cooperatives, Getting Started, and Financing.*

National Council of Farmer Cooperatives. 1969. *Directory of Cooperatives of the United States*. Washington, DC: National Council of Farmer Cooperatives.

National Council of Farmer Cooperatives. 1995. *Journal of Cooperatives* (entire issue) *10*.

NCDC (n.d.) All India Conference on Co-operative Rice Milling Industry. New Delhi: National Co-operative Development Corporation.

Nelson, 2000, available at www.prout.org

Nelson, R.E. "Promotion of Small Enterprises", in small Enterprise Development: Policies and Programmes, Eds. Neck, P.A. and Nelson, R.E.,ILO, (Genva, 1987), p.3

Nelson, R.E. and Nguiru, R.G.: "Training for Entrepreneurship", pp. 103-106.

Nor, Radziah. 1995. *Member Communication Methods Used by Selected Agricultural Cooperatives in the Eastern North Central Region of the United States*. Unpublished Master's Thesis (M.S.), Ohio State University, Columbus.

Novkovic, S. 2008. Defining the Co-operative Difference. Journal of Socio-economics 37: 2168-2177.

Otu, MF.1988. Cooperative Extension: The Missing Ingredient in Nigeria's Cooperative Development. Land Reform, Land Settlement and Cooperatives. 1988, No. 1/2, pp. 69-77.

P.E. Lambert. 1963. Studies in Social Philosophy of Cooperation, Manchester: Cooperative Union Ltd.

P.Y. Chinehankar and M.V. Namjoshi. 1977. Cooperation and the Dynamics of Charge, Bombay, Somaiya Publication Pvt., Ltd.

Parliament, Claudia, Yacov Tsur, and David Zilberman. 1989. Cooperative labour Allocation Under Uncertainty. *Journal of Comparative Economics 13* (December): 539-552.

Parnell, Edgar. 1995. Reinventing the Co-operative Enterprise for the 21st Century. United Kingdom.

Patrie, Bill. "Critical Organisation Steps-Cooperative Development." *Gives Four Major Steps in Cooperative Development*. Phases of Co-op Development." Author Unknown. *Gives the Four Phases as Organising, Start-up, Growth, and Consolidation*.

Patrie, William. 1998. *Creating "Co-op Fever": A Rural Developer's Guide to Forming Cooperatives* (RBS Service Report 54). Washington, DC: U.S. Department of Agriculture, Rural Business-Cooperative Service.

Patwardhan, V.S. 1969. "Distribution of Consumer Goods by Co-operatives in Rural Areas". Economic and Political Weekly, 4, pp. 361-370.

Paul Roy, Ewell. 1964. Cooperatives: Today and Tomorrow Illinois; The Interstate Printers and Publishers.

Payne, Malcolm [Reviewer]. 1998. The Myth of Mondragon: Cooperatives, Politics, and Working- Class Life in a Basque Town [Book Review]. *Human Relations 51*(9): 1179-1193.

Pencavel, John, and Ben Craig. 1994. The Empirical Performance of Orthodox Models of the Firm: Conventional Firms and Worker Cooperatives. *Journal of Political Economy 102*: 718-744.

Peterson, Christopher, and Bruce Anderson. 1996. Cooperative Strategy: Theory and Practice. *Agribusiness 12* (July/August): 371-383.

Ploughing for Profits. 1991. *Economist 320* (July 20): 84-85. Porter, Philip, and Gerald Scully. 1987. Economic Efficiency in Cooperatives. *Journal of Law & Economics 30* (October): 489-512.

Pope, Jeffrey L. "Practical Marketing Research." American Management Association. 1993. Siegel, Eric S., et al., "The Ernst & Young Business Plan Guide." New York: John Wiley & Sons, 1987.

Poter, P. And Scully, W. 1987. Economic Efficiency in Cooperatives. Journal of Law and Economics 30(2): 489-512.

Pritchard, William N. 1996. Shifts in Food Regimes, Regulation, and Producer Cooperatives: Insights from the Australian and US dairy Industries. *Environment & Planning A 28*: 857-875.

Pritchard, William N. 1998. The Emerging Contours of the Third Food Regime: Evidence from Australian Dairy and Wheat Sectors. *Economic Geography 74*(1): 64-74.

Randall, Donna, and Mike O'Driscoll. 1997. Affective versus Calculative Commitment: Human Resource Implications. *Journal of Social Psychology 137*(October): 606-617.

Rasmussen, Wayne. 1991. *Farmers, Cooperatives, and USDA: A History of Agricultural Cooperative Service* (Agricultural Information Bulletin #621). Washington, DC: U.S. Department of Agriculture.

Regan, Donald. 1980. *Utilitarianism and Co-operation*. Oxford, UK: Clarendon Press.

Reynolds, Bruce J. 2001. *A History of African-American Farmer Cooperatives, 1938-2000*. Washington, DC: U.S. Department of Agriculture, Rural Business-Cooperative Service.

Rhodes, James. 1983. The Large Agricultural Cooperative as a Competitor. *American Journal of Agricultural Economics 65*(December): 1090-1095. (Related Material: Discussion in 65: 1096-1098, December 1983).

Risto, Tainio. 1999. Strategic Change in the Evolution of Cooperatives. *Journal of Finnish Business Economics*: 484-490. Retrieved May 3, 2007, from www.pellervo.fi/finncoop/material/tainio.pdf.

Rooney, Patrick Michael. 1992. ESOPS, Producer Co-ops and Traditional Firms: Are they Different? *Journal of Economic Issues 26*(June): 593-603.

Rosow, Stephen, Naeem Inayatullah, and Mark Rupert. (Eds.). 1994. *The Global Economy as Political Space: Critical Perspectives on World Politics*. Boulder, CO: Lynne Rienner Publishers.

Rothburd, Carrie. 1986. Co-opted. *The Progressive 50* (May): 27-29. Royer, Jeffrey. 1987. *Cooperative Theory: New Approaches* (ACS Service Report 18). Washington, DC: U.S. Department of Agriculture, Agricultural Cooperative Service.

Roy, Ewell Paul. 1964. Cooperatives: Today and Tomorrow. Danville: The Interstate Printers and Publishers.

Russell, Raymond, and Robert Hanneman. 1992. Cooperatives and the Business Cycle: The Israeli Case. *Journal of Comparative Economics 16* (December): 701-715.

Samuli Skurnik. 2002. The Role of Cooperative Entrepreneurship and Firms in Organising Economic Activities – Past, Present and Future, The Finnish Journal of Business Economics, 103.1.

Sando,RA. 1986. Implications of Development Policies for Agriculture in Taiwan. Practicing Development Anthropology [edited by Green,E. C.]. 195-210. Boulder, Colorado: Westview Press.

Sazama, Gerald W. 2000. Lessons from the History of Affordable Housing Cooperatives in the United States: A Case Study in American Affordable Housing Policy. *The American Journal of Economics and Sociology 59*(4): 573-608.

Schilthuis, Gijs. 2001. *Continuously Reinventing Cooperatives*. Marshall, MN: Southwest State University Center for Rural and Regional Studies.

Schroeder, Ted. 1991. *Multiproduct Scale and Scope Economies for Agricultural Cooperatives* (Staff Paper, 92-5). Manhattan: Kansas State University, Department of Agricultural Economics.

Sexton, Richard. 1984. Perspectives on the Development of the Economic Theory of Cooperatives. *Canadian Journal of Agricultural Economics 32* (July): 423-435.

Singh, Mohinder. 1970. Co-operatives in Asia. New York: Praeger.

Sommer, Robert, and Sandra Nelson. 1986. The Use of Survey Results by Democratically Controlled Organisations. *Journal of Applied Behavioural Science 22*(2): 113-125.

Staber, Udo. 1992. Organisational Interdependence and Organisational Mortality in the Cooperative Sector: A Community Ecology Perspective. *Human Relations 45*(November): 1191-1212.

Staber, Udo. 1993. Worker Cooperatives and the Business Cycle: Are Cooperatives the Answer to Unemployment? *American Journal of Economics & Sociology 52*(April): 129-143.

Stanglin, Douglas. 1990. Front Row at the Revolution. *U.S. News & World Report 108* (March 26): 35-37.

Stans, Maurice. 1984. Running Dogs of Capitalism. *National Review 36* (December 14): 38. Staub, Ervin. 1984. *Development and Maintenance of Prosocial Behaviour: International Perspectives on Positive Morality*. New York: Plenum Press.

Svsrdsrum, K.F. 1969. Agricultural Marketing for Co-operators. Bombay: Allied Publishers.

Taimni, K.K. 1998. "Cooperative Entrepreneurship: Concept, Design and Approaches to Development", Unpublished Working Paper.

Tanzer, Andrew. 1996. Small is Beautiful. *Forbes 158* (September 23): 90-92.

Torgerson, Randall. 1990. *Agricultural Cooperative Issues for the 1990s* (Working Paper Series, Number 5-A). Davis: University of California at Davis, Center for Cooperatives.

Texier, J.M. (1978). The Promotion of Cooperatives in Traditional Rural Societies. In Policy and Practice in Rural Development (Edited by Guy Hunter, A. Hugh Bunting, Anthony Bottrall), p. 215. London: Croom Helm Ltd.

Thompson, David (n.d.). Weavers of Dreams.

[Authors address for copies: David Thompson, 516 Rutgers Drive, Davis CA 95616, USA]

U.S. Department of Agriculture (USDA). 1997. *Co-ops 101: An Introduction to Cooperatives*. Washington, DC: USDA, Rural Business-Cooperative Service. USDA. 1998. *Cooperative Historical Statistics* (Cooperative Information Report: 1, Section 26, April). Washington, DC: USDA, Rural Business-Cooperative Service.

Umeki,T. 1989. Marketing of Processed Farm Products of Agricultural Cooperatives. Marketing Farm Products in Asia and the Pacific. pp.149-159, Tokyo: Asian Productivity Organisation.

University of Wisconsin Centre for Cooperatives. "Steps in Forming a Cooperative." Online. World Wide Web. Available at http://www.uwcc.wisc.edu/info/startc.htm. *The Article gives Seven Steps Informing a Cooperative. The Steps include Establishing a Steering Qommittee, Conducting a Feasibility Study, Draft Articles of Incorporation and bylaws, Prepare a Business Plan, Secure Financing, Recruit Members, and Recruit Personnel.*

USDA, Rural Business and Cooperative Development Service, Understanding Cooperatives: How to Start a Cooperative, Cooperative Information Report 45, Section 14. *Gives Fourteen Steps in Organising a Cooperative. Steps include such things as Determining Economic need to Important Factors for Success.*

USDA, Rural Business/Cooperative Service, "How to Start a Cooperative," Cooperative Information Report 7. *A Detailed Booklet Explaining what a Cooperative is, Organising Steps, Investment, Membership, and General Rules for Success.*

V.L. Mehta, Towards a Cooperative Socialist Common Wealth, Bombay: Maharashtra State Cooperative Union, 1965.

Valentionov, V. 2007. Why are Cooperatives Important in Agriculture? An Organisational Economics Perspective. Journal of Institutional Economics 3(1): 55-69.

Van Ginkel, Rob. 1996. Cooperating Competitors: Texel Fishermen and Their Organisations (c.1870-1930). *Anthropological Quarterly 69* (April): 51-65.

Vercammen, James, and Murray Fulton. 1996. Non-linear Pricing Schemes for Co-operatives: The Equity/Efficiency Trade-off. *Canadian Journal of Economics* (Special Issue) *29* (Pt. 1): S303-S307.

Wade, Robert. 1987. The Management of Common Property Resources: Collective Action as an Alternative to Privatization or State Regulation. *Cambridge Journal of Economics 11*(June): 95-106.

Wadsworth, James J. 1998. *Cooperative Restructuring, 1989-1998* (RBS Service Report 57). Washington, DC: U.S. Department of Agriculture, Rural Business-Cooperative Service.

Wagner, Ralph D. 2004. A history of the Farmington Plan. *Libraries & Culture 39*(4): 473-475.

Warman, Marc, Larry Stearns, and David Cobia. 1997. *Strategies for Survival by Cooperative Country Elevators: Revisited*. Washington, DC: U.S. Department of Agriculture.

Whatmore, Sarah, and Lorraine Thorne. 1997. Nourishing Networks: Alternative Geographies of Food. In *Globalising Food: Agrarian Questions and Global Restructuring*, ed. David Goodman and Michael Watts, 287-304. New York: Routledge.

Wilkins, Paul. 1980. *Marketing and Farm Supply Cooperatives Livestock Producer Membership and Use, 1980* (ACS Research Report 23). Washington, DC: U.S. Department of Agriculture, Agricultural Cooperative Service.

Williams, Ned. 1993. *The Co-op in Birmingham & the Black Country: 150 Years of Co-operation, 1844-1994*. Wolverhampton, UK: Uralia Press.

Williamson, Lionel, and Forrest Stegelin. 1989. *Successful Co-ops don't just Happen* (Staff Paper 262). Lexington: University of Kentucky, Department of Agricultural Economics.

Wills, Robert. 1985. Evaluating Price Enhancement by Processing Cooperatives. *American Journal of Agricultural Economics 67* (May): 183-192.

Wisconsin Center for Cooperatives, Cooperatives: A Tool for Community Economic Development, Madison.

Won, HS. 1989. The Agricultural Co-operative Movement in Korea. Review of International Co-operation. 82: 4, pp. 65-74.

Young, Kun Shim. 1989. Korea Republic. Marketing Farm Products in Asia and the Pacific. pp. 257-271; Tokyo:Asian Productivity Organisation.

Youngjohns, B.J. 1978. Cooperative Organisation. In Policy and Practice in Rural Development (Edited by Guy Hunter, A. Hugh Bunting, Anthony Bottrall) pp. 236-238. London: Croom Helm Ltd.).

Yun, KH. 1987. Agricultural Cooperative in Korea. Seoul: National Agricultural Cooperative Federation.

Zimbelman, Karen. "How to Start a Marketing Co-op." Second Draft. June 29, 1995. An Informational Booklet on how to Start a Marketing Coop. *It includes Sections on "Making your Co-op Successful, Steps to Starting a Marketing Coop, and Tips and Hints for Success.*

Index